A Day Late and a Dollar Short

High Hopes and Deferred Dreams in Obama's "Postracial" America

Robert E. Pierre
and Jon Jeter

WILEY

John Wiley & Sons, Inc.

For general information about our other products and services, please contact our Customer Care Department within the United States at (800) 762-2974, outside the United States at (317) 572-3993 or fax (317) 572-4002.

Wiley also publishes its books in a variety of electronic formats. Some content that appears in print may not be available in electronic books. For more information about Wiley products, visit our web site at www.wiley.com.

ISBN 978-0470-52066-6

Printed in the United States of America

10 9 8 7 6 5 4 3 2

To Daisy Mae Francis and Harrison Francis Sr.
and all of their people:

Our People

Contents

Contents

Acknowledgments

I want to thank two of my most consistent nags, Tim Kelly and Linda Botts, who have never failed to ask when I was going to write a book. Perhaps this is that book; perhaps it is one not yet written. But Tim and Linda—who do not know each other—never let me forget this goal. In fact, it was Linda who planted the seed for this endeavor.

Thanks as well to family and friends who listened to kernels of ideas, read over chapters, suggested chapters, and remained friends even as I blew them off for several months during the writing and reporting process. I hesitate to mention other names for fear of leaving someone out, so to everyone who helped (you know who you are), thanks so much.

Finally, Jon and I send a heartfelt thank-you to all of the people who allowed us into their homes and lives, sharing intimate, funny, and embarrassing details that help shine a light on black America as it struggles to understand what it means to live under a black president.

—Robert E. Pierre

Introduction

It was November 2008, a few days after Americans had chosen a black man as the nation's forty-fourth president. The head of a New York–based nonprofit, Maya Wiley, sat on the dais in the center of a cavernous symphony hall in Dallas, Texas, staring out into a sea of white faces, hundreds upon hundreds of the city's wealthiest elites, oil money mostly, but some finance and real estate types, too. She had been invited to serve on a panel with *New York Times* columnists David Brooks and Nicholas Kristof, *New Yorker* writer Elizabeth Kolbert, and Ron Kirk, the first African American mayor of Dallas. The topic was the intersection of race and American life in the Barack Obama era. She was a last-minute replacement for retired Supreme Court justice Sandra Day O'Connor, though for the life of her, Maya couldn't imagine how anyone would've thought of her—a fortyish, dreadlocked, leftist African American intellectual—as a replacement for the conservative and white O'Connor.

But there was something in the air. Maya could feel it.

The Center for Social Inclusion, which she founded, takes a particular tack on civil rights issues, which is that class is no proxy for race and that as well intentioned as some Americans may be in thinking that the country should focus its efforts on helping the poor rather than on remedying discrimination, that approach misses the point almost entirely. Half of all Americans without health insurance are people of color; the subprime loan market, which sank the entire economy, targeted, with radarlike accuracy, blacks and Latinos; no successful social movement in the history of this country failed to integrate into its central narrative African Americans and their specific grievances. This idea—that racism is America's original sin and until the country speaks its name it's destined to continue to curse one generation after another—was uncomfortable stuff, especially among white folks, and uniquely among the elite, white, blue-blood Republican crowd like the one she faced that day. But from the moment that the moderator, historian Michael Beschloss, turned to Maya twenty minutes into the program and asked her what impact the Obama presidency would have on race and the law, Maya sensed the earth shifting beneath her.

"The short answer is that we don't really know. If Barack Obama uses his leadership as the most visible African American in the world to plug into the dangerous and misguided notion that everything is all right and we are indeed a postracial society that has moved beyond racial disparities and deeply rooted racial injustice, then the law, as a tool for inclusion and creating opportunities, will suffer gravely." This is when she noticed it. Usually, with an audience peopled with heretics and unbelievers in the notion of racism as America's design flaw, the turning off and tuning out is unmistakable.

"They lean back in their chairs, they fold their arms across their chest, they *shake* their heads," Maya said. "They make it very clear, with their body language, that they are not with you." But this audience leaned *forward*. They uncrossed their arms; they nodded their heads, as though in agreement, or at least in recognition of something that struck them as closing in on the truth. "I was prepared to be pilloried, but they were very clearly engaged by what I was saying. It's like the election had stirred this dormant part of

2

their brains and their consciousness and we had an opportunity to talk, openly, about race and racism in America." In that moment, the possibilities inherent in the election of the first black president of the United States became almost giddily clear.

And then just a quickly, the moment slipped away. Minutes after Maya spoke, Beschloss turned to the local panelists on the dais for comment. This group included Kirk, the only other African American on the panel and soon to be appointed U.S. trade representative for the Obama administration. He lit into Maya.

"I just want to say that Maya is wrong," he said, as though he were a prosecutor and Maya a defendant in the dock. "What Barack Obama does for black America is to let black people know that they"—and Maya remembers that he paused here for dramatic effect—"have no more excuses."

And that was it. The moment passed, the opportunity slipped away, the audience exhaled a sigh of relief, and when the panelists divided to lead separate workshops, most of the whites went with David Brooks. Maya doesn't doubt that Kirk was sincere. He wasn't just playing to the crowd like some Uncle Tom trying to assuage his white benefactors. She had seen that before, and this was not that. Still, his retort short-circuited, in her estimation, what could have been an electric conversation on the most intractable issue in America's history. "It was like there was this breakthrough, and then another wall just went up in its place."

What does Barack Obama mean to black America? This is a running debate taking place somewhere in the country every day, and the answer so far is this: everything and nothing; transformative change and elegiac stasis; a stark symbol of how far we've come and a painful marker of how far we've yet to go; a Rosetta stone that can help decode the distinctly different languages spoken by blacks and whites in this country; or a looming Tower of Babel that will encumber communication, corrupt speech, and scatter tribes like leaves. He is a repository for joy and sorrow and rage, a movie screen that runs the length and breadth of the country onto which young and old, rich and poor, socialists and conservatives, the ambitious and the demoralized, project their lament for the dead, their dreams for the unborn, and their nightmares for the living. He exemplifies what blacks can achieve when they quit whining, study long, and work hard, or alternately, just how comfortable white folks are with light-skinned blacks who never raise their voices and never try to wrestle the white people from their sweet spot atop a trash heap of privilege and denial. He is a messianic figure and a minstrel, the Good Black, the Blackness That Dare Not Speak Its Name, the torchbearer for Martin Luther King Jr., and the modern-day Booker T. Washington exhorting blacks to cast down their buckets where they are. He is the Dreamcatcher.

That mythical character is an Ojibwa legend and refers to an amulet meant to ward off bad dreams. Woven from twigs, sinew, and feathers, the talisman is dangled above a baby's crib in the hope that good dreams will find their way into the baby's thoughts while bad dreams will get tangled in the web and trapped, so as not to disturb sleep. As the idea spread to other tribes, the materials and the meanings changed, and the concept became commercialized and bastardized into a generic representation of faith and family and hope, packaged and peddled as a clichéd inspiration for paintings, books, and even tattoos.

"We are the ones we've been waiting for," Obama said again and again. He implored us to dream, with "Yes we can" uttered so often and so loudly that it became at once an invitation to believe in a country far better than we'd dared imagine and to mock, like the vague, innocuous message unfurled in a fortune cookie: *We are the ones we've been waiting for—in bed*, or *Yes we can—in bed*. The ascendancy of the nation's first black president comes at a time when the American Empire is in decline and African Americans are more estranged from one another than at any time in history. There are more black millionaires than ever before, and more black prisoners, too. A black man is in the White House, but black women, more than ever before, are the breadwinners in the house. There is a black first lady, but the number of HIV infections is growing fastest among black women. There are two beautiful black girls who live at 1600 Pennsylvania Avenue, and yet one in three children who live in the surrounding neighborhoods of Washington, D.C., is poor. A coterie of Ivy League–educated African Americans are among the top power brokers in the world, but in the president's hometown of Chicago, thirty-five schoolchildren have been slain in the first hundred days of his tenure, and only three out of one hundred black freshmen who enroll in a Chicago public high school will graduate from college—*any* college—within ten years.

This is black America in the age of Obama: On the day after Christmas 2008, at a strip bar known as the Players Club in Greensboro, North Carolina, a twenty-two-year-old woman who called herself Sade danced nearly naked on the stage to the delight of men two and three times her age. She was slim and lean, earning twenty dollars for a racy lap dance. She was also a college student, studying journalism at the historically black college North Carolina A&T and feeling hopeful about Obama's election. Neither her mother nor her boyfriend liked her chosen job. And, when she was truthful, Sade hated it, too. But where else could she earn as much as two hundred dollars a night to pay for tuition, books, gas, rent? She certainly couldn't rely on her father; he was in prison, and more men than she cared to count had called her bitch or whore as if it were her name. But Sade remained focused, and Obama was her North Star, her Moses, leading her out of the wilderness with his example. What was it that Hillary Clinton had said in her speech at the Democratic National Convention, invoking Harriet Tubman's directives to slaves fleeing to freedom? "Children, when you get tired, keep going. When you get hungry, keep going. When you hear the dogs barking, keep going."

And so Sade kept dancing, kept going, kept searching for a better life. The following month, she would join the masses headed to Washington for the inauguration. *Yes We Can.* She wanted, needed, to believe.

And *this* is black America in the age of Obama: As the one-hundred-day mark of Obama's presidency drew near, a woman in her fifties slowly made her way back home from the corner store in southeast Washington, D.C., with a small plastic bag in her hand. Her community of Anacostia is a mostly black neighborhood, a river and a world away from the White House and the gleaming monuments of Washington. Young professionals and businesses are slowly moving in, but the area remains the city's poorest, with higher crime and the worst schools. But on this splendid spring afternoon, with the famed cherry blossoms attracting throngs of admirers downtown, the grandmother lamented that she had no money to make the trip to Delaware to play the slots. People are hurting, she said, losing their jobs and their homes. She couldn't understand why the new president and first lady were overseas on an eight-day foreign trip, visiting the Queen of England and European capitals. On her block of W Street SE, across from the historic home of Frederick Douglass, there had been a shooting earlier in the week. Blood had pooled on the sidewalk, but mercifully no one was killed, this time. Her grandchild hid in a closet after the shots rang out. When the election results had rolled in, she had allowed herself to be sanguine, to believe that change, finally, was on the way. The rat-a-tat-tat of gunfire had awakened her, as though from a long, unproductive daydream. She wondered: "Had I expected too much? Had I wanted too much?" She knew only this: "I'm not going to vote next time. Why are they in Germany? Those people don't like us anyway."

There are surely good reasons to visit foreign lands, but none of them seemed relevant to this woman. She wasn't tearing Obama down, she just wasn't sure how the jubilation she had seen at her

6

polling place six months earlier mattered anymore. She could no longer see how the election of the nation's first African American president actually had any bearing on her life, her neighborhood, or the chances that she might have to bury her grandchildren before their time.

Wherever Obama travels, whether across the Anacostia River or the Atlantic Ocean, people want to know what he can do for them.

An informal poll of black America would reveal a population in the midst of an identity crisis, torn between hope and despair, pride and shame, an evangelic peace and a biblical rage. America elected a black man to the most visible position in the world, but at a time when many blacks feel as powerless and invisible as ever. On the night of Obama's election, those burdens seemed a tad lighter, after a lifetime of hearing "No, you're not good enough," "No, I wasn't following you around the store," and "No, you can't have this or that job. " No, No, No.

And then, finally: "Yes."

But an election doesn't wipe the slate clean.

The implosion of the housing market has triggered the greatest loss of wealth for African Americans in history. Life expectancy for black men in cities like Washington, D.C., Baltimore, Oakland, and New Orleans rivals that for black men in Port-au-Prince, Sierra Leone, or Kinshasa. Black women are half as likely to marry as white women, twice as likely to die from a chronic disease like diabetes, three times as likely not to have health insurance, four times as likely to have a doctor amputate a limb. An African American infant is twice as likely to die before his or her first birthday as a white infant in America. A black child is twice as likely as a white child to be diagnosed with asthma; a black teenager is four times as likely to be suspended from school, and in cities like Los Angeles and Houston and Boston, nearly half of all black high school freshmen drop out of school. By May 2008, the economy had claimed so many jobs that nearly a fifth of all black workers were out of work, a figure that rivals the nation's unemployment at the peak of the Great Depression. There are more black millionaires than ever, and yet, Bill Gates annually earns more in investment income than every black man, woman, and child in America put together.

And in places like Selma, Alabama, which became a national symbol of racial intolerance during the 1960s, residents got on a bus to Obama's inauguration hoping that some of the hope in Washington would change their reality. Selma may be seared into America's image as the catalyst for the Voting Rights Act of 1965, but there's plenty of unfinished business. Ride across the Edmund Pettus Bridge, where peaceful marchers had their heads bashed in for trying to cross, and you'll find a main drag struggling to maintain businesses. The place that looms so large in American history seems quite small to the first-time visitor. To the young people who attend Selma High School, the old struggles seem so passé: the right to vote, the right to walk on public streets, the right to sit at the front of the bus, the right to eat in a restaurant. They want jobs, they want money, and they want to participate in the society they see on television.

So they leave Selma in droves, as do people in small towns across America, because they don't see a way up and a way out. Prior to 2000, the town experienced double-digit unemployment for twenty years. The unemployment rate in Alabama in the spring of 2009 was 9 percent. In Dallas County, where Selma is located, it was 18.2 percent. A cigar factory closed the month Obama was elected, putting three hundred people out of work. Other plants announced layoffs and reduced hours. There are no race riots here, but there is hardly peace. The town markets its ties to both the Confederacy and Civil Rights, an uneasy coexistence at best.

Go to a basketball game at Selma High, and you'll search hard to find a single white face. Visitors to Selma stop to hear the old stories retold again and again: people ran to this church for cover, they were beaten right here, look at this picture of me standing next to Dr. King. The stories feel triumphant—the unarmed, in the end, defeating the armed and dangerous segregationists. But stop to look around Selma today, and many residents, young and old, ask: how does all that relate to now?

"For 2009, you really see how separate we are," said Denise Roy, who works at Alabama State University in Montgomery and made the inaugural bus trip with a contingent from Selma High. "It's so divided to be such a small town. We have maybe three churches that are integrated. The high school is not the greatest anymore. Instead of progressing, we're regressing."

Will black people progress or regress under Obama? The fear is that America, black and white, will breathe a sigh of relief and declare that the racism that created a permanent underclass is dead and that people like James von Brunn, an avowed racist and anti-Semite, are merely part of the fringe. In June 2009, on a slightly overcast afternoon, the eighty-eight-year-old double-parked his red Hyundai outside the United States Holocaust Memorial Museum in downtown Washington. Carrying a .22-caliber Winchester rifle nearly as old as he was, von Brunn shot to death the security guard who'd been kind enough to prop open the door for an elderly man who had murder on his mind. The guard, Stephen Tyrone Johns, was shot in the chest and died a short time later. Von Brunn was wounded in the face by other security guards but survived the gunshots. In von Brunn's car, investigators found notes that included this rant: "The Holocaust is a lie. Obama was created by Jews. Obama does what his Jew owners tell him to do."

Weeks earlier, von Brunn had shown up at the gates of the U.S. Naval Academy in Annapolis to demand a meeting with the commanding officer, who had proudly observed that the incoming class was the most diverse in the institution's history. "A crackpot who spewed venom" is how the media described von Brunn, who had a history of violent episodes. But take away his most vile comments about blacks and Jews, and the underpinning of his argument—that America was greater when it was pure and not so politically correct—is what right-leaning politicians have used to get elected for decades and what made Rush Limbaugh a mighty rich man. Von Brunn, many argued in the immediate aftermath, may be an extremist, but he was egged on by the so-called mainstream.

Obama, for now, gets the benefit of the doubt from black America. But the paradox of the first black president is that it is not enough for him to merely be the first black president. Black America is pregnant with expectation. They want better schools, better jobs, better health care, lower taxes, more unions, and fewer casualties in Iraq and Afghanistan and in Brooklyn and Los Angeles. Many black Americans fully expect that the first black president will finally make them citizens of the country of their birth. If that doesn't happen, the experience of David A. Paterson, the first black governor of New York, may be instructive. A year after being warmly received by two thirds of black voters, Paterson found himself in the unenviable position of receiving the approval of only half of the state's black voters for his failure to deliver on bread-and-butter issues. "There is some letdown from people who were so proud of his ascension," Charles Barron, a New York City Council member from Brooklyn, told the *New York Times*. "People have to realize that when we invest our aspirations in you, we expect more. We expect better."

Another example of black voters' political pragmatism is the 2006 campaign for the U.S. Senate run by Michael Steele, in Maryland. Steele, an African American and currently the chairman of the Republican National Committee, ran for an open seat against the charmless Democratic nominee, Ben Cardin, who is white. Even though black anger was still simmering over the failure of the 2002 Democratic gubernatorial nominee, Kathleen Kennedy Townsend—daughter of the late Robert F. Kennedy—to choose an African American running mate, Steele lost badly, as Cardin won three of four black votes in the state.

This tension, between elation and expectation, between hoping for the best and fearing the worst, underscores the precarious high-wire act required of the nation's first black president and provides one clue to the question, What does Barack Obama mean to black America?

"In the end," said Maya Wiley, "it's not really about Barack Obama."

It's about us.

Daisy Mae on the Bayou

The Past Is Still with Us

We have helped to build America with our labor, strengthened it with our faith and enriched it with our song. We have given you Paul Lawrence Dunbar, Booker T. Washington, Marian Anderson and George Washington Carver. But even these are only the first fruits from a rich harvest, which will be reaped when new and wider fields are opened to us.

—MARY MCLEOD BETHUNE, NOVEMBER 23, 1939, "SAY IT PLAIN,"
AMERICAN RADIOWORKS, AMERICAN PUBLIC MEDIA

The mood was festive, like a Friday afternoon before a three-day weekend. Trays of chicken fingers, meatballs, and assorted fruit filled the tables. My family was celebrating the sixty-first birthday of my mother, whom everyone called Peaches. But on Tuesday, November 4, 2008, the birthday cake was decorated in red, white, and blue, and carried the message: "Obama '08." Commentators had been buzzing all day long, and for months before that, that

13

Barack Obama was cruising toward victory as his Republican opponent stumbled through the final weeks of the campaign. The presidency, many at this party and throughout the nation felt, was now assured.

My grandmother Daisy Mae was among the handwringers, both fascinated and frightened by the campaign. She remembered vividly the day Martin Luther King Jr. was killed and wondered whether the country was ready for a black man and his family in the White House.

"I want him to win and I don't," she said. "I pray that he will be strong enough to clean up this mess, but I am afraid these people are going to try to hurt this man. Obama got a little white in him too, but he's a black man. I want him to win, but thinking about what may happen to him, I am praying for him and his family."

Two weeks shy of turning seventy-nine, the family matriarch had learned not to take anything for granted. Her life and her family were relatively secure by now, with steady jobs, houses they owned, and a feeling of confidence that her massive brood had advanced further she had. The year Daisy Mae came into the world, 1929, the stock market crashed, plunging the world into the Great Depression. People her age remembered that even when the nation emerged from the fog more than a decade later, the vast majority of black people remained poor, subject to the whims of whites and certain only that equality with white people was a fantastical notion. So on Election Night, as history hung in the balance, Daisy Mae waited until the words flashed across the screen announcing that Obama would be the next president of the United States before passing out hugs and kisses and joining in the cheers.

We won. We actually won.

Daisy Mae grew up on a sugarcane plantation on the banks of Bayou Teche in southwest Louisiana, waking each morning in the same clapboard shacks where her bonded ancestors had slept. She cleaned white people's homes, washed and ironed their clothes, and pampered their children before going home to put supper on the table for her own. She married when she was fifteen, gave birth to fourteen children, and worked in the backbreaking sugarcane fields. Whites mistreated her because she was black, and her husband mistreated her because there was no one else to lash out at when he'd been called "boy" or "Uncle Tom" one time too many. He drowned his sorrows in liquor and women while she kept the family going.

Faith had seen her through, certain a better day would come. It did, though it came slowly. Her experience was not that of the angry South epitomized by George Wallace and Bull Connor, who unleashed dogs, fire hoses, and angry mobs on men, women, and children in Montgomery and Selma. People in Franklin, Louisiana, and in nearby nooks and crannies like Baldwin and the Alice C Plantation didn't buck the established hierarchy and sometimes seemed oblivious to the racial unrest in other Deep South cities, where blacks were sitting in at lunch counters, boycotting public buses, and marching to protest the systematic denial of voting rights through poll taxes and unfair tests required for voter registration.

But Daisy Mae, who knew her place in those difficult times, changed right along with the times. Blacks won the right to vote and to seek public office. One of her youngest children, Harrison Jr., won a football scholarship to Louisiana State University, which had been off-limits to blacks most of her life. Affirmative action and scholarships led to college degrees as her brood inched their way into middle-class lives in San Francisco, Atlanta, and Austin. And I, one of her oldest grandchildren, was a writer for the *Washington Post* and a budding author. Daisy Mae herself had risen far above her original station in life and was now living in a white brick house partially paid for by one of her sons, who had played nine years in the National Football League. But when a black man, about the age of her youngest son, walked across a stage in Denver and, to thunderous applause, accepted the Democratic nomination for president of the United States, it was beyond her wildest dreams. Now he was president.

"I never thought I would see it," she said. "Not in my lifetime."

"Not in my lifetime" became a cliché during the campaign. Everybody said it.

Ever since I was a small boy, my grandmother and I had one continuous conversation that always involved my pushing her and her pushing right back. I would say things like, "When I grow up, I'm leaving this place and never coming back." She said I would change my mind, that I was just young. But I was adamant. Franklin always felt too small, an accidental stop on the road to somewhere else. I never got too attached. I never had a girlfriend in the town because I didn't want to be one of those people who had children young and got stuck. Most days, after school, I walked the few blocks from her house to Bunche Branch Library at the corner of Fourth and Willow streets. It was my personal portal to New York, the Kremlin, or wherever Toni Morrison, Maya Angelou, or the Hardy Boys would take me.

I jumped out of the car when my parents dropped me off at LSU and was at home immediately. With all the new people and the wide-open spaces, the sprawling campus was everything that Franklin wasn't: a daily intellectual adventure. I traveled the two hours home when prodded to do so or on holidays. After I graduated, I would visit four or five times a year to see my people, mainly my parents and my grandmother.

When Daisy Mae was diagnosed with cancer of the ovaries in July 2006, those trips acquired a new sense of urgency. My grandmother asked God why he'd given her the disease she had long dreaded. She suspected the answer lay in the foods she'd eaten, so she started juicing, tediously grinding up and drinking carrots, spinach, and apples. She prayed for a miracle and wondered when she would die. We encouraged her to focus on life. Dying, we told her, would take care of itself.

Her mind remained sharp, and she followed the 2008 election closely. Like most African Americans, my grandmother considered the nation's forty-third president a clown. Louisiana and the Deep South as a whole make up the most reliably Republican voting bloc in America, with most whites taking a dim view of the Democratic Party's stance on such issues as affirmative action, gun control, and the rights of states to determine their own course without interference from the federal government. These issues have remained essentially unchanged since the post–Civil War Reconstruction era, and it's no surprise that blacks see things quite differently. In St. Mary Parish, where my family has lived for generations, snug against the Gulf of Mexico, whites and blacks work side by side and clamor for good-paying union jobs at carbon-black plants, in the shipyards, and on oil rigs. But like the rest of the nation, they go their separate ways when they socialize, worship, and vote for governors and presidents.

"George Bush is a fool," Daisy Mae told me, spitting the name like it was rancid. "He looks crazy."

"That's the president of the United States. George *W*.," I said, egging her on.

"The one that got us in this mess we in now," she said.

"He said he was going to smoke 'em out, get 'em running," I said theatrically.

"I hope they smoke him out first," she said. "Look at those poor people, no legs, no arms, can't do a thing for themselves, or for their family. A lot of people say he's trying to get revenge for whatever happened to his daddy. Whoever gets in there next is going to have to clean up the mess he made."

At the time, in March 2007, she didn't think Barack Obama had a chance, nor did I. Within months, his African name would come easily and often to her lips. She would become familiar with his policies. She would pray for him, even though she could hardly recognize the world he spoke about, a world in which white youth by the thousands shouted, "Race doesn't matter." It had always mattered in Daisy Mae's world. Barack Obama was not black like her. She couldn't imagine his Indonesian childhood or the Kenyan village of his father. But she understood quickly that he was black enough for some whites to want to kill, black enough for her to see her own children in him, and black enough, surely, to be proud of.

For most of Daisy Mae's life, free expression was not an option. On the plantation, everyone understood the rules: white people talked, black people did what they were told.

Alice C Plantation was named for Alice Calder, the wife of the man who once owned the property and the black slaves who worked in its fields. The main plantation, or Big House, is an 1850s Greek Revival–style structure with a grand foyer and august columns.[1] At the rear is a sweeping lawn that rolls right up to Bayou Teche. Stately oaks, dripping with moss, oaks that shaded my grandmother, my mother, and me as we each played under them as children. We all hid from the sun under those trees, ran up those steps, and rolled in that dirt, oblivious to all that had gone on before.

This is the Deep South, its principal cleavage that between black labor and white wealth. In 1860, St. Mary Parish was home to 13,057 slaves, more than just about any other parish in the state.[2] My grandmother was born there on November 22, 1929. There are no records of her birth, but she knows that to be her birthday because a family friend remembered that her own daughter had been born the same day. When she was two months old, my grandmother was given away by her mother, who worked for a white family that was moving to New Orleans and forbade the young woman to take the child along.

Daisy Mae ended up with Willis "Papa" Jones and his wife, Ma Bertha, who died when my grandmother was five. Ma Bertha was a faint memory for my grandmother, but Papa's second wife, Kizzie, remained a source of raw contempt more than a half century later.

"She was an old devil," Daisy Mae said of her stepmother. "That old girl was mean. She never had any children of her own. I was just something that if she felt like she wanted to beat on, she did it. Papa didn't know about all of that. I never told him. I don't blame him. He was a good old soul." Papa's house was "down the quarters," in the vernacular passed down from slavery, referring to the original slave quarters. Their house had two rooms, a bedroom and a catchall room where Daisy Mae slept on a sofa bed and the family ate its meals and socialized. The black farmworkers—like Papa, my great-grandfather—raised a little of everything. "Mustard greens, turnips and okra, chickens, hogs, and turkey," my grandmother said. "Most of the time, we had meat to go along with gravy and rice."

Big families were the norm. Schoolchildren walked an hour each way to attend school in Franklin, the closest town. My grandmother wanted to be a nurse but quit school in the eighth grade to help out on the plantation. At Alice C, the sugar-grinding mill churned nonstop October through January until it was dismantled in the 1950s. During grinding, every hand was needed to bring in the crop. Slavery might have been outlawed after the Civil War, but life on the plantation for Daisy Mae moved to the same cyclical rhythms that her ancestors had known.

On the plantation, long after slavery had ended, blacks were treated like children, with whites as their wiser guardians. Workers paid no rent or utilities. If they got sick and went to a doctor, the bill was sent to the office manager at the plantation, who took it out of their pay a little at a time. At the company store the store clerk decided when the unannounced credit limit had been reached. Discrepancies involving pay or store charges went unchallenged, and workers were not expected to know or care about politics. It was not until 1968—three years after the Voting Rights Act—that a majority of black citizens participated in a national election. But participating, for Daisy Mae, did not necessarily mean free choice.

"The overseer would say, 'There's an election coming up and this is who you're supposed to vote for,'" Daisy Mae told me.

Now, she was free, no longer a washerwoman, her body failing but her faith intact. Obama was proof, living proof, that God answers prayers and that he does not want black people to ever abandon hope, to ever surrender to despair, because in his kingdom, change is possible, and as imminent as the sunrise. In 1961, as Obama entered the world, Daisy Mae could not even imagine the five-mile journey that would take her fifteen years later from the plantation of her birth to a home that she owned. She doesn't know quite when the light turned, but by the spring of 2008, my grandmother began to dream the impossible. It changed her. Where once she took in only game shows, baseball games, and the local news, she began watching CNN, Fox, and MSNBC religiously, hoping to get her daily fix of Barack news. Where was he? What did he say?

For eight years, she had been told that the number-one threat to America was terrorism. But in her lifetime, the people who terrorized black people didn't have foreign-sounding names, and they didn't wear masks. Their dirt was done in the light because their authority was exercised with impunity. It wasn't physical abuse she feared, but being stuck, as a poor black woman with little education, on the bottom rungs of society, dominated at home and an afterthought to politicians and policy makers.

The Franklin of my grandmother's formative years was much the way Obama, in *Dreams from My Father*, described the empty plains towns that reared his grandmother, "a place where fear and lack of imagination choke your dreams so that you already know on the day that you're born just where you'll die and who it is that'll bury you."[3]

Daisy Mae could relate. "I never watched that much politics," she said. "There was always something else to do. This is the first time I have had time to watch and listen to comments, just to show these people who never did give black people that much credit. I just didn't think he would do well enough to have a chance to win this election."

She had always voted, or at least for as long as white folks allowed, but she had never felt really vested in the outcome, and with good reason—Louisiana politicians like Representative Hale Boggs, who headed the Dixiecrats, the white, southern Democrats who vehemently opposed desegregation and equal rights for black people. But during the final stretch of the 2008 campaign, she proudly wore a bright multicolored Obama T-shirt proclaiming "Change." She began rethinking race, and she marveled at the unbridled enthusiasm of Obama's youthful white supporters and his endorsement by the Kennedys. Conversations with one of her closest neighbors exposed a rift—Daisy Mae realized that her long-time neighbor was a not-so-closeted Republican, a black woman who actually felt sorry for Sarah Palin when she was criticized by the media.

Harrison Francis was born in 1906 on the nearby Oaklawn Plantation, but when he was in his teens, he found work driving trucks and running errands at Alice C. He didn't read much but was pretty good with numbers, and at the sugar mill, he blew the horn to mark the shift change. Unlike the other workers who were tied to their posts, he occasionally traveled the state on errands and was allowed to take a work truck home with him at night and on weekends. All in all, it was a pretty good job for a black man. Other blacks on the plantation took a more dim view: Uncle Tom.

He met Daisy Mae Jones when she was thirteen or fourteen years old. Anxious to get away from her stepmother's abuse, she quickly took up with this man who was twenty-three years her senior. "The condition I was in with that woman, I was ready to get out of there," she said. "I thought maybe he was the one who was supposed to take me out of the situation at home." A year later, they were married by a justice of the peace.

They moved to Houston to live with my grandfather's aunt, and Daisy Mae had envisioned a place where she would have her own room and new adventures. But this place was even more isolating than the plantation. The aunt lived in a home far from the city center and, to make ends meet, had boarders moving in and out of the house all the time.

"You'd wake up and two new people had replaced the people you'd met the day before," Daisy Mae said. "We were on top of each other. You always think the grass is greener. But when I got the letter from Papa telling me that he needed help because his wife had taken sick, I was never more excited to get back to the plantation."

Her first child, Harold James, was born in 1945, followed by the rest in quick succession: Carol Ann; my mother, Louise (Peaches); Raymond (Blackie); Michael (Weechie); Wallace (Boley); Octavia (Taye); Willie; Samuel Joseph; Harrison Jr. (June); Herman; Gerald; Darrell; and Ray Anthony, who died at birth. In the family's early years, they lived a meager existence without electricity or indoor plumbing. Water had to be fetched from a well. The children recalled that white people would stop their cars and take pictures of them all the time.

With both parents working into the late afternoon and evening, the older kids took turns skipping school to care for the younger siblings. From early on, the power relationship was clear: Daddy—even his grandchildren called him that—came and went as he pleased. Daisy Mae raised the children and kept quiet. She leaned on her two oldest daughters to help with the chores. Carol Ann was a Daddy's girl, getting him to give her special meals or win her favor with moon cookies, pig's feet, and soda. Peaches, meanwhile, stuck close to her mother. She was the only one of Daisy Mae's children never to move away.

Society was in turmoil. The landmark Supreme Court ruling in *Brown v. the Board of Education* was followed by the Montgomery bus boycott, the murder of Emmett Till, and the budding civil rights movement. Blacks' anger and frustration had reached a boiling point. Daisy Mae didn't join the protests; no one on the plantations did. They had work to do and kids to feed, and cities like Selma and Montgomery and Birmingham seemed far away from Alice C. Daisy Mae worked in the cane fields for a while, but when she saw a snake lurking in the rows of cane, it was her last day. The following morning she went looking for work in white people's houses. She took whatever pay they offered.

Daisy Mae and Daddy—his friends called him Bruh—were disciplinarians at home. They loved their children but didn't spare the rod. Tree switches and belts often left welts. For some reason, Blackie was the one who most frequently caught whippings. Once when he was young, Blackie ran from Papa instead of submitting to a whipping. Papa picked up his double-barreled shotgun and fired. He missed but sent a clear message: respect your elders and take what's coming to you.

For girls at that time, the primary goal was to marry someone who would take them away from their parents' house, where they had an inordinate share of the household duties. For fun, they jumped rope, played hopscotch, and braided tall blades of grass, adorning them with ribbons or barrettes to make dolls that they played with for hours. And all of the children worked. Boley, for instance, had part-time summer and weekend jobs in the cane fields and the salt mines. He worked as a bricklayer's apprentice and a construction worker, and after work he would go to the local segregated high school to run bleachers to get into shape. His dream was to play pro football. "If I didn't get a scholarship," he said, "I was going to the marines. I didn't want to work on the plantation. I didn't want to be a welder. I wanted to get away."

He did get away, following two brothers to the University of Arkansas at Pine Bluff. He got a scholarship and starred in football, sometimes with family members watching from the stands. But one moment from Boley's collegiate career is seared in Daisy Mae's memory. She had received a letter from the university and needed to respond. Postage was three cents at the time. She had two.

"I searched all over the house and couldn't find a penny," she said.

After that, even as the value of the penny diminished to nearly nothing, she said could never pass one without picking it up. As a result of her penny-pinching ways, she became the equivalent of the family banker, telling each of us to always put something aside and bailing out many of her children and grandchildren when they had spent beyond their means. No matter how tough times were, she always had a stocking, a coin purse, or a bank account somewhere with a little something in it.

President Lyndon B. Johnson's Great Society programs had an impact on Daisy Mae's family. The passage of minimum wage laws meant that white women who normally kept her working from early in the morning until six at night began to dismiss her hours earlier to avoid paying extra. Food stamps were a big help. Around the same time, the family moved from the brown clapboard plantation houses that all the black farmworkers lived in to a large boarding house right next to the big white plantation house, which everyone called the office. It was painted white, with an expansive porch. It had been used for seasonal workers and to dispense meals. The kitchen had two large metal sinks and an industrial stove. It had an indoor bathroom and running water in the kitchen, and had served as a gathering place for people up and down the quarters.

But before the family moved in, the plantation owners made one significant change to the house. They enclosed the porch, converted it into a bedroom, and moved the main entrance to the other side of the house. No one said so, but the message was clear: a white house and a huge porch filled with black children would've offended whites with business at the plantation. For years it was the only house on the plantation without a porch, and years later, when Daisy Mae's family bought their first home and left the plantation, the original porch was restored.

On moving day, Daddy initially refused to go. He had lived on the plantation all his adult life. When he needed an advance on his paycheck, he shuffled to the office to ask Mr. Mac for the money. As the move got closer, Mr. Mac asked him a pointed question: How much did you pay for the house? Daddy hadn't put any money into the deal, but he knew how much the house cost, and he told Mr. Mac, "Thirty thousand dollars."

Daddy was a hard drinker of cheap liquor. He smoked Pall Malls and could be assertive, even abusive, at home. But change scared him. As a boy, I wondered why he said "Yes, sir" and bowed his head in the presence of teenage boys not much older than me. Once, much later in life, when one of his sons introduced him to a white woman he was courting, Daddy shuffled away apologetically, afraid that someone would kill him for such an offense. In reality, he thought very much like a slave, so when his boss told him that the new house was too good for him, he told his family to make the move without him. That was in 1975. "You shouldn't have told him anything," Boley scolded his father. "He didn't pay a penny on it." When the old house was emptied, Daddy went along with the last load.

Two years earlier, the family had hit the lottery, or at least it felt like it at the time. My uncle Boley, an all-American receiver in college, had been selected in the fifth round of the National Football League draft by the Buffalo Bills. Weeks before the draft, on January 5, 1973, the *Franklin Banner* ran an article that filled an entire inside sports page. The headline read: "The Francis Family—An Athletic Legend." On the page were nine of the ten boys, seven of them wearing letter jackets from high school or college. Harold, the oldest, had been an all-American in track at the University of Arkansas—Pine Bluff for four years. He had broken the National Association of Intercollegiate Athletics record in the 440-yard dash and was the sixth-best quarter-miler in the world in 1968.[4] At the Olympic trials, Harold ran his best time ever, but failed to make the team.

In the middle of the newspaper photo was a proud but unsmiling Harrison Francis Sr., standing tall and lean next to his boys. "There was no football around for me when I a kid," he told the newspaper. "I did play baseball, and I guess ever since then I wanted my kids to participate in athletics. I pushed them hard, but I believe they are glad of it."[5]

At the time, Daddy was still on the plantation, rising early to drink black coffee next to the gas heater with white-hot bricks. He was responsible for keeping up the yard, and he would take us with him to tidy up around the office next door, which never seemed dirty when he took me along. But all around him, the world was changing. Several of his sons had gotten athletic scholarships to college. Blackie had gotten married. Carol Ann was overseas in England with her husband, a local boy. Now Boley was moving the remaining family members off the plantation and into town. He would play nine years in the NFL, for the Buffalo Bills alongside O. J. Simpson and later for the Atlanta Falcons. During his rookie year, he led the league in kickoff-return yardage and ran two back for touchdowns.

His first contract was for $35,500 over two years, with a $6,000 bonus. One thousand went for a down payment on a bright red Toyota Celica, $3,700 to purchase a lot next to Park Avenue High School, where he planned to build his parents a new home. Instead, more than a year later, he put $6,000 down on a $30,000 home that he bought from his former high school football coach. It was the first home anyone in the family owned. Daddy was proud but didn't like that his son had taken to giving him advice. On one weekend trip home, Boley told his father, "You have to stop that drinking. You been wrecking cars. Slow down on that drinking." This was the same son who had ruined two cars, one in a car accident, the other by driving twenty miles to Jeanerette in low gear. Daddy nodded, pretending to agree. No sooner had his professional-football-playing son pulled away than he grumbled to the other children: "Goddamn boy come here telling me what to do. Think he some kinda goddamn Philadelphia lawyer." Daddy kept drinking, and running into things, for another decade.

"Poor Bruh," Daisy Mae said. "He never got out of that slave mentality."

But to the family, he was no caricature. Later in life, he would take the grandchildren fishing and hunting on Saturday morning, pointing out things to avoid, like snakes. He was a binge drinker on weekends but a breadwinner who rarely drank during the workweek. He never missed work, and his bosses trusted him more than they did the field hands. "He never drove tractors," Daisy Mae said. "He never worked in the fields. There were a lot of people who would have liked to have had that job. But for whatever reason, he got the job. I don't know how he got the job. It was a good job. They trusted him. He did whatever they told him to do."

. . .

Daisy Mae could justifiably have complained about the way my grandfather treated her. Daddy rooted for the Dodgers, and my grandmother rooted for the Atlanta Braves. He took particular glee when the Dodgers beat the Braves. It's unclear whether his love was a nod to Branch Rickey's decision to bring Jackie Robinson into the fold or just another petty dig at his wife. But two decades after his death, she took a more compassionate view. His bedroom, across the hall from hers, remained much as it was when he died. It was the only one with an attached bathroom, but she never moved into it. Their relationship was never all it could or should have been. They talked at, not to, each other, about the children and about money.

"I'd get so angry," she said. "I'd be sitting there counting on my fingers and he'd come up with the answer. He worked it out from the top of his head and I would get angry. I think about the old boy all the time. I think that I could have helped him through what he was going through. But I didn't know how. There were things we should have talked about. You're supposed to be able to talk."

The move from the farm to town was a life changer for Daisy Mae.

"It was great," she said. "It was a joy. The one thing I appreciated about that was you could have hot water. Before, you had to heat up your water. It was a different way of life."

She was no longer isolated on the farm. She still didn't drive, but now she could walk places. One of those places, just across the street, was Willow Street Elementary, the former Negro school she had attended as a child. She was hired as a cook. Her boss was a black woman. "I never dreamed of that," she said.

White people in town were jealous of her house with the soaring picture window. A white woman who had once hired her to clean her house was shopping in St. Mary's Hardware Store, on Main Street, on the day Daisy Mae went in to buy a new vacuum cleaner. It cost ninety dollars. She paid cash. The woman, who had never telephoned her before, called shortly afterward. "She asked if I knew anyone who could clean her house," Daisy Mae said. "She said, 'You're probably too busy with your new house.' I told her yes I was and that I didn't know anyone. She wanted to put me in my place."

Daisy Mae was no longer a washerwoman. She could pull in a hundred dollars on the days she baked sweet potato and apple pies. Daddy still worked on the farm, doing less and less but still collecting his paycheck every two weeks. They still needed the money to pay the mortgage of $234.34 a month. The plantation owners continued to pay Daddy years after he had stopped going to work. But when he died in 1986 of prostate cancer, Daisy Mae was on her own.

Her life had been put nearly on hold as Daddy languished in bed, shriveling into nothing in his back room. Once he was gone, she traveled more, visiting children and grandchildren all over the country, including a trip to Hawaii to visit her granddaughter Rhonda and Rhonda's husband, Fred. It was a bittersweet trip. She and Rhonda's mother, Carol Ann, had planned the trip to celebrate a new addition to the family. The baby died at birth. Both mother and grandmother knew Rhonda's pain, as each of them had lost a child at birth.

For Daisy Mae's seventieth birthday, family members came from all over the country for a surprise party at the Broussard-Harris Recreation Center in Franklin. It had been named for two young black boys who drowned in 1972 while swimming in the bayou. They had gone there because the recreation center with a pool—the white rec as it is still known—didn't allow black children to swim there. But on November 22, 1999, the place was decked out for a party. There were balloons, white tablecloths, and a deejay. Her children and grandchildren gave her money, delivered tributes, danced, and recited poetry in her honor. She cried, posed for pictures, and cried some more. "I had never had a birthday party before. I didn't think that would ever happen to me. I just remember all the family, all the food, everything that was done. I enjoyed every bit of it."

Daisy Mae was an elder, a deaconess, at Triumph Baptist Church. People would flock when she arrived to take her seat, stage right, front row, one pew in front of the pastor's wife. She was a member of the pastor's aid society and helped to cook dinners for funerals and celebrations. Her favorite pastor for many years was Reverend Moore, but in 1990, just as the prayer service was about to begin one Wednesday night, his estranged wife shot him in the head as he exited the pastor's study. He died in the hallway. Church members were traumatized.

By the fall of 2008, Daisy Mae was thinking often of her own mortality. As always, her thoughts returned to the sacrifice of Jesus, who spilled his own blood to wipe away her sins. It had become difficult to rise in the morning. Her right side, where the bulk of the tumor was located, ached. The tips of her fingers and toes felt like they'd been stuck with needles. Her right ankle was chronically swollen. Still, she would put on black dress shoes, stockings, a stylish grayish white suit with an ankle-length skirt, and a shiny brown silk hat. When we arrived just before eight in the morning, the church was nearly empty. The organist was setting up, the deacons huddled in the back. She hummed and nodded her head to one of the first songs highlighting the trials of a Christian, who, through good and bad days, remains steadfast in his beliefs, unwilling to complain.

"Thank you, Jesus," she said, nodding her head.

It was pastor appreciation day, and the pastor, Clarence Stewart, was about the same age as her eldest boy. She loved him like a son, but at the moment, she was at odds with him. He was leading the charge to build a new sanctuary, and my grandmother and several older members felt it unnecessary. The guest preacher that day might have been talking to her.

"Church members going one way," the guest preacher said, "Pastor going another. That's disobedience. That won't be tolerated. The pastor is the overseer of the flock."

She had dutifully done what she was told for so long that now Daisy Mae had become a bit of a maverick. This "overseer" talk was the language of the plantation, of masters and slaves. She had always been more of a peacemaker than a rabble-rouser, but in the sunset of her life, her tongue loosened to speak. And later she confided that she doesn't like it when people—authority figure or not—don't tell the truth. She didn't like it when people got up at Daddy's funeral and talked about how nice he was. We loved him, but he was just as likely to curse you out as look at you. She didn't like it when George Bush told lies. And she didn't like being bullied from the pulpit into thinking a certain way. That's why she was so enthralled by Obama's promise of change and hope. She had become resigned to the reality that her days on earth were numbered, that perhaps she wouldn't survive another year. She gave away things that she treasured most, including a blue and white ceramic bowl that belonged to Papa. It now sits atop a cabinet in my kitchen.

"When I first discovered that I had cancer, I was amazed at myself," she said. "I have always been afraid of cancer. Oh, yeah, I was upset at first. But I don't worry about this because it's there. Worry is not going to remove it. And when the time comes that I got to, well hey, I gotta go."

It's not that she wanted to die. But she had an abiding hope that she would go to heaven, and that her family would prosper after she was gone. Obama represents part of that hope. With his victory, her life has come full circle. Her life embodied his message. She understood that lives and countries can be transformed over time and with determination. As a little girl with a lazy left eye, she was made to feel like a nobody by her peers. Her dreams of becoming a nurse were doused by the reality of an early marriage, children, and piles of ironing for white people. But in her later years, she had a seat in the front pew at church. She flew first-class in airplanes. Her thirteen children all have owned homes. Her children and grandchildren—her blood—work in jobs that take them all over the world. Even those who've faltered, she once said, have had opportunity.

Daisy Mae was most thankful that she was not alone. Peaches, my mother, picked her up every evening and took her to our home five miles away. She would eat dinner there every night, sleep there, and then spend the daylight hours in her own home, receiving visitors and taking phone calls. She was no longer a lonely plantation girl. When those in authority spoke, she no longer had to submit. Her pastor thought they needed a new church. She wasn't so sure. Her president said the Iraq War was a good and necessary thing. She vehemently disagreed. When either of them spoke a truth that wasn't her truth, she would call them on it. Obama said a change was going to come. For her it already had.

Election night, November 4, was Peaches's birthday, and about twenty relatives and friends arrived for the festivities. Applause, cheers, hugs, and tears flowed as the returns came in, and shortly after ten o'clock central time, Obama was projected to become the forty-fourth president of the United States.

The next afternoon, the headline in the *Banner-Tribune*, the one that years earlier had trumpeted her family's athletic prowess, read: "McCain favored by state voters."[6] The article did not mention that Obama would soon become the next president. There was no picture of Obama and his family, only a sidebar that said he was to begin receiving intelligence briefings. The local news program, *Teche Talk*, didn't mention Obama's victory at all the next morning.

It was a reminder to Daisy Mae that the past was still with us. A week later, Louisiana was again in the news for the wrong reason. In Bogalusa, sixty miles north of New Orleans, eight people were arrested after an Oklahoma woman was shot to death when her initiation into the Ku Klux Klan went awry. Photographs of white robes, large Confederate flags, and confiscated weapons were beamed across the airways as a stark reminder of how the South's racist and violent past was still present.

Daisy Mae couldn't get over her hometown newspaper.

"They're not admitting that he's president," she said. "It shocked me. I didn't think they were that bad. I don't know if it's racist, but they didn't mention it. If it would have been McCain, it would have been all over the front page."

She canceled her subscription to the newspaper, even though her son continued to buy single copies and bring them to her.

In February 2009, a month after the inauguration, Daisy Mae had just returned from the wedding of a granddaughter in Atlanta. Remarkably, she was still able to travel and to feed and bathe herself. She had begun wearing adult disposable underwear as a precaution, and her navel bled periodically. But her oncologist, who had long ago said there was nothing more he could do, had invited her back for return visits, marveling at the vigor with which she was living life. He had wanted to debulk—or surgically remove—as much of the tumor as he could when she was first diagnosed, but he didn't spare his grim prognosis once the chemotherapy had stopped holding the tumor at bay. Now when she visited, the doctor couldn't stop smiling, and he even called in two other oncologists to take a look at what to him seemed like a medical anomaly. But on the day of a scheduled visit in late February, she woke up in pain at her daughter's apartment in Houma, Louisiana, halfway between Franklin and New Orleans and serving as her regular pit stop for doctor visits. But instead of going to New Orleans, she went to the nearest emergency room for a steady pain.

A doctor took a look and said there was nothing to be done: the pain was the result of the cancer. All he could do was prescribe pain medication. It was a turn, family members realized, for the worse. It was the first time she hurt too much to take all of her calls. She began spending large parts of each day in bed, getting up only to use the bathroom and to eat. She took the pain pills that she'd vowed not to take. Her children decided to hire someone to sit with her every day and began regular weekend conference calls to get updates on her progress. Daisy Mae got on the phone each week to give updates and listen to her thirteen children clown around like they did when they were all under a single roof. "Is Blackie on the line? What about Taye? Now don't y'all start all that joking around already. Is anybody coming to visit this weekend?"

"It felt like we were all in the same place," she said of the calls, looking forward to them and commenting when a week or two went by without one. Even when she wasn't feeling well enough to talk, she popped on to say hello and tell everyone she loved them. Peaches also stopped taking Daisy Mae home to her house each night. As they had done when she was first diagnosed, Peaches started living with her again, even though her husband—my father—has heart problems, diabetes, and liver disease. Weechie stayed with Daisy Mae each afternoon while my mother went home after work to cook and relax for a couple of hours.

One afternoon, when Peaches was at work, Daisy Mae fell asleep in the tub. She woke up disoriented, with water all around her, and immediately yelled, "Peaches! Peaches!" A granddaughter who had come to stay for a few days came running to calm her. At that moment mother and children officially switched places—the protector of her brood for nearly eight decades was now in their hands.

On good days and evenings they continued their campaign routine of watching the news. All around Franklin, McCain/Palin signs still dotted yards. But most of the world, like Daisy Mae, had settled in to the reality that Obama was president. "Everywhere you look," she said, "Obama, Obama, Obama." But more important, each day brought some new, or at least more pronounced, sign of her ailment: her fingers felt like there were pins sticking in them, her left side was sore all the time, her stomach protruded now as the unwelcome guest pushed against her organs. She felt full all the time. She felt constipated. She could still laugh, but her mind, now, was stayed on Jesus, an oft-repeated phrase in the Baptist church and gospel songs. One Sunday, when she was too sick to go to church, she gathered everyone for a small service in her room. After a Bible reading, she sang this old spiritual, in the drawn-out way of the Baptist Church:

> Jesus, keep me near the cross;
> There a precious fountain,
> Free to all, a healing stream,
> Flows from Calvary's mountain.
>
> In the cross, in the cross,
> Be my glory ever,
> Till my raptured soul shall find
> Rest beyond the river.

A steady stream of children and grandchildren began to make what felt like final trips home. But Daisy Mae's mind remained sharp as she counseled one grandson to get his anger problem in check and work things out with his estranged wife. She lamented that two other grandsons continued having babies without, she felt, considering what it took to raise such large broods these days. A daughter and a granddaughter were supposedly dieting, but she noted, "I looked every whichaway and I can't see where they lost weight." She had long lacked a filter for her words, but her directness grew as she aged. She spoke without malice, saying exactly what she saw. "I could never look down on anybody," Daisy Mae said, her body racked with pain, stomach bloated with a cancerous growth and fluid buildup. "My mother gave me away. I had a husband who was there when he was there and when he wasn't, well, he wasn't. I had low self-esteem. When somebody said something about me, I would cry."

But her days of crying over idle talk had ended. Her children were still alive, none of them in jail. She owned her own home. She was debt-free and kept her taxes paid. She marveled that in all her years as a daughter, wife, and mother, she never thought she'd have days when she had no one to cook and clean for and didn't have to feel guilty about it. She spent days lazing in her front yard, looking at the flowers or, when the sun was scorching or rain pouring, sitting in the shade of her screened back porch. She had done all she could. Even her funeral, when the time came for that, was paid for. She had never wanted to be a burden. And, to boot, a black man had been elected president in her lifetime. Lying in her bed in the wee hours one morning, unable to sleep, she thought back through her good days and her bad days and concluded confidently, "I had a good life. I'm satisfied."

| 2 |

Made in America

Union Organizing in Chicago

I asked her if there were black people in the land where she came from. She burst out laughing: Oh, Fortin, you ask such questions! I was astonished: if there were no black people in the land then who did all the heavy work?

—MOZAMBICAN WRITER MIA COUTA, FROM THE SHORT STORY
THE RUSSIAN PRINCESS"

Shorty!"
Ricky Maclin bellowed at the secretary in a stairwell at Republic Windows and Doors, trying to get her attention. She was one of the few black temps in the secretarial pool; he was vice president of the union local, the lone black on its executive board. They were both upbeat, jovial personalities and usually got along like a house afire. Just a week or so earlier, the two spotted each other in the cafeteria on the morning following Election Day and giddily broke out in an impromptu two-step, celebrating, cheek-by-jowl, Barack Obama's unprecedented triumph. More than once, Shorty had even shared with Ricky the contents of a memo that

37

she'd come across, or a conversation she'd overheard, when the plant's management was dragging its feet or flat-out lying to the union about some issue or another.

But on this morning, the week before Thanksgiving, as the pair walked past each other on the stairs, Ricky's greeting went unacknowledged. So preoccupied was the diminutive secretary that she had barely even lifted her gaze from the ground.

"Shorty!" Ricky repeated, almost shouting this time.

"Hunh?" she said, as if she had dozed off for a moment but was now coming to.

"What is wrong with you?"

"Nothing."

"*Something* is going on," he said. "You didn't get the ax, did you?"

"No," she answered. "But Ricky, I don't know if I'm going to make it through the day. When we got into work this morning, everything was gone: our desks, our computers, the file cabinets. We didn't even have chairs to sit on. We had to go to the cafeteria, grab some folding chairs and carry them upstairs just so we'd have a place to sit."

The equipment had begun disappearing from the factory on Chicago's North Side just days before Halloween. At first, it was big-ticket stuff: a punch press, the big industrial saws that cut fiberglass, the machines that spat out the plastic moldings for the windows, another that wrapped them for shipping, and yet another that cleaned hard-to-reach corners. Management was mum, but the disappearances were hardly a mystery. That same month, the company let go thirty workers; in November, another fifteen.

With the first shift buzzing on the morning after machines first turned up missing, Ricky, an engraver, decided to stick around after quitting time to compare notes with Armando Robles, a machinist who worked second shift and is president of Local 1110 for the United Electrical Radio and Machine Workers of America, or the UE, as everyone calls it. The two men decided to assign two workers from each shift to keep an eye out for anything suspicious and, when possible, to follow any equipment removed from the plant, which sits on an island that juts into the Chicago River like a floe of ice.

What they reported back was that U-Haul trucks were appearing at the loading dock in the dead of night, loading, leaving, and then unloading their payload onto trailers parked near railroad tracks on the city's South Side. Labels provided a clue to where the inventory was headed: Red Oak, Iowa, where Republic's principal owner had another factory that made replacement windows for industrial buildings. All 102 employees there were nonunion.

"We *had* to go detective on them," Ricky would say later, "because you see everyone's job is tied to those machines. When the machines leave, sooner or later, we leave."

Which is why, when the secretary finished telling Ricky that their offices had been cleaned out the night before, he asked the obvious question: "Did you say anything to the bosses about it?"

Shorty's answer was muffled, her words punctuated with a grimace, as if to say to Ricky he should know better. She wanted to shout but did not dare: "Hell *no*, we didn't say nothing, Ricky. We don't have a union like y'all do."

Ricky started to respond but thought better of it. His first impulse, when it came to dealing with management, was to slug it out, because after seven years on the job, he'd learned that confrontation was the only language they understood. But Shorty was right, and he knew it. Capitalism is a declaration of war, work an act of violence—these are articles of Ricky's faith—and without a union to represent them, the secretaries were unarmed, defenseless, voiceless. You don't need to read *Das Kapital* or Chairman Mao's *Little Red Book* to know that. Ricky knew it because he was fifty-four years old and punched a time clock every weekday at six in the morning and again at two in the afternoon, all for fourteen measly dollars an hour and benefits, which meant he was doing a damn sight better than most black men who lived on Chicago's South Side. Even with the union's backing, working for hourly wages in America was akin to getting smacked in the mouth five days a week. Joining the union just meant that the boss couldn't sucker punch you, and he had to provide you with a clean handkerchief to wipe away the blood, and maybe, *maybe*, if you had a good union, they'd even pay for the doctor to mend your split lip.

Local 1110 was a good union, and Ricky had done as much as anyone to make it so. He enthusiastically endorsed the employees' 2004 effort to oust as their representative the corrupt, mobbed-up union that was led by pinkie-ring-wearing white boys with slicked-back hair who never seemed very interested in negotiating pay raises for Republic's Latino and black workers or coaxing the company to increase their contributions to the health insurance plan but always seemed to have their hands in the employees' pension fund. The Central States Joint Board was so chummy with Republic's management, in fact, that they once joined the bosses in exhorting striking workers to return to their jobs. And it was the company's owner who led the campaign—complete with company picnics, ice-cream socials, and a remodeled cafeteria—against the workers' ultimately successful campaign to decertify the union and replace it with the progressive UE, which had a long-standing reputation for transparency and aggressively representing workers of color, as well as women.

In his first three years on the job, Ricky hadn't done much for the union other than pay his dues and vote. In this regard Ricky was like virtually every other black worker at Republic who had, it's fair to say, a certain ambivalence about organized labor. Across the nation, polls consistently indicate that none of America's tribes is more supportive of trade unions than blacks[1], and here in Chicago, the birthplace of the nation's organized labor movement, the struggle of the Brotherhood of Sleeping Car Porters, civil service employees, meatpackers, steelworkers, and autoworkers to create a local black middle class is the stuff of legend, even today. In terms of career moves, getting hired at the Post Office is as good as it gets for wide swaths of the black community. As recently as the early eighties, it wasn't uncommon to see black UAW men wear their washed and pressed Ford or GM uniforms to the speakeasy on Saturday night or church service on Sunday, to announce to the single ladies, and maybe a few married ones, that they were a good catch. And the first lady's father, Fraser Robinson, had a good job as a city pump operator, and you'd be hard-pressed to find a black Chicagoan who doesn't believe that the American Federation of State, County and Municipal Employees Council 31 didn't put at least one of the rungs on that ladder used by Michelle Obama (née Robinson) to climb from a one-bedroom apartment on the South Side to Harvard Law School to the White House.

"You ask any organizer what they think when they go to a job site for the first time and they see mostly black people working there," said James Thindwa, the executive director for the Chicago chapter of Jobs with Justice, a coalition of labor unions and community activists, "and they will tell you that they breathe a big sigh of relief because they know it's going to be an easy sell. The resistance—and any union organizer will tell you this—almost always comes from the white workers."

To prove the point, Thindwa pointed to the example of the world's largest slaughterhouse, Smithfield Packing Company in North Carolina, which unionized in December of 2008 after a nearly twenty-year campaign by management to sway company-wide elections in their favor through the use of firings, the threat of mass layoffs, and other propaganda. Then, in the midst of another union drive in 2006, the plant's management notified more than five hundred workers that their names and Social Security numbers didn't match, and several weeks later, federal immigration agents raided the plant, arresting twenty-one Latino workers with the

41

intention of deporting them. This triggered an exodus of Hispanic workers—many of them illegal Mexican immigrants—from the Smithfield plant. Virtually overnight, the number of Latino workers dropped from about twenty-three hundred to one thousand. In most cases, African Americans were hired to replace them. When the ballots were counted two weeks before Christmas, Smithfield had approved the union by a vote of 2,041 to 1,879.[2]

Had Ricky had a vote at Smithfield, he most surely would've voted in the affirmative, he says. He had toiled away on someone else's farm or in someone else's factory or warehouse long enough to know that the boss, *any* boss, generally speaking, didn't give two shits about workers, and especially a black worker. Of course, Ricky had lived in Chicago long enough to know that neither did the typical blue-collar building and construction trade unions in the city, until election time, when they wanted to crank up the Daley machine for some Irish or Italian or Polish candidate campaigning for alderman or mayor or state representative. But once the politicians were in office, they could never seem to fix the lightbulb at the Forty-seventh Street El, and it was the hard hats from ethnic enclaves like Bridgeport who made the decision to move the union's apprenticeship training programs from Chicago's South Side to the faraway suburb of Elk Grove, while maintaining that the only way to join the union is to graduate from their training program. And it was many of the same union men who voted Republican rather than cast a ballot for the city's first black mayor, Harold Washington, the staunchly pro-union Democratic nominee. How's that for proletariat solidarity?

Hell, a few unions had even joined Old Man Daley's son, Mayor Richard M. Daley, in opposing proposals out of City Hall requiring big-box retailers like Wal-Mart and Target to pay their workers a living wage, despite public opinion polls that showed that a clear majority of Chicagoans—and nine of ten blacks in the city—backed the legislation. Angered at the aldermen who voted against the bill, some of the more progressive city unions—most notably AFSCME and the Service Employees International Union—spent $3 million to unseat seven aldermen who had sided with Daley.[3] Endorsed by the largely black and Latino rank and file from those unions, who knocked on doors, distributed fliers, and raised cash, all seven pro-union candidates won their campaigns. Three of the aldermen vanquished for their opposition to the big-box ordinance were black, including Dorothy Tillman, who was particularly blunt, telling an audience that the proposal would have crushed job opportunities for African Americans who badly needed the work, and that the unions didn't care one way or the other what happened to blacks, unemployed or otherwise, as long as they could keep collecting dues and rifling through pensions to pay their salaries. When Wal-Mart and other retailers had taken their jobs elsewhere, it would be black folks who would be left holding the bag, she said.

"Dorothy Tillman and [those] other aldermen, they needed to go," said Ricky. He was not involved in the effort to unseat the aldermen, but he supported it and voted for the union-backed candidate who ran against the alderman who represented his ward. In a country where workers haven't seen a pay hike since the Nixon administration, he says, how in God's name does a labor union oppose a pay raise for workers, any workers, particularly one that squeezes it, in dribs and drabs, from some of the wealthiest corporations in the country?

And so, unfortunately, most of the more than three dozen blacks who worked at Republic saw the Central States Joint Board's mishandling of their affairs as quite typical of how things went down in the city, rather than some sort of aberration. And yet, change was in the air, and it was blowing in from the South. A wave of Latino workers who began pouring into Chicago from the Mexican countryside in the mid-nineties had transformed Republic. By the winter of 2008, nearly 200 of the plant's 240 workers were Latino, and many of them, like Armando, had been radicalized by the peasant and workers' movements back home for land and wages.

Impressed with their ferocity and with the UE's responsiveness to the local's black and brown rank and file, Ricky decided he didn't want to sit on the sidelines anymore and allow others to do battle for him, especially when there was so much at stake. He ran for steward.

There was initially some tension between the plant's black workers and the Mexican workers, many of whom did not speak English fluently. Some black employees fully expected that Local 1110 and its newly elected Latino leadership would merely do as the previous union had done, which is to ignore them, and, indeed, management tried to manipulate this friction by, among other things, deploying most of the black men who worked at Republic to the shipping department, which was physically demanding and backbreaking work. Conversely, many of the Latino workers openly wondered why some of the black workers seemed so ground down, so demoralized, that they refused to do battle for what was rightfully theirs.

Ricky was the bridge between the two camps. When the first contract between the UE and Republic included a "bumping" clause, which required that employees with the most seniority had first dibs on all overtime hours, many black workers—typically the low men on the totem pole in terms of years on the job—complained to Ricky that they were drawing the short stick more often than not. And because they had less seniority, blacks were hardest hit by layoffs, and a few threatened to report their illegal immigrant coworkers to Homeland Security on their way out the door, Ricky said. Ricky told them that he understood how they felt, but explained that seniority was a pillar on which organized labor was built to stamp out favoritism and nepotism. As he put it, they would appreciate it when they had a few more years on the job and their seniority prevented bosses from bypassing them for overtime in favor of their pets with less seniority.

Similarly, some of the immigrant workers were a bit leery as well. Before he ran for steward, Ricky had befriended a Mexican worker named Polo, and the two men had, for a while, become thick as thieves, going for drinks after work and watching Bears games together on the weekends. Then, almost as quickly, they had a falling out. Still, when Polo needed someone to represent him at a grievance hearing over some back pay he was owed, he turned to his estranged friend.

"I tore them a new asshole," Ricky said. "I mean I went in guns blazing. I think even Polo was surprised, but my feeling was that whatever disagreements we had was personal. This was business. And when it comes to business, I'm in it to win it." Polo won his grievance and sang the lone black steward's praises to his Latino coworkers. In no time at all, many of the plant's Latino workers were asking for Ricky to represent them in their disputes with management, and they remembered that when Ricky ran for vice president of the local. "Black or brown," he said, "it didn't matter. We were all getting the shit kicked out of us. I told everybody: 'Look, we need to look at what we have in common more than what divides us.' Just like Obama, I knew I couldn't win with just the black vote so I had to let everybody know that I had their back."

Months after he became Republic's majority owner in 2007, Richard Gillman initiated round after round of layoffs, and complained to one of his bosses that one of the union reps at the bargaining table was a thorn in his negotiators' side. "Who's the little skinny black dude at the table?" he asked his manager. "He talks more shit."

"That," the manager responded, "would be Slick Rick."

Ricky's given name is Melvin, but everyone calls him Ricky or some variation thereof. He has a bantamweight's physique, features that are delicate, almost prim: a neat, thin goatee, close-cropped hair impossibly barren of gray. He was raised mostly on a farm in Mason, Tennessee, just outside Memphis, where his grandfather worked as a sharecropper all his life, until the day he died. He was poor and black and had only a third-grade education, but he looked white people in the eye when he spoke to them, didn't apologize if he didn't do anything wrong, didn't smile if he wasn't happy, and stood his ground when the white landowner tried to cheat him out of his wages or when the local elections board tried to deny him his vote. If he was ever afraid, Ricky never heard him say it.

"Granddaddy used to always tell me: look, you don't always win when you fight, but if you don't fight you are guaranteed to lose."

And so Ricky fought. When he was in eighth grade, he got into a fight with a kid named Jesse, who towered over him. "He whupped me Monday. Tuesday morning I was right back in his face." Ricky moved to Chicago to live with his mother while he attended high school, and in the late sixties he helped organize student demonstrations and sit-ins at Jones High School to protest the absence of any kind of African American cultural curriculum. The students won that battle. Later he ran with a street gang and earned a reputation for being hard as nails, the first one to swing in combat, and always taking aim at the other side's biggest guy. Once, in the late seventies, Chicago police officers were questioning Ricky about a convenience store robbery. Ricky had an idea who was responsible, but no one had been hurt in the robbery, and he refused to give the two white police officers a name. Frustrated, one of them hit the unsuspecting Ricky in the back of the head—to this day Rick is not sure with what, but if he had to guess, he would say it was the Chicago Yellow Pages. The blow left him unconscious for hours and hospitalized for a day.

But he never gave them a name.

46

"My grandfather showed me what it means to be a man," Ricky said. "I tell people all the time: I don't even know what it *means* to fight a motherfucka my size."

In the days following Election Day, the workers became almost certain that management would try to close down the factory without paying the employees all they were owed. Not surprisingly, Ricky was the first of the local's seven officers to give the thumbs-up to Armando's proposal to occupy the factory if that happened. By this time, the union was requesting documents to show the workers where the missing equipment was going. Management stuttered in response. "We're going through a rough patch and selling off some equipment to make payroll," one of the managers said to Armando and Ricky during a meeting. They didn't buy it for a second.

During an aimless drive along Lakeshore Drive, Armando spoke with the UE's top organizer in Chicago, Mark Meinster, about what options were available to the local, and it was Meinster who first proposed the idea of an old-school sit-in, like the wildcat strikes in the thirties that the UAW used to prevail over General Motors. Armando wasn't sure. Would Republic's management just call the police and have them arrested for criminal trespassing? What if they just ignored the workers? Could a bunch of working-class Mexican immigrants and blacks win any kind of popular support, with seemingly a third of the country out of work already, another third breathlessly excited about Obama's inauguration, and yet another third so staunchly conservative that the workers' plight would be cause for celebration, if anything? Meinster said occupying the factory was fraught with risk, but it was a big, bold idea, and if ever there had been a situation that required something radical, outsized, different, well, this was it.

Armando decided to take the idea to his executive board just days after Election Day in a meeting at the UE's Chicago union hall. In the second-floor conference room, Armando laid out the idea but said he didn't think it was even worth the attempt if they weren't certain they could get at least forty workers to participate in the sit-in. Could they get that many to sign on? Armando wanted to know. They went down the list of workers, ticking off the names of Latinos who might not be able to risk a trespassing charge because they were illegal aliens, and who, without proper documents to work, risked both jail and deportation.

A woman named Julia chimed in. She was not one of the officers and, in fact, had been laid off just a few weeks earlier. She had come to the union meeting to discuss her grievance about unpaid vacation time with the local's executive members. When Armando had ended the general meeting and moved the meeting upstairs so that the officers could strategize before making a proposal to the entire rank and file, Julia, who was from Mexico, simply tagged along.

As they spoke of the considerable risks of occupying the plant, Julia gave an impassioned speech in favor of the sit-in. Management, she said, thought they could do whatever they wanted to a group of poor "spics and spooks" and suffer no consequence. "The darker-skinned people had taken too much already off of these sons of bitches," she said, and they were obliged to make a stand, not just for themselves, but for their ancestors and their children, to draw a line in the sand and say *"not one inch further."*

Ricky had, by this time, already endorsed the idea of occupying the factory, but Julia's impassioned speech left him even more convinced it was the right thing to do. He was ready to go right then and there. After Local 1110's board members had gone down the list of Republic's Latino employees and were convinced that they could satisfy their minimum requirements to stage a sit-in, Ricky raised his hand to speak.

"A lot of the brothers might be hesitant to do this because you know, quite a few of them might be on probation or parole and they might not want to risk getting arrested again, even for something minor like trespassing," he said.

One of the officers asked Ricky: Did he think they could count on enough support from the blacks to give their plan at least a shot at success? Ricky answered: "Let me work on them." Armando pressed the issue. For their plan to work, he said, they would need at least half the black employees to participate as a show of solidarity. "Can we do this, Ricky?" he said.

Ricky smiled impishly and said: "*Sí. Sí se puede.*"

"It sure is good to be here with you all on this morning. You know my grandmother used to always say, 'I can only find peace in two places in the world: when I am in the house of the Lord, and when I am in the house of labor.' And I can tell you that I am just like my grandmother in that respect."

This was Letitia Taylor speaking. Everyone called her Tish. She was sixty-two, black, a former AFSCME organizer, and a member of the Coalition of Black Trade Unionists, or CBTU, which played a central role in electing Chicago's first black mayor, Harold A. Washington, in 1983. She was speaking from a dais to an audience of about fifty people assembled inside the Charles A. Hayes Labor, Cultural and Community Center in Chicago's historic Black Belt, on the city's South Side. With more African Americans than any patch of land in the country, the South Side of Chicago is the capital of black America. For much of the twentieth century, if you were an African American and wanted a good job, "there weren't no better place in America for your black ass than right heah," one elderly African American man in the audience said to a friend sitting next to him, as they chatted before the program started. The South Side ghettoes were first peopled mostly by the Irish, who'd begun moving to Chicago in the mid-nineteenth century to build the canal and work the factories and rail yards, but they left it to the blacks when they began pouring in from Mississippi, Georgia, Alabama, Tennessee, and Louisiana.

The South Side, the saying here goes, built Chicago; the North Side owns it.

It is deep winter, and a bitter wind howls hauntingly outside the converted union hall for packinghouse workers, which once had a capacity of fifteen hundred people but now holds fewer than three hundred, mirroring the decline of organized labor over the past thirty years. Chicago is where the American labor movement was born on May 1, 1886, when a bomb detonated in Haymarket Square on the city's North Side as thousands of demonstrators marched in the streets for legislation limiting the workday to eight hours. Three police officers were killed, and three trade union leaders were hanged for their murders; a fourth committed suicide in prison. The incident became an international cause célèbre that led to the May Day holiday celebrating workers' rights, observed almost everywhere in the world except for the United States.[4]

At the height of the postwar economic boom, trade unions represented nearly a third of the country's workforce; now the figure is 12 percent. The loss of manufacturing jobs has hit black workers the hardest: 55 percent of all union jobs lost in 2004 were held by blacks,[5] despite their being only 12 percent of the population nationally. Taylor is one of four panelists gathered at the Hayes Center to discuss, among other things, whether the proposed Employee Free Choice Act, which would make it easier for employees to join unions, could do for President Obama's legacy what passage of the 1935 Wagner Act did for Franklin Roosevelt. And, the mostly over-forty audience wanted, much like a congregation, simply to bear witness to their struggle and to the evolution of organized labor into an institution so integral to the African American experience that it's rivaled only by the church.

"As black people, as workers, as union men and women, we hold *these* truths to be self-evident," Tish Taylor says to the crowd. "With God and each other we can achieve anything. Alone, we will achieve nothing. Dr. King knew that at our best, we are in this together. Never forget that he put his life on the line while working on behalf of AFSCME and the striking black garbage workers in Memphis."

Since Africans and whites first made eye contact more than four hundred years ago, the matter of labor, and the question of its price, has always stood between them. In southern Africa, the country of Zambia was, for the first thirty-six years of its existence, a corporate subsidiary, wholly owned by Cecil Rhodes's mining empire,[6] its population valued as no more than depreciating assets on a balance sheet, human lives reduced to black ink in a ledger. Similarly, to Zambia's north, Congo's entire population of thirty-eight million people was owned by Belgian King Leopold II's private holding company for nearly forty years, their labor conscripted in a genocidal campaign of torture, amputations, kidnappings, rape, and murder. To save money on bullets, Leopold's mercenaries—the middle managers of their time and place—reduced overhead by using machetes to cut off the hands and feet of workers who did not meet quotas for harvesting rubber trees.[7] Across the Atlantic Ocean, Portuguese settlers imported more African slaves to Brazil's shores than were brought to any country in the Western Hemisphere, because their quite explicit nationalist ambition was to create a nation in which white men would never have to do a day's work as long as they could get someone else to do it for them, free of charge. "The Brazilian dream was to have one or two slaves whose labor could be hired out for a price high enough to free the dreamer from ever having to work," wrote the country's first post-independence leader, Pedro I, in 1836. "Begging was preferable to work. Even beggars had slaves."[8]

Here in the United States, slaves—led by women—were among the pioneers of the trade union movement, organizing plantation-wide work stoppages to bargain with their owners for a day off, or the freedom to make regular visits to friends and relatives on neighboring farms. As freed slaves and their progeny fled the South for jobs up north in the factories, slaughterhouses, and railroads, they discovered an almost feudal workplace where the boss unilaterally decided how much you were paid, how long you worked, and under what conditions. And yet their efforts to strengthen unions by joining them were thwarted again and again by white coworkers, specifically those represented by the building trades. The 1935 passage of the National Labor Relations Act, or the Wagner Act, opened the door for workers to choose their representatives on the job, tripling the number of union members within ten years, and dramatically increasing the numbers of blacks in trade unions, from one in every one hundred to twenty-five in every one hundred by the mid-seventies.[9] This happened despite provisions in the law that specifically exempted railroad workers, domestics, and farmworkers, written in as a concession to white Southern lawmakers who did not want to see their good supply of dirt-cheap labor dry up. "But, as integration led whites to abandon inner-city neighborhoods and public schools by the millions, their involvement with labor unions and their traditional political sponsor, the Democratic party, rapidly fell. Today, even as the percentage of unionized workers in the labor force has plummeted from a postwar high of 30 to 12 in 2009, the percentage of blacks, Latinos and Asians in labor unions has swollen to more than 30 percent of the total number nationwide."[10]

As a result of this history, many people of color, not surprisingly, see, in attacks on labor, if not an all-out race war, then certainly a series of racial skirmishes, with the battlefield tilted heavily in favor of the capital class. The former professional basketball player Sam Cassell said as much during the National Basketball Association's 1998 lockout of its union, when he accused management of failing to make a good-faith effort to negotiate because they viewed the Players Association as a "bunch of ghetto guys." More recently, many labor activists and organizers cite the 2006 decision by a New York State Supreme Court judge to sentence the African American president of a largely black and Latino transit workers' union to ten days in jail for leading a strike that shut the city down for three days. The strike was the union's only effective option for beating back the transit authority's demands for concessions from the union, in a year when union officials contend the transit authority had a $1 billion surplus on its books.[11]

The law throws labor leaders in jail for using the only real bargaining chip workers have—withholding their labor—but when was the last time the owner or CEO of a company went to jail after workers were injured in a mine collapse or explosion? That guy who ran that Union Carbide plant in Bhopal, India, when a dangerous gas leak in 1984 resulted in the deaths of twenty-five thousand people? He never spent a day in jail even though the courts in India ruled that he was criminally responsible.[12] And, have you ever, ever, heard of employers going to jail for forcing their employees to regularly work off the clock, or for locking workers inside the plant or warehouse in a feeble effort to prevent theft, only to have someone badly injured—or even killed—when a fire or accident occurs and no one can get out in time?

Which is not to say that organizing a union, or joining one, is an exercise in futility. Consider, as one example, the country of Sweden, where 79 percent of all workers belong to a trade union,[13] and, not coincidentally, Swedes enjoy free health care, free university education, at least five weeks of paid vacation time, virtually inexhaustible jobless benefits, the highest wages, and a narrower gap in income between the rich, the middle class, and what few poor people there are than in any other industrialized country in the world.[14] Here in the United States, that chasm yawns more widely than in the rest of the industrial world and rivals that of some developing countries.[15] Health care and higher education are anything but free, any kind of public assistance is tenuous, and employers are not legally required to pay for even one day of vacation. Unionized workers are able to cut a better deal. Across all industries, union workers in the United States earn $4.23 more per hour than nonunion

workers, according to the Bureau of Labor Statistics. Black workers earned $190 more per week than black nonunion employees,
and Latinos $220 more per week. Unionized female workers earn
11.2 percent more than nonunion female employees, and a woman
who has gone no further than high school but belongs to a union is
far more likely to have health insurance benefits and a pension than
a woman who has earned a four-year college degree but does not
belong to a union.

But blacks aren't in it merely for the money. Historically, workers of color have viewed unions not merely as a means for negotiating an extra week of vacation or a few cents more per hour (to
paraphrase the longtime UAW leader Walter Reuther), but as an
articulation of their citizenship, a vehicle for transformative, democratic change. Throughout Africa and Latin America, unions
were the engines of the liberation struggle against colonial rule
and against the unholy alliance between the U.S. government and
right-wing, anticommunist dictatorships. This partly explains why
anticommunist purges, particularly during the Reagan administration, almost always resembled some kind of race war, with wealthy,
mostly white, Nicaraguans, Colombians, Salvadorans, or South
Africans (take your pick), represented primarily by the military,
facing off against usually darker-skinned Nicaraguans, Colombians,
Salvadorans, or South Africans (take your pick), represented, in the
main, by trade unions. It was in the early years of the Reagan era
that longshoremen in California turned up the volume on democracy by refusing to unload ships carrying South African cargo.[16]

In Chicago in the 1980s, a coalition of black trade unionists,
welfare rights advocates, and clergy approached a then-little-known
African American congressman named Harold Washington to run
for mayor. Frustrated with a municipal government that hoarded
jobs and city contracts for whites and couldn't be counted on to reliably deliver to black and Latino neighborhoods even the most basic
services—such as trash collection and snow removal—the activists

turned to Washington, a gifted orator, a staunch union supporter, and a progressive whose ties to the antiwar and environmental movements demonstrated his skill at bringing together diverse constituencies. Washington had already run for mayor in 1977, but he'd been soundly defeated in the Democratic primary, and while he was flattered by the offer, he thought it a nonstarter in a city so polarized by race and so dominated by the white, ethnic Democratic machine. Thinking it would put the matter to bed, he told his suitors that he would entertain the notion only if the activists could raise $100,000 and register 100,000 new Democratic voters.[17]

Led by the CBTU and African American rank-and-file union members, Washington's supporters knocked on doors, visited churches, set up telephone banks, and twisted arms. In the end, they registered 200,000 new Democratic voters and raised the money necessary for Washington to win City Hall in a bitterly contested campaign that saw the white chairman of the Democratic Party vote for the Republican nominee rather than for Washington.

Backed by a multiracial, or "rainbow," coalition of black, Latino, and white voters, Washington brought a reformer's zeal to City Hall. One of his first acts as mayor was to repeal a puritanical law banning street musicians. He repaved roads that hadn't been touched in decades, got the garbage picked up on time, plowed snow, created a city environmental agency, and formally recognized the unions representing city employees.

For decades, unions, and especially the building trades, did business with City Hall using a wink and a nod, enabling Chicago's good ol' boys network of Irish, Italian, and Polish aldermen to collaborate with their high school classmates, friends, brothers, and cousins, while cutting blacks, Latinos, and women out of the deal. Washington, by officially acknowledging city employees' collective bargaining rights, cut them in, effectively opening the doors on the backroom deals that served as political caucuses in Chicago's political machine. The process was more transparent, and unions more accountable. In particular, the American Federation of State, County, and Municipal Employees Council 31, of which Michelle Obama's father was a member, really managed to take advantage of the new arrangement and carve out more space, higher wages, and better benefits for its rank and file.

Two key Washington supporters were labor leaders Rudy Lozano and Charles Hayes, for whom the South Side community center is named. Hayes was one of the tens of thousands of African Americans who poured into Chicago's stockyards in the years following World War II to replace whites who left for the better-paying jobs that opened up in the postwar economic boom. Hayes led an interracial faction that challenged, and ultimately replaced, the meatpackers' conservative union leadership, and eventually he rose through the ranks to become the international vice president of the United Packinghouse Workers of America, the forerunner to the United Food and Commercial Workers Union. Hayes's imprimatur on organized labor took the form of an aggressive civil rights agenda; under his leadership, the union supported Martin Luther King Jr. in the 1955 Montgomery bus boycotts and was a fundraiser for the Southern Christian Leadership Conference's voter registration efforts in the Deep South. In 1959, Hayes testified before the House Un-American Activities Committee, denouncing communism but refusing to say whether he had any dealings with the party, and in the seventies, he partnered with Jesse Jackson Sr. to start Operation Push. Hayes also supported Washington's failed 1977 mayoral campaign and was one of the leaders of the contingent who approached Washington about a 1983 run. He was instrumental in raising the money, creating phone banks, and mobilizing precinct workers to register the voters Washington needed to win, and when the Chicago Federation of Labor balked at supporting the Democratic nominee for mayor, it was Hayes who convinced them that an endorsement for a Republican mayoral candidate would be tantamount to political suicide in Chicago.[18]

Lozano was a Mexican American, a labor organizer for the International Ladies' Garment Workers' Union, and a prominent figure in Chicago's Pilsen neighborhood, the heart of the Latino community. Lozano's support was widely credited with providing Washington with his narrow margin of victory in the Democratic primary by heightening turnout among Latino voters, most of whom cast ballots for Washington. The Latino community's alliance with Washington's black political base was a harbinger for the burgeoning political relationship between the two groups in the post-NAFTA era. Polls show that African Americans are far more supportive of extending citizenship rights to Latino immigrants than non-Hispanic whites,[19] and while there is certainly some feeling of unease about competition for scarce jobs, many blacks, particularly those involved in the organized labor movement, understand that unemployment for blacks is as high in cities with very few Latino immigrants as it is in cities with very high Latino immigrants. "I don't think," said Thindwa, "that you are ever going to see any African American minutemen-like movement patrolling the Mexican border for illegal crossings."

Washington's appeal to blacks, Latinos, and progressive whites, his charisma and skill as an orator, and the against-all-odds triumph for African Americans not only inspired Jesse Jackson's Rainbow Coalition and transcendent 1984 and 1988 presidential campaigns, but also, years later, invited most comparisons with Obama's meteoric political rise. But there are fundamental differences between America then and America now, and, just as important, between the two men themselves.

Washington's success was the product of a movement in which black workers and their trade unions played a seminal role. Simply put, had there been no organized labor, there would have been no

Mayor Washington, and, during his brief reign, he governed the city accordingly, as a man with a debt to pay to his principal benefactor. He marched, politically speaking, in virtual lockstep with organized labor.

Obama marches to the beat of a different drummer. With their cash, phone banks, and get-out-the vote efforts, trade unions certainly played an important role in Obama's success, but the unions' dwindling ranks and declining significance in American public life means that Democrats—the traditional party of the working class—have divided loyalties. In the 2008 election cycle, as just one example, organized labor donated nearly $1.1 million to Democratic presidential candidates; the finance, insurance, and real estate industries together contributed almost $70 million.[20]

Looking at politics purely from the perspective of horse trading, Obama's electoral success owes relatively little to organized labor. And unlike Washington, Obama has not clearly chosen a side in the running battle between labor and capital. He has rewarded bankers' misbehavior with billions of dollars in taxpayer money and attached few strings to the purse strings. But he has not been nearly so forgiving of the auto industry's sins, doling out a relatively paltry sum of taxpayers' cash, but with many strings attached, including demands for tremendous concessions from the UAW. His administration's economic stimulus package included tax credits and other incentives for creating new, sustainable, and decent-paying "green" jobs, and during his campaign, he repeatedly professed his support for the Employee Free Choice Act, which, many trade unionists believe, could be the most transformative piece of labor legislation since the New Deal. Essentially the proposal would allow workers to join a union simply by checking a box on a card—hence its shorthand designation as the "card check bill"—and forgo the need for costly, time-consuming plant elections, which management often uses to harass, intimidate, and straight-out deceive workers into rejecting union representation. Studies have shown that one in five workers involved in union organizing drives on the job are later fired.[21] Many trade unionists believe that removing that barrier to unionization would rebuild the postwar middle class in America, because, as one activist said, "you can't offshore jobs at Wal-Mart and Home Depot."

Initially, Obama seemed intent on delivering on his campaign promise, with the appointment to his cabinet of California congresswoman Hilda Solis, a Latina and an ardent supporter of organized labor. But as big business has poured millions into lobbying against the legislation, more and more Democratic lawmakers on Capitol Hill have caved to the pressure and peeled away from the EFCA. Rather than flexing his administration's political muscle to lobby Democratic lawmakers to support the bill, Obama, in the first hundred days of his presidency, seemed increasingly reticent about using its clout, and Vice President Joe Biden indicated that a watered-down version of the bill may be in the works.

Local 1110 voted overwhelmingly for Obama, according to Ricky and Armando Robles, and both men said they would be shocked if Senator John McCain got a single vote from any of Republic's employees. That support was based largely on the simple fact that Obama's policies represented a greater departure from those of the Bush administration's than did McCain's, they said, but a significant chunk was predicated on Obama's support for the EFCA. "It's great that we have a black president of the United States, and black kids need to see that to know there's nothing we can't do," Ricky said. "But I can't lie: I know that a lot of us will be real disappointed if we don't get [the EFCA] passed."

But Ricky has been disappointed before and expects that he will be again before it's all said and done. This is what Armando and many of the other Latino workers at the plant didn't get at first about their black coworkers. Armando and the Mexican immigrants understood that America's playing field was tilted and uneven, but the black employees understood something else: that the ground was constantly moving underneath them and that even victories were likely to be wiped away when the earth shifted, as it inevitably would. During the battle over Chicago's living-wage ordinance, for instance, busloads of unemployed blacks replied to fliers promising them jobs, only to discover that it was a ruse orchestrated by a local black church, sponsored by Wal-Mart, to boost the crowd at a rally against the proposal. And, after union workers had volunteered their time to knock on doors, distribute campaign literature, staff phone banks, and raise money to unseat the offending politicians at City Hall, nothing happened. And to this day, it is the worst-kept secret in Chicago that the CFL and the building trades met with Daley sometime after the election, offering to not push for the big-box legislation in exchange for a favorable contract. This, it was understood, would give Daley the labor peace he needed as he courted the 2016 Olympic Games.

"It's very clear what happened," said organizer James Thindwa. "The mostly white construction trade unions sold out the mostly black and Latino workers in the lower-paying service industries. So the sad irony is that they made a truth-teller out of Dorothy Tillman. She played the race card, and she was right. The unions, or at least some of them, didn't care what happened to black people. So, you see the whole reason that we don't have a living-wage ordinance in Chicago today is race."

Thindwa and Ricky agree that immigrants from Mexico are reenergizing black workers and the labor movement in America, but there is an old story that explains why a certain lethargy has settled in. In 1952, a group of white prisoners at Louisiana State Penitentiary—know as Angola—cut their Achilles tendons to protest the harsh conditions, mistreatment, and beatings. The gesture led to reforms at the former plantation turned prison, but when researchers asked a group of black inmates why they had never considered such a gesture, one of them looked quizzically at his questioner and said simply: "Because don't nobody care nothing about no crippled niggas."[22]

"Armando and them couldn't quite understand at first that there are a different set of rules that apply to black workers," Ricky said. "They understood injustice because they had seen plenty of that back in Mexico, but they didn't understand injustice when the whole system thrives off that injustice and has for two hundred years and they plan on keeping it up for another two hundred years. They can't let you win. Different rules apply to black people. Mexicans got it bad; we got it worse. When you fight and fight and fight and never come away with a victory, you become hopeless."

And hopelessness, he said, breeds inertia. And that's what he was up against when he made the rounds in mid-November, telling black workers what was in the works and trying to coax them into participating in the plant occupation if it came to that.

"I don't know, Ricky," a few of the black workers said to him.

Ricky had no shame. He invoked Julia's remarks at the executive meeting when she committed to the plan.

"Here's a woman who has children and she stands to be deported back to Mexico if she goes through with this," Ricky said to a number of his black coworkers, "and she's ready to go balls to the wall. And here you are legal, and you're telling me that you're not going to fight?"

Finally, on Monday morning December 2, management sent down word that there would be a companywide meeting at noon. Thinking that the workers might have to chain themselves to plant equipment, Armando was out buying some industrial-length chains at Home Depot when the call came. At the meeting, management let the other shoe drop. The bank had frozen their line of credit, and they could no longer make payroll. The employees' last day would be Friday, and all employees were to come in that morning at nine to pick up their final paychecks.

Ricky was confident that he had sold the idea of a sit-in strike to at least half of the black employees, but his wife, Cynthia, was another story. The two had been married just six months earlier—Ricky's second marriage—and Ricky went home from work that day and broke the news to her that the plant was closing for sure and that the union planned to occupy the plant until they received the two months' pay and benefits they were entitled to under a labor law that required sixty days' notice for plant closings.

Cynthia was skeptical. "Baby, I don't know about this," she said as they sat in their living room watching television underneath the wall that Cynthia had decorated with dozens of photographs cut out of newspapers and magazines of Obama, Michelle, and the girls. "You gonna do all this and you gonna catch a case for trespassing, and you know everybody does background checks these days. What you gonna say when you applying for your next job?"

Ricky acknowledged there was risk involved. "But I got to do this," he said. "You just have to trust me on this. I am going to do what's best for me and my family."

They barely spoke the rest of the week, and on Friday morning Ricky went to work. It was cold and gray, and a fine snow had begun to fall, whipped like confetti by a stiff lakefront wind.

The workers were milling around in the cafeteria after they had collected their paychecks, and Armando searched for Ricky in the throng. His English was good, but just in case it failed him, he wanted his vice president by his side.

Finally, they two of them found the plant's manager in the center of the cafeteria. Armando cleared his throat and said: "Barry, we're not going anywhere."

"Say what?" Barry asked, clearly puzzled.

"We're not leaving the plant until we get what you owe us by law," Armando said, loudly and clearly.

Local 1110's members had already agreed to man the plant in shifts of fifty or so. This was not to be a Haymarket sequel. Two people from each shift would sweep and clean and pick up trash. When the snow fell, they shoveled it. There was to be no smoking in the plant, no drinking. Meinster, the EU's chief organizer, had alerted the local television news broadcasts earlier that morning, as well as the police precinct.

"It's going to be a peaceful protest," he said he told the precinct commander. "There will be no violence, no destruction of property, no vandalism. We've told our people we don't even want them swearing when they're on the property."

The captain, Meinster said, was clearly sympathetic. "Well, I guess as long as you don't cause any disturbances, it's okay."

Workers picketed in the parking lot holding placards that read: "Bank of America: You Got Bailed Out; We Got Sold Out." The television news reporters and cameramen began showing up by late morning to hear the workers marching in the parking lot and chanting. "What do we want? Justice. When do we want it? Now." Ricky was shown on local news broadcasts saying defiantly: "It's time for the little man to stand up. We are not going anywhere."

Luis Gutierrez, a Democratic congressman representing Illinois' Fourth District on Chicago's West Side, came by that afternoon. He had helped the workers decertify their union five years earlier. Jesse Jackson Sr. showed up with a turkey and blankets and words of encouragement that evening. The following morning, residents from the neighborhood began showing up, bringing food, water, and blankets, and fathers showed up carrying their young children on their shoulders to get an admiring glimpse of what the workers were doing. The state's Democratic governor, Rod Blagojevich, made an appearance Saturday and announced that he had suspended all state contracts with Bank of America, worth tens of millions of dollars.

Before that first weekend was over, every single unionized worker at Republic Windows and Doors would do at least one shift at the plant, and about forty other former employees showed up to participate in the sit-in as well. One African American named Johnny, who'd lost his job months earlier in a round of lay-offs, was watching the sit-in on television with his grandmother Saturday afternoon when she said, "You need to go support your ex-coworkers." He turned up Sunday morning.

That same day, from his home on the city's South Side, President-elect Obama expressed his support at a news conference. "When it comes to the situation here in Chicago with the workers who are demanding the benefits and payments they've earned, I think they're absolutely right. What's happening to them is reflective of what's happening across this economy."

That afternoon, Cynthia called Ricky on his cell phone as he sat on a chair inside the plant. Her tone was markedly different from the past few days. She was upbeat, asking Ricky how things were going, urging him on.

Ricky had to know. "What's gotten into you?" he asked her.

"Did you see Obama was just on television? He said he supported what you were doing," she said.

Ricky laughed. "Oh, so that's why you're acting so supportive. Because you got Obama's approval."

Cynthia laughed sheepishly. She had never expected that Obama would even notice what was happening at Republic, much less endorse it. Shit, if the president-elect had the workers' back, she thought, maybe they actually had a shot.

"Well, yeah," she said, answering Ricky's question, "when you put it like that . . ."

.   .   .

"Man, *fuck* your country home in Connecticut."

Ricky slammed his fist, hard, on a marble conference table so big and beautiful and flawless it looked unreal, like a slab of Kryptonite. It was two weeks before Christmas, a week after Local 1110 began their protest, and the union leadership had managed to finagle a meeting at Bank of America's corporate headquarters in Chicago, to try to coax the executives to extend to Republic the line of credit it needed to pay what they owed the workers.

Things had gotten off to a bad start. As they waited for the meeting to begin, the bankers in their dark tailored suits, with their salon-styled hair, chatted between sips of coffee, discussing their travel plans for the Christmas holidays.

"How in the fuck are y'all standing over there talking about going skiing when I can't even get my granddaughter a doll for Christmas?"

There must've been twenty people in the big conference room overlooking downtown Chicago, and Ricky was one of only two blacks. When he exploded angrily, Mark Meinster, the UE's top organizer who was sitting next to him, squeezed his knee and said, "It's all right, Ricky."

But Ricky wasn't having it. "No. It's *not* all right," he said, and slammed the table again. Luis Gutierrez, the congressman who played an instrumental role in arranging the meeting, walked over to where Ricky was sitting and rubbed his shoulders and said softly, "It's okay, Ricky. I was just about to say something myself."

Just then, one of the bankers spoke up. He apologized and agreed that it was insensitive for the executives to be discussing their extravagant plans when the Republic workers assembled in the room were in such dire financial straits. "We want to make this right," he said.

Ricky's outburst seemed to put the executives on the defensive and set the tone for the rest of the meeting, which led to an agreement to extend a $1.7 million line of credit to the company to pay the workers about seven thousand dollars each in salary and benefits. A deal would've been struck sooner, but Republic's majority owner, Gillman, got wind of the deal and initially insisted that the line of credit include enough money for him to make the monthly payments on his leased BMW.

In February, a California manufacturer of energy-efficient windows purchased Republic Windows and reopened the plant in May, rehiring all 260 workers at their same salaries. The new owners said they were spurred to do so by the tax credits for green jobs included in Obama's economic stimulus package. Vice President Joe Biden spoke at the ceremony celebrating the plant's reopening.

Encouraging growth in a promising new industry, said Jobs with Justice organizer James Thindwa, provides a clear rebuke to left-leaning critics who contend that there is no significant difference between Obama and McCain, or Democrats and Republicans. "Say that to one of the two hundred and sixty people who are going to get up and go to work tomorrow, making fifteen, seventeen, and as much as twenty dollars an hour, as a clear consequence of a policy undertaken by the Obama administration. I agree I would like to see more done, but it's just not true to say that there's only a dime's worth of difference."

And yet, there is something in the time that has lapsed between Harold Washington and Barack Obama that underscores the growing divide between politicians and ordinary working people, and demonstrates, in the Democratic Party specifically, a slowing of the party's reflexes due to the degenerative influence of big business and its cash. A populist, grassroots movement identified Harold Washington as the leader who could help advance their agenda, and he responded in kind. A month after his inauguration, Obama continued to endorse the aims of the Employee Free Choice Act.

"I don't buy the argument that extending to workers collective bargaining rights somehow weakens the economy or worsens the business climate," he said. Still, far more than Washington or the Democrats of yesterday, Obama and Democrats on Capitol Hill serve two different masters. Their relentless attention to business interests puts at risk any real change for America's workers, whose wages are plummeting while the cost of everyday living soars. It is not the banks' balance sheets that triggered the world's gravest economic crisis in at least eighty years; it is the balance sheet of ordinary Americans. Or to put it another way, what good does it do to replenish the bank's ability to loan money, if there is no one who can afford to borrow?

This is Obama's dilemma. The shift in the American economy over the past quarter century has triggered an almost biblical plague, and the scope of the crisis will not allow his administration to straddle the fence. Which side is Obama on?

The EFCA would begin to put more money back into workers' pockets, stimulate the economy, and, maybe, rebuild democracy in the United States by amplifying the voices of workers, long downsized and diminished. No country has adopted, as one example, a national health insurance program without organized labor's playing a central role.

Moreover, politically, the nation is changing. By 2050, the country will resemble Local 1110, a majority brown and black nation, whose shared grievances far outnumber their differences. One way or another, as the eight-day occupation of Republic Windows illustrated, they will have to be reckoned with.

"I really think that what the workers at Republic Windows did was a model for the nation," Ricky said weeks after the standoff had ended. "Just think about it. *We* led; the politicians followed."

He Doesn't See What We See

Diop's Protest in St. Petersburg

Harvard has ruined more Negroes than bad whiskey.

—ADAM CLAYTON POWELL

Inside the basement of the First Unitarian Church, a regal one-hundred-year-old ivy-covered limestone building in downtown Philadelphia, an integrated audience of seventy sits on folding chairs and listens to a succession of speakers discuss racism, police brutality, the crisis in capitalism, environmentalism, and imperialism. This is the Uhuru Solidarity Movement's National Conference, a day of workshops and panel discussions intended to foster solidarity between whites and blacks. "We in the white community can't just continue to sit in our nice Victorians in University City and peek out the window when we see another police car buzzing by on its way to put another black man in jail," says Allison Hoehne, one of the organizers. "We have to say stop: not in my name."

Penny Hess of the African People's Solidarity Committee put on a Power Point presentation, illustrating efforts to grow community gardens in America's inner cities and West African villages. "From Brazil to Brooklyn, Guinea to Ghana, Africans live the same everywhere." Diop Olugbala, the Uhuru Movement's top international organizer, leads a panel discussion on how communities can politically engage local governments, and introduces the final speaker, Umar Abdullah-Johnson, a psychologist who leads an organization called the International Movement for the Independence and Protection of African People.

"The mother of all crimes is miseducation," Abdullah-Johnson tells the crowd. "The father is economic castration. And they work hand in hand. They are holding our children in psycho-slavery to make them good slaves, good workers, unquestioning, unwilling to fight for their citizenship. Our children are being set up. You disagree with me?"

People shout, "No!"

"Ask yourself why all these children are being put on Ritalin and Prozac and all these psychotropic drugs that are expensive and untested and we don't know what effect this stuff will have on children. No, check that, we know that Prozac and some of these other so-called antidepressants actually make some young people suicidal. And yet, if the school systems and the child welfare authorities tell a mom that her child needs to be taking this drug and she refuses to give it to him, they can take that child away from her."

The crowd of white college students and baby boomers, and blacks in suits, T-shirts, and West African garb, applauds. One black woman recounts her own struggle to fight her Philadelphia public school's efforts to medicate her son.

"Who in the world ever came up with the idea of a nine-year-old child being hyperactive," the woman says. "You should be concerned if a nine-year-old boy *ain't* real active." From the podium, Diop, a clean-shaven thirty-one-year-old African American with a cruiserweight's physique and a resemblance to Marlon Wayans, advises her to get in touch with some local affiliates of the Uhuru Movement. "You don't have to go through this alone, Sister," he says to her. "We're here for you."

So much of being black in America is seeing things that no one else sees, or wants to see. Sometimes, it turns out, there is indeed nothing there. For instance, it is not difficult to find African Americans of a certain age in Chicago who believe that the white political and business elite poisoned Harold Washington when all evidence suggests that the late mayor's lethal heart attack was caused by too much bad food, too much stress, and too little exercise.[1] Did the government invent the AIDS virus? Probably not, but there are African doctors educated in U.S. medical schools who question whether South Africa's white-minority government and its biological weapons program played a role in creating a disease that is a right-winger's wet dream.

And yet, many conspiracy theories are eventually proven true. The late Detroit mayor Coleman Young used to always say: "Just because you're paranoid, don't mean ain't nobody out to get you." Black people all over the world know that there are people out there who mean them harm and who have a vested interest in writing off their claims as craziness, conspiracy theories, fantasy.

Thomas Jefferson *did* father Sally Hemings's children;[2] the CIA *did* help introduce crack cocaine into America's inner cities;[3] those doctors at Tuskegee Institute *weren't* healing those black men infected with syphilis;[4] white folks in New Orleans, Chicago, and Washington, D.C., *were* plotting to reclaim neighborhoods from blacks.[5] The Chicago Police Department and the FBI *did* execute Black Panthers Fred Hampton and Mark Clark while they slept.[6]

Many wonder why Michael Vick went to jail for killing some dogs when George Bush and Dick Cheney are responsible for the deaths of more than a million men, women, and children and neither has spent so much as a day in jail. Detroit's Mayor Kwame

Kilpatrick went to jail for lying about having an affair with an aide and costing his broke-ass city some loot, but no one died.[7] And those poor white soldiers in Iraq who just did what they were told went to jail, but no one in the top brass did.[8] Why are the feds prosecuting as terrorists three African Americans in Miami who talked a big game but didn't have a pot to piss in, or four convicts in upstate New York who agreed to a terrorist plot only because the government informant offered them money to do so?[9] Yet, the United States refuses to extradite Luis Posada Carilles, a white Cuban émigré who has acknowledged blowing a Cuban plane out of the sky and who was called the "biggest terrorist on this continent" by Venezuelan president Hugo Chavez.[10] In North Carolina, many blacks find it more than a little odd that the white prosecutor who charged three white, affluent Duke University students with the rape of a black stripper was disbarred after the charges were dropped and even spent a night in jail for contempt of court,[11] when not once, *not once*, in North Carolina or Illinois or Texas or anywhere, has a prosecutor, police officer, or judge been charged or sanctioned for any of the numerous cases in which a black or Latino was convicted of rape or murder, only to be cleared years later by DNA evidence or witnesses who recanted their statements and said they had been pressured to testify against the defendant. Similarly, it's not difficult to find blacks in New York or Illinois who believe that their respective disgraced governors, Eliot Spitzer and Rod Blagojevich, signed their political death warrants by taking on the powerful banking industry that was raking in record profits by targeting blacks and Latinos with fraudulent, predatory home loans.

And even Abdullah-Johnson's assertion here in Philadelphia that drug companies are conspiring with government to drug black kids has a whiff of truth to anyone who is paying attention. According to a 2006 article in *Mother Jones* magazine, Pennsylvania is one of nine states that have adopted rigid guidelines for prescribing experimental drugs known as atypical antipsychotics to patients at state hospitals, clinics, and other mental institutions. These guidelines call for the newest and most expensive medicines to be used in the treatment of mental disorders like schizophrenia and depression. And the writing of these guidelines is financed and heavily influenced by big pharmaceutical companies, who stand to make millions on the sale of powerful, untested drugs that sell for as much as ten times the price of older, more commonly used psycho-tropic medicines. Here in Pennsylvania, two state investigators sued the state in 2004 after they were fired for exposing the industry's undue influence over the state's prescribing practices and the inap-propriate medication of vulnerable patients, particularly children. In 2004, atypical antipsychotics were the fourth-highest-grossing class of drugs in the United States, with sales totaling $8.8 billion—$2.4 billion of which was paid for with state Medicaid funds.

Every month Texas authorities prescribe the drugs to nearly twenty thousand patients who are undergoing treatment at state institutions, including one fourteen-year-old African American girl who was committed to a state psychiatric hospital in 2004 against her parents' will and injected with nine different drugs, including two anticonvulsants, although she did not suffer from convulsions.[12]

In Philadelphia in 1985 police bombed a northside row house following complaints from neighbors about noise. The row house was occupied by MOVE, a communal organization of mostly dreadlocked, vegan blacks who substituted garlic for Western medicine. The resulting fire consumed nearly an entire city block and killed six adults and five children.[13] The incident remains one of the most storied of many cautionary tales reinforcing the belief that it is unwise for blacks to completely ignore their paranoia.

This is the vexing duality that makes hip-hop relevant, even urgently so, to so many blacks, by bearing witness to the barbarous incongruities and grueling injustices that remain largely invisible in mainstream American culture. The everyday grind of inner-city life rarely makes a sympathetic appearance on the news.

"Rap," the rapper Chuck D once said, "is black America's CNN."

The schism does not fall entirely along the black-white divide. Eminem is widely recognized by blacks as a gifted, authentic MC. Whites widely dismissed the abolitionist John Brown as nuts; Frederick Douglass regarded him as a greater hero than even Abraham Lincoln. And many blacks see, in the West's mistreatment of Muslims in general and Palestinians in particular, a rather recognizable kangaroo court.

As just one example of sympathy for the Palestinians, take the case of Sami Al-Arian, a University of South Florida computer science professor charged by federal prosecutors in 2003 with heading up the American wing of a Palestinian terrorist organization. The son of Palestinian refugees, Al-Arian was an outspoken champion of Palestinian causes and a top fund-raiser for Palestinian charities. After a six-month trial that included eighty witnesses and four hundred transcripts of intercepted phone conversations, Al-Arian's defense team, led by an African American attorney, rested without offering any witnesses or evidence to challenge the prosecution. The jury of three blacks and nine whites acquitted him on eight of the seventeen charges and deadlocked on the remainder, with ten favoring acquittal.[14]

Local attorneys agreed that the prosecution's case was weak, but that wasn't what lost it, one African American lawyer in the area would later say. "They lost that case the day they allowed three blacks to be seated on the jury. You can't find ten black people in all of America who would side with white folks trying to send a Palestinian to jail for trying to help his people beat back the Middle Eastern version of the Jim Crow South."

. . .

In her 1993 book *Volunteer Slavery*, the African American journalist and former *Washington Post* reporter Jill Nelson wrote that urban police departments across the nation went on hiring sprees following the 1967 riots in Detroit and Newark, integrating what were, at the time, their nearly all-white ranks. But white police officers were suspicious of their new coworkers. Would they be loyal to the blue? Or, would their allegiance lie with their friends and family and high school classmates who were in the sights of law-enforcement officials? Consequently, Nelson wrote, many white officers encouraged—subtly at times, expressly at others—black officers to shoot their own, to *prove* their fidelity. The same, Nelson argued in her book, was true for black journalists hired on at big-city newspapers and television stations following the 1968 Kerner Commission Report identifying the media's role in sowing America's racial divisions. In ways both subtle and explicit, white journalists encouraged their black coworkers to gun down blacks in news stories that singled out the pathology, criminality, and recklessness of African American welfare moms, politicians, and institutions.

This tension, and ultimate betrayal, contend Diop and many other blacks, dates back to slavery and extends far beyond law enforcement or journalism into virtually every sector of American life, with black politicians, especially, prodded by their white benefactors to slay the Angry Negro, who raises uncomfortable truths and inconvenient grievances that threaten the privileged and their way of life. *First, pretend they're not there, and maybe they will go away. And if that doesn't work, attack.*

"Malcolm X used to talk about the difference between the house Negro and the field Negro," Diop says weeks before the Philadelphia Uhuru conference. "The house Negro lived relatively well. He ate food from the master's table, had a lighter workload, indoors, away from the sun. Consequently, when the master's house caught fire, the house Negro came running with a bucket of water. The field Negro on the other hand, he suffered the lash and worked

75

hard every day, outdoors in the elements from sunup to sundown. He had no interest in the preservation of slavery or whether the master's house survived the fire. So when the master yelled fire, sometimes, the field Negro came running too—with matches."

Understanding this peculiar American dilemma, and that yawning chasm between the nation's ideals and its practices, fuels the only art form to have originated in America in a century, the musical genre known as rap. Like America's only other recognized art forms, the blues and jazz, rap—and the culture it inspired, hip-hop—is a way of dealing with sorrow, spoken in the language of the dispossessed and the uncelebrated. It articulates what America looks and sounds and feels like from the vantage point of the slave ship, and this is why it resonates most in sojourner communities, estranged from their homelands and their countrymen: Palestinians in Gaza and the West Bank, Brazilians in the favelas, South Africans on their Bantustans and in their townships, even the Romani people—commonly referred to using the slur "gypsy"— across Eastern Europe. Consequently, you don't just listen to rap music; you have to *feel* it, live it, to really appreciate it. The black comedian Chris Rock used to tell a joke in which he commented that white people don't like rap music. "That's because it's not for you," he said. "Chances are if you like a rap song it is the worst song in rap history."

Similarly, in searching for the genre's historical roots, the African American poet Nikki Giovanni wrote: "In 1822, a slave named Denmark Vesey used the talking drum as a code to call his people to fight for freedom. His freedom run was unsuccessful, and the slave owners outlawed the drum to prevent further trouble. But the enslaved had a secret weapon: creativity. They lost the drum so they drummed on themselves. It's called hamboning. Snap your fingers, that's a hambone; hit your thigh; that is hamboning. Beat your chest; stamp your feet. That's a rhythm and a silence: you don't need a drum, you can be a drum."[15]

It is no coincidence that most people date the creation of rap to 1973, the last year that U.S. workers received a pay raise (in real, inflation-adjusted terms) following a stock market crash, an oil embargo, and inflation that led Nixon and the business elite to begin fundamentally restructuring the American economy, eating away at workers' wages and widening the inequality between rich and poor.[16]

To that end, a constant in hip-hop is its preoccupation with the themes of alienation: identity, invisibility, authenticity, and loyalty, reflected in lyrics such as "who you with?" or "keep it real" or "all eyes on me"—which are like rallying cries, framing what is, to the generation reared on hip-hop, the defining reality of life in the twenty-first century: there is a war going on.

"The situation that working-class people find themselves in at the beginning of the twenty-first century is much bigger than Obama or any one man," Diop says. "The problem is the system. What is your relationship to the system? That determines how you move in the world. We in the Uhuru movement were always suspicious of this black man who just seemed to come out of nowhere right after Hurricane Katrina and leading up to this whole subprime crisis, and if you listen carefully, you understand why." Barack Obama and the Democratic Party in general have a program that represents the white ruling elite. Barack Obama is actually the desperate response of imperialism trying to save itself, the last kick from a dying mule. "He is not the answer to imperialism; he is the mother lode of imperialism," in Diop's words.

Diop is, to use a phrase used by the comedian Rock, "a child of hip-hop," a believer in its transformative power, and a witness to its prophecy. A graduate of the University of Texas, he considered enrolling in a doctoral philosophy program but opted to become a labor organizer instead, because he thought that the dire, deteriorating condition of the black community required him to step up his game. Diop is sober, thoughtful, almost stoic.

He seldom smiles. If he thinks he may be even a few minutes late for, say, a Friday appointment, he will call ahead on Thursday. He uses words like "Uncle Tom" and "sellout" to describe Obama and other African American elected officials like Philadelphia mayor Michael Nutter, but the phrases sound off-key when he speaks them, largely because he is typically precise with his language and seldom resorts to the kind of lazy shorthand that is commonly heard on talk radio or bad sitcoms. He is, much like Obama, more intellectually ambitious than that and can talk at length about the ethnic slur that is the etymological root of words like "patrol" or "paddy wagon," or the writings of revolutionary thinkers like the slain prime minister of Guinea-Bissau, Amilcar Cabral, or the late Martinique poet and mentor of Franz Fanon, Aimé Césaire, or the assassinated South African icon Steve Biko and, of course, his American avatar, Malcolm X.

Similarly, he can talk at length about hip-hop and its role in the movement. "I grew up listening to Public Enemy and the Poor Righteous Teachers, whose music was clearly inspired by [Marcus] Garvey," he said. "Art isn't produced in a vacuum. It is a product of the material conditions in society. Dead Prez came up in the Uhuru movement so they obviously have something to contribute to the struggle."

He refers to a video on YouTube of the rapper KRS-One speaking to a group of black youths sometime before the election. "Yeah, y'all like Barack Obama now, but what about when he bombs and kills a million Iranians?" he asks. Juxtapose that against rappers like will.i.am or Jay-Z, who publicly supported Obama, and "you can see what a powerful tool that the music can be for engaging people in the real political debates that are relevant to our communities." Hip-hop represents both the greatest champions of, and the greatest challenge to, Obama.

"Somebody like Biggie [The Notorious B.I.G.] wasn't overtly political, but he was the narrator for his generation, like James

Baldwin was for his, breaking down what life is like in this community at this moment in time, almost like an anthropologist."

"Tupac [Shakur]," he says, "obviously had political consciousness. He was raised in the movement [his mother was a member of the Black Panthers, jailed while pregnant with Tupac] and was exposed to philosophy, which had a lot to do with the quality of his music. He elevated consciousness and surprised you at the same time. There was never anything predictable about Pac."

As evidence, he refers to one song, "You Wonder Why They Call You Bitch," which at first sounds like a misogynistic screed. Despite the ugliness of the language, it is in fact, quite the opposite, a plea for black women to liberate themselves from the patriarchy's narrowly drawn boundaries for what women should do and be.

"The way that they [Tupac and Biggie] articulate their ideas are completely different," Diop explains, "but both of them spoke for an entire generation, not just blacks but women as well. These are the types of figures we don't have in the rap game anymore because imperialism controls the music community as well as the community at large. We only have five major record labels, and they handpick the artists and send them out to speak on behalf of the empire. It's okay to say 'bitch' and 'ho' every other word, but don't raise questions about why Israel jails Palestinians and demolishes their homes, and yet we call the Palestinians the terrorists. The whole philosophy now attempts to liquidate something that once attempted to articulate the aims and aspirations of our people. But now we see clearly that hip-hop is being stripped of its essence. In terms of who has control of the music industry, we in the hip-hop game are finding a postracialization of hip-hop itself."

Asked to explain, he reloads: "You can take someone like Little Wayne, who doesn't have a political bone in his body, and he is unable to articulate the reality of the African American community, much less articulate a solution, and his inability coincides with the inability of Barack Obama to address our reality. Little Wayne has a song about having sex with a female cop. For any black person to entertain such a notion with all the havoc that the police have wreaked on our community, it's just unconscionable. It's the same with Jay-Z. Jay-Z represents a different social force; don't nobody in the hood own a Bentley. We need artists who are on the ground, who live with the people, and this is something that we used to have, but imperialism got hip to the game and began to conscript artists and use them as their tools. The reason Obama can listen to Jay-Z is because he won't say anything challenging. In that same way, Obama reinforces the lies of colonial rule: Our failures are personal rather than structural. Have a good work ethic and follow the rules and you will be a success. We live in a postracial society. Barack Obama *liquidates* any kind of revolutionary consciousness in our community."

Consider, he says, Obama's sycophantic support for Wall Street, which targeted African and Latino communities with predatory subprime mortgages. "This is a scheme that has made millions for people like Obama's chief financial adviser, Penny Pritzker," Diop says, invoking the scion of the Hyatt hotel chain and a prominent Chicago family who was one of Obama's key early financial backers and a key figure in Superior Bank, which was shut down in 2001 and sharply criticized by regulators for its deceptive lending practices. "Black families have been stripped of billions of dollars, the greatest loss of wealth our community has suffered since being brought in chains to this country, and he will not denounce one of the prime beneficiaries of this exploitation."

Asked to elaborate on the full range of his objections to Obama, Diop can speak endlessly, recounting in almost encyclopedic detail the votes Obama has cast and remarks he has made, like the contents of a dossier kept on his brain's hard drive: "This is a man who has criticized African fathers for abandoning our children, although a recent study showed that black fathers stay more involved with their children after a split from the mother than white fathers. He says nothing of the unjust imprisonment of one in nine black men of child-bearing age, the overwhelming majority of whom are locked up on minor drug or other nonviolent economic violations stemming from conditions of desperate poverty.

"Moreover," he says, "Obama has failed to achieve any meaningful program of economic development for the African community and yet, speaking to a group of black legislators in South Carolina, he told them that 'a good economic development plan for our community would be if we make sure folks weren't throwing their garbage out of their cars.' He plans to increase military spending; praised Reagan, a homicidal, genocidal madman, who dreamed of creating a Star Wars–like shield to protect us from a Russian missile attack and who armed and trained right-wing, corporatist militias all over the world to torture, jail, and kill workers, many of them African, who only wanted a decent wage, a decent future for their kids. He praised Clinton for abolishing AFDC [Aid to Families with Dependent Children] and welfare. He wants to escalate the U.S. military presence in Afghanistan and has threatened Venezuela and Iran with military aggression. Here is a man who was a professor of constitutional law at one of the country's finest institutions [the University of Chicago], trained at one of our finest institutions [Harvard Law School], and yet he has backed wiretapping and the U.S. government spying on citizens. His advisers on foreign policy include war criminals like Richard Holbrooke (whom some accuse of giving Indonesian authorities the green light to massacre thousands of East Timorese dissidents and civilians as a U.S. diplomat in the seventies), Trilateral Commission founder Zbigniew Brzezinski, and Madeleine Albright, who once said that the Clinton administration's efforts to impose sanctions against Saddam Hussein's despotic regime were 'worth the price of one million dead Iraqi children.'

"Here is a man who is so careful not to offend, yet, in Miami, he promised the Jewish community that he supports turning all of Jerusalem over to Israeli control, despite an international consensus that the city belongs to both the Palestinians and Israel. He goes before the rabidly right-wing, mostly white, Cuban community in the same city and says that he plans to continue to support a murderous embargo against poor, many of them black, Cuban people, who have done nothing to the United States. In forty-five years, what has this policy wrought, other than the impoverishment of the Cuban people?

"This is why we in the Uhuru movement believe that Barack Obama is a danger to the African community. Instead of asking how we can demand justice for the people who were devastated by Katrina, he's got us all chanting 'Yes, we can.'"

When Diop was thirteen, his father, a lieutenant in the U.S. Army, was arrested in a department store in a Dallas suburb where the family lived. The police were looking for a slender, short, fair-skinned black man who was wanted for fraudulent use of a credit card. Diop's father, dark-skinned, broad-shouldered, and well over six feet tall, apparently fit the bill well enough.

It took three months before he was released.

Today, Diop's mind is a Rolodex of the dead young black men killed in confrontations with police. Among them are Javon Dawson, whose story is told in the next section, and Sean Bell, who was accosted by three plainclothes New York City detectives—two of them African American—while leaving his bachelor party at a Queens nightclub in November 2006. As the twenty-three-year-old Bell was pulling away from the parking lot, the officers squeezed off a fusillade of fifty shots, killing Bell and injuring the two passengers in his car. Lawyers for the officers chose to permit a judge to decide the case, rather than seeking a jury trial, and Judge Arthur J. Cooperman acquitted the officers of all charges.

Obama did issue a statement following a judge's acquittal of the three officers in the Bell case, but many blacks were stunned to see that it offered no sympathy for Bell's family. Even Hillary Clinton had managed to offer condolences to Bell's fiancée, mentioning her by name. By comparison, Barack's statement urged support for the court's verdict, saying that "we are a nation of laws."

"Here is a young man, a law-abiding citizen, a father, who is gunned down in the prime of his life, and all Obama can do is to warn black folks not to riot," Diop said in an interview. "He condoned the killing of Sean Bell."

Another fatal police shooting that the Uhuru Movement protested was that of Oscar Grant by a Bay Area Rapid Transit officer in the early-morning hours of New Year's Day 2009. Grant, twenty-two and the father of an infant son, was one of several young black men rounded up by BART officers responding to calls reporting a fight on a subway outside Oakland, California. Recorded on digital cameras and cell phones, Grant can be seen lying face down, his hands handcuffed behind his back, when the officer, Jason Mesherle, draws his weapon and fires a single shot into Grant's back.[17]

The shooting sparked weeks of protests, some violent, in and around Oakland leading up to Obama's inauguration, and came on the heels of another controversy surrounding the Election Day victory of a California bill expressly prohibiting gay marriage in the state. In the days that followed, gay rights activists and mainstream media punditry blamed California's black voters for the setback, citing a CNN exit poll that indicated, incorrectly, that 70 percent of the blacks who went to the polls voted in favor of the antigay measure.

Later analyses of the results showed that black support for the legislation, known as Proposition 8, was somewhere between 53 and 57 percent, a majority, but still the lowest of all of California's ethnic groups. And, if any group should have been singled out for supporting the discriminatory legislation, why not Mormons or Catholics, who supported the legislation by margins of close to 9 to 1? What's more, many blacks here say, is that while whites want to make scapegoats of blacks when they don't get their way, they don't want to support issues that are important to blacks, like gentrification or police brutality. This is part of the vilification of African Americans that seems both gratuitous and hypocritical to many blacks. Blacks are more homophobic than they need to be, but still not as homophobic as any other racial group in the country, so why does it fit the popular narrative to single out blacks, Diop and others in the Uhuru and similar movements say. Diop points out that even though Obama chastised all-black audiences for their homophobia during the campaign, he asked a famous white clergyman who *had* made antigay comments to deliver the high-profile invocation at his inauguration. He had a well-known black minister who has never made antigay comments to deliver the much less prominent benediction.

"Look around you," one black protester said just days before Obama's inauguration, during a demonstration outside the BART station where Oscar Grant was killed. He was twenty-nine, with waist-length dreadlocks and black-rimmed eyeglasses, and described himself as an artist and gave his name only as Enoch. He said he voted against the ban on gay marriage but knows many friends and relatives who voted differently, and he understands why. "Do you see the white gay community represented here?" he asks, almost theatrically, shoving his sunglasses down on his cheek and turning to peer out into the crowd. "I frankly don't give two shits whether two men want to get married, but we got a lot more pressing problems to worry about, and the gay community always wants to tell us what we should do but they never stand up for us. Most black people really aren't openly homophobic—they just see things like Proposition 8 as 'white people shit' that got nothing to do with us.

"You see this is what it means to be black in America. We're invisible until someone wants to assign blame, and then, all of a sudden, they see no one but us."

. . .

Diop got his chance to air his concerns directly to the candidate around the time Barack Obama was closing in on the Democratic presidential nomination. Obama appeared at a town hall meeting at Gibbs High School in St. Petersburg, Florida. Amidst the throng of maybe three hundred supporters was a contingent of the Uhuru Movement. Just two months earlier, not two miles from Gibbs High, a white police officer and U.S. Marine named Terrence Nemeth, who had only recently returned from a tour of duty in Iraq, had shot and killed an unarmed seventeen-year-old African American youth named Javon Dawson, who was attending a high school graduation party. Described as a "good kid" by his classmates, friends, family, and teachers, Dawson had never been in trouble with the law before, and was, by all eyewitness accounts, complying with officers' demands to raise his hands when he was gunned down.[18] Obama's campaign stop in Florida coincided with weeks of protests and demonstrations led by the Uhuru Movement, which compared the Clinton administration's 1996 omnibus crime bill putting 150,000 additional patrol officers on America's streets to the Bush administration's occupation of Iraq, both targeting communities of color. If government did not address these concerns, the movement's leaders warned, the black community would boil over in anger, just as Iraqis have in response to their American occupiers, or as the city of St. Petersburg responded years before, following the fatal police shooting in 1996 of another unarmed black youth, Tyrone Lewis.

"Javon Dawson attended Gibbs High School," said Diop. "Obama's campaign only announced that he was coming to Gibbs High School forty-eight hours in advance, so the moment we heard that, we just immediately thought it our responsibility to use the opportunity to bring into the national political debate the serious issues experienced by African working-class people across this country."

Diop and his aides weren't looking for a major confrontation. But an hour into the event, frustrated by what they regarded as empty, monotonous campaign rhetoric and Obama's failure to even acknowledge their presence, Diop and his colleagues began heckling the candidate, stomping on the bleachers as if they were at a pep rally and shouting at the top of their lungs: "What about the black community, Obama?"

The usually unflappable Obama was visibly unnerved as he tried to answer a question from the audience.

"And when our government fails . . . hold on a second," he said into the microphone, "hold on a second . . . what's happening?"

Regaining his composure, Obama told his hecklers to wait their turn, and he would address their questions shortly. Finally, a few moments later, a campaign aide raced up the bleacher steps and shoved the microphone in Diop's face. Diop leaned into the microphone and spoke slowly, calmly, with an almost professorial tone that is not unlike Obama's own speaking manner.

"So my question is in the face of the numerous attacks that are made against the African community or the black community by the same U.S. government that you aspire to lead—and we're talking about attacks like the subprime mortgage which you spoke of and it wasn't just a general ambiguous kind of phenomenon but a phenomenon that targeted the African community and the Latino community, attacks like the killing of Sean Bell by the New York police department and Javon Dawson right here in St. Petersburg by the St. Petersburg Police Department and the Jena Six and Hurricane Katrina and the list goes on—in the face of all these attacks that are clearly being made on the African community why is it that you have not had the ability—not one time—to speak to the interests and even speak on behalf of the oppressed and exploited African community or black community in this country?"

Knocked off balance, Obama momentarily sounded like his predecessor, stammering badly when he initially attempted a response. After a few seconds, he collected himself. "Well, I've been talking about predatory lending for the last two years in the U.S. Senate, and I worked to pass legislation to prevent it when I was in the [Illinois] state legislature, and I have repeatedly said that many of the predatory loans that were made in the mortgage system did target the African American and Latino community."

He continued, answering, almost pedantically, each of the points raised by Diop. He was the first presidential candidate to issue a statement following a judge's acquittal of three New York City Police officers who had fatally shot Sean Bell. "Jena Six," he said, referring to the six black teenagers charged with felony assault charges when their peaceful protests against a noose hanging from a tree outside their Louisiana high school resulted in a series of racial skirmishes with several white youths, none of whom were charged, "I was the first candidate to get out there and say this is wrong. There's an injustice that's been done and we need to fix it."

And then, almost as though you could see his brain calibrating the "Sista Soulja" effect that would be achieved with white voters by using this moment to prove his bona fides as the *un*-Jesse Jackson, to show that he was *their* man, Obama, his tone turning sharp, surly, said: "Now, that doesn't mean that I am always going to satisfy the way you want these issues framed," he said.

He concluded with as condescending a dismissal as he could get away with by telling his hecklers that they could always run for office themselves if they didn't like his answers.

Even with Obama surging in the polls in the weeks leading up to the election, many blacks still feared that a conspiracy would keep the first black president from taking office or remaining in it for very long. In private conversations and on radio call-in shows, the talk turned quickly and repeatedly to assassination attempts and shenanigans like the maneuvers that kept Al Gore out of the White House following the 2000 election. On Bill Maher's show, the comedian Chris Rock joked: "They'll look him dead in the face and go 'Hey man, you got the most votes. Too bad you lost.'"

To Rock, the powers that be weren't going to let him win. To Diop, the powers that be made sure he couldn't lose.

| 4 |

Where the Grass Is Greener

Linda in the Promised Land

Bernie Mac: Hey baby, the phone bill kind of high this month. Look at that.

Wanda: Vanessa was doing good in school, so I let her call some friends.

Bernie Mac: Vanessa?

Wanda: Mmm-hmm.

Bernie Mac: You still got to watch her, baby. I mean, she already think we rich.

Wanda: Well, compared to where she's from . . .

Bernie Mac: Yeah, but she think we're old country club rich— old money rich. Shoot, we just nigger rich.

—SCENE FROM THE BERNIE MAC SHOW

Linda thought surely she had misheard her daughter, so she asked again.

"*Where* are you staying?"

"Red Roof Inn," was barely out of Ashley's mouth for the second time when her mother laughed out loud. Linda had nothing against the family- and budget-friendly chain of hotels, which once advertised itself with the slogan "Sleep Cheap." But Ashley, her youngest, learned early that the family had more than others, and when she was a teenager, she preferred first-class to coach, the Surf and Turf to Mickey D's, and the Ritz Carlton to roadside inns. Neither Linda nor her husband, Sam, had come from wealth, but they built a successful business, and their income places them in the top 2 percent of the nation's wage earners. Averse to debt, the Bottses own a condominium in Atlanta and a weekend home on the water in southern Maryland, and their primary home overlooks a golf course in the most exclusive neighborhood in the black American mecca, the Washington, D.C., suburb of Prince George's County, Maryland, the most affluent population of African Americans in the country.

Ashley, at twenty-two, was just starting out. It was the spring of 2009, and she was nearing completion of her bachelor's degree from Old Dominion University in Hampton, Virginia. Her parents spared not a dime on her education, paying for private elementary and high schools and an expensive private college. But for a pregraduation spring break cruise out of Fort Lauderdale, Ashley was on her own.

Linda could easily have written the check, but she wants her children to live within their means, which, in the case of the Red Roof Inn, resulted in a good laugh.

"I couldn't even talk to her," Linda said, giggling again. "Ashley said, 'Why are you acting like that?' She told me to stop laughing. I said, 'But it's not the Ritz.' I couldn't stop laughing."

Ashley explained the incident this way: "When I'm with my family, I want more of the nicer things. But when I'm with my friends, I can appreciate that they are not as well off as we are. I'm not too bougie [bourgeois] that I can't stay at a Red Roof Inn. I'm fine with it. I'm not ungrateful or spoiled about money."

.   .   .

As a child, Linda was taught to feel like a little princess who had a standing lunch date with grandma. Back then, her family wasn't rich, or even well off, but her grandmother was emulating what she saw in the houses where she had worked as a maid much of her life. The white mothers didn't work, and the children were pampered and cleaned up to await their father's return from work. Linda's grandmother adopted that *Leave It to Beaver* sensibility to set her granddaughter on a path to prosperity.

"She would cut the crust off the bread and she would have it on nice china, and I would have a little lunch with her," Linda said of her grandmother. "When I got up from a nap, she would powder me and put my Sunday best on, and I would dress up for the afternoon."

"It's all about the journey," Linda likes to say. Her personal journey began in the Lincoln Homes projects in Trenton, New Jersey. Whatever image public housing conjures for others, Linda remembers this: "For me it was happy times. You knew everyone. Everybody was like a relative who looked out for you."

The family's next stop was a middle-class white neighborhood of neat homes in West Trenton, which had been her mother's dream. They had more room to stretch out: she and her grandmother shared a room; her brother and her mother had their own rooms, even if there wasn't enough furniture to fill the place. Her father, an alcoholic and a waiter, was great when he was around, but he wasn't around often. "We were so happy. I was coming from an environment where it was like family. I moved into this neighborhood, and it was a big deal. I think the house might have cost nine thousand dollars in 1957 when we moved in. The white couple next door had a mean brown dog. There was another white family with two kids, and the kids were our age. We were so excited. They had a beautiful yard with a beautiful swing set, a little kiddie pool, all the things a kid would want, little plastic toys out there. We would kind of size each other up and so on. I remember going into the yard, and they called us niggers and told us they couldn't play with us. I learned to be friends with the dog next door, Corky. Corky became my best friend. 'For sale' signs went up, and the white folks moved out and blacks moved in."

As a teenager, Linda got a glimpse of what it was like to be rich, or her concept of it. She was fourteen, her grandmother had died recently, and Linda was sent to live for a year with a family friend, whom she called Aunt Leola, in Detroit. She headed the music department at Burroughs Junior High School. To Linda, Aunt Leola appeared to have everything and, with no children of her own, not a soul to share it with. She doted on Linda. While other students ate cafeteria food, Linda's aunt prepared her gourmet lunches like shrimp salad that she reheated for Linda in the teacher's lounge. Aunt Leola even took her to see one of Marian Anderson's farewell concerts in 1965, when the singer said a year-long goodbye to her fans. Linda got involved in church and various other activities.

"She just introduced me to a whole lot," Linda said. And then, "You understand why I say I can't relate to a class kind of thing? So am I middle class, low class, or upper class?"

That's a question that could be applied to Prince George's County, where the Bottses live. It occupies an unusual place in American demographics, an entire county for people like George and Weezy Jefferson, moving on up, to that dee-luxe apartment in the sky.

Prince George's doesn't offer much in the way of East Side Manhattan élan, but with its proximity to the U.S. capital, a black majority that accounts for two-thirds of the population, and sprawling old mansions, brick colonials, and modern townhomes rising like hallucinations from the old tobacco plantations, this former slaveholding county is a beacon for blacks who cashed in on government jobs and contracts to live the American dream.

If Prince George's is the promised land, then its Moses is Wayne K. Curry, who was forty-three in 1994 when he was elected the first African American county executive. When he made his way to the podium inside a hotel conference room on that election night, well-wishers danced and dabbed tears from their eyes, in a scene that was like a low-budget production of the scene that unfolded outside Grant Park in Chicago fourteen years later as Obama strode to the podium. Just a few years before, it seemed, a white woman county councilor with a blond beehive hairdo had fought bitterly against school busing, and the county's police department was widely viewed in much the same way that black Chicagoans, Philadelphians, and Angelenos regarded their local law enforcement. "Don't get caught after dark," residents of Washington, D.C., used to say of the county mounties. And now, people said in 1994, a black man is running the joint. "A bit of this campaign reminded me of the civil rights movement," said Dorothy Bailey, elected that same evening to the Prince George's County Council.[1]

Curry's victory, in some ways, gave Prince George's black population a fourteen-year head start on the rest of black America in answering the question: What does black political leadership mean to black people on the ground? If Prince George's is any indicator, then the answer is unequivocally equivocal: it depends on which black folks you're talking about.

Across the country, the election of black politicians has produced optimism that growing political power would translate into economic power and lift all boats. But the same historical forces that catapulted many African Americans into elected office left them to manage jurisdictions laden with problems and limited sources of revenue. Not everyone had an oar in the water.

In a stark departure from other white-to-black transformations that followed white flight from the cities, the overall income and educational level of the county *rose* as blacks moved in. But this was deceptive, because the county has essentially expanded along two very different tracks, creating a local jurisdiction that resembles an almost monochrome apartheid state. Prince George's is, in fact, two very different counties: one affluent, mobile, connected, rising, and living in the archipelago of communities that are outside the Beltway; the other poor, isolated, plummeting like stones, and living in the blighted neighborhoods closer to the District's city limits inside the Beltway.

Charming, handsome, and a gifted orator, Curry, a millionaire attorney and developer, entered office with a constituency that sometimes made competing demands. The outside-the-Beltway crowd wanted in on the action; they wanted the contracts that went to white folks; they wanted safe streets, schools that could get their kids into Ivy League universities, and good shopping—Macy's and Saks Fifth Avenue—like white people had in Montgomery County and northern Virginia. The inside-the-Beltway folks wanted jobs, not contracts; decent housing; and schools that prepared their kids to go to trade school or community college or, maybe, a historically black college; they wanted safe streets, but that meant getting a handle on the police as well as the outlaws, and good shopping meant a place where they could by fresh greens and grapes, not Gucci.

Curry felt that Maryland Democrats, mostly white, took black voters for granted, offering them little more than pats on the back and a few crumbs. But he had grand plans. As the former president of the Prince George's Chamber of Commerce, Curry knew the political and the business game. He raised money from developers and their lawyers, and he established a campaign organization that tapped into a wellspring of black pride in both poor and affluent areas. Everyone, no matter their address, wanted less crime and better schools—also essential to attracting business. His aim was also to build black wealth, which he considered the equalizer that would trump all the social issues that black leaders had spent too much time marching and praying about. He wanted to grow millionaires who could bid on and win large government contracts and have as much impact outside of government as he was hoping to have inside it. Curry became a salesman, telling folks about the county's advantages—proximity to Washington, a good transportation system, and a well-heeled populace ready to spend their money. He traveled to meet with business executives and took every opportunity to be the county's cheerleader. He irked developers by demanding that they build more expensive homes, and the poor by attempting to close down garden apartments that he felt hurt the image he wanted to project. He also hosted ritzy $1,000-per-person fund-raisers at his executive mansion near the county seat of Upper Marlboro.[2]

"If you want to be upscale," Curry said often, "you've got to act upscale."

But that wasn't much help to residents just trying to get through the day. Throughout his first term, budget cuts forced the reduction of the social service safety net. Seniors too sick to leave their homes stopped receiving "friendly visitors" at the county's expense.[3] Groups serving the homeless and those on welfare had their grants slashed. When the county moved to close the Manchester Square Apartments in 1997 as part of an effort to rid itself of six thousand substandard apartments, residents balked, even though roofs leaked, windows were broken out, and vagrants and prostitutes squatted in vacant units. "People are poor," said resident Thornell Johnson, who organized meetings to save the complex. "Poor people don't have a lot of selection. They don't have the option of moving somewhere that is not as dirty."[4]

But Curry said the county had done enough balancing. Prince George's had far more affordable housing than any of its neighbors, and if it was going to move forward, its image as the low-rent district in the Washington metropolitan area had to go. Easier said than done, countered one of Curry's staunchest critics at the time, County Council member Walter H. Maloney.

"It's simple enough to say, 'Bulldoze them all,'" Maloney said. "The problem is, where are these people going to go? And I can't answer that. You can't eliminate the problem without harming the people who live there."[5]

The class divide was also at play during the case of Jeffrey C. Gilbert, who was badly beaten by police as he was arrested on charges that he killed Corporal John J. Novabilski in April 1995. Gilbert was treated for a broken nose, a concussion, and hemorrhaging. He was released a month later, after another man who had the officer's stolen weapon killed himself in a shootout with police. The county's black up-and-comers said a collective, "So what?" Media reports harkened back to the county's earlier days when white police officers regularly brutalized blacks, including thirteen-year-old Terrence Johnson, who in 1979 managed to wrestle a pistol from one of the two white cops who he said was beating him, and shot the two men dead. But the typical response to Gilbert's case was like this one from Barbara Valentine, who was unfazed by the beating: "He's no hero," said Valentine, a middle-class black homeowner. "These kinds of stories are going to destroy our property values. This kind of coverage is going to keep businesses from moving here. He probably got some of what was coming to him."[6]

The twenty-five-year-old Gilbert, with a criminal record, represented the low-class past that Prince George's was trying to move beyond. Back and forth, forth and back, the conversation has gone. Curry served his two terms and was replaced in office by another black man, and development, at least theoretically, remains a priority.

The latest attraction is National Harbor, a sprawling riverside complex of offices, condominiums, restaurants, and shops that opened in 2008 on the county's southern edge. What Prince Georgians longed for was upscale retail shopping, which had been slow to arrive. And when it has, success has not always followed. Take, for instance, the Boulevard at Capital Centre, the former site of a basketball and hockey arena, which was envisioned as one of the sites in the center of the county that would bring the midrange stores to match the neighborhoods like Linda's. Six years later, in the spring of 2009, anchors including Linens 'n Things, Circuit City, and Office Depot were closed, and many of the remaining retailers sold T-shirts, jeans, and cell phones, stores that resemble those found in run-down retail strips in low-income neighborhoods. More disturbing, however, is the fact that five people have been killed there in four years.

"The operation has clearly suffered actual and image setbacks that are inconsistent with the lofty vision we set at the outset and the kind of product our citizens deserve," said Curry, who, as county executive, led the effort to build the Boulevard. "It's off the track, clearly, and needs to be firmly redirected."[7]

This derailment describes the county's hopes and dreams as well. Curry's election ushered in an era in which Prince George's top three elected officials—county executive, chief prosecutor, and the county's representative in Congress—are all black. By the time Obama was sworn in as president of the United States, the era had reached fourteen years and counting. Here is what Prince George's has to show for it: the highest rate of foreclosures in Maryland;[8] the Washington, D.C., metropolitan region's second-poorest population; the state's worst-performing school district, with the exception of Baltimore; three times as many liquor stores per capita as in neighboring Montgomery County, Maryland;[9] no Macy's, Whole Foods, or Saks Fifth Avenue; and the second-highest rate of HIV infections in Maryland.[10]

"It doesn't offer an awful lot," Linda Botts said. "I don't feel like I'm so connected. When I was in public service, at that point in time, there was hope this could be a great place. There was hope that it was going in the right direction, hope that it would be a wonderful place for family and kids to come back to and a place of opportunity, a place you could look at with pride and a sense of belonging. But that's gone."

During more optimistic times, when the Bottses still believed, they were active in everything, especially their children's lives. Nothing was more important.

Their oldest, Sammie, was an only child until he was fourteen. Before he became a man, confident in his own skin, Sammie had been a somewhat nerdy kid who felt like an outsider and desperately wanted to fit in. Most of his troubles in the early years emanated from the schools. His parents believed in public education and sent Sammie to public schools until third grade. His first- and second-grade teachers had been a joy. But in third grade, one day Sammie came home with twenty-five paper airplanes and spitballs that he'd made.

"I said, 'Man, what's all this?'" Sam Sr. said. "He said he finished his work and his teacher said he could do whatever he wanted. She didn't make him go on to the next lesson."

But the decision to move him to private school was the result of the kind of slight that seems small but isn't. Sam Sr. knows that in children, particularly black boys, seeds get planted in which teachers and other adults foist their negative thoughts about black men onto boys who are still finding their way. Sam would not allow that for his son, particularly when the quality of education was marginal.

"The teacher was black, and some white kid said Sammie had his pencil," Sam said. "The teacher took it from Sammie and gave it to the white kid. That did it. I went up to the school and said my son is not getting an education up here. I am a proponent of public schools. I believe in them. But we took him out of there."

98

Private school was no panacea. Wherever he went to school, Sammie, a future mechanical engineer, had shown himself to be something of a whiz at mathematics and science, but that didn't shield him from racial stereotyping. The Key School in Annapolis, for example, had been founded in 1958 by college professors from nearby St. John's College based on the premise that "children possess inherent intellectual vitality that schools generally do not reach."[11] He wasn't big on writing and the arts—things that fascinated his parents—but he gravitated to the sciences. Once, when he signed up for the most advanced math class the school offered, school officials balked, even though the curriculum expressly allowed students to advance through courses at their own pace.

"He felt he could handle it," Linda said. "For no apparent reason they didn't want to put him in the class." Linda and Sam—as would become their typical response—went to the school and demanded he be placed in the class. Sammie excelled. "You have to be really careful with male children that they don't have subtle kinds of things happening to them to make them feel insecure or less than."

High school was no different. Sammie went to Dematha Catholic High School, the same prestigious, college preparatory high school his father attended. There, he quit playing soccer when some of his black friends told him it was a white-boy sport. "Dumbasses," Sam said of those former friends. "If he would have talked to me, I would have told them, let me show you who won the World Cup for the last three years, an all-black team from Brazil."

But the most serious incident occurred days after the family adopted Ashley, who was an infant. Sammie was fourteen. Instead of soccer, he'd now taken up lacrosse and one of the assistant coaches, a white man, had taken to calling him Sambo. Sammie told his parents—as he always did—but he wanted to solve the problem himself. He told the coach that Sambo was a derogatory term to black people and that he'd rather be called Sam or Sammie. The coach persisted. Ashley had been home for a day when Linda went to the school to pick Sammie up after practice.

"I was sitting in the car getting angry at this coach," she said. "I put Ashley in her little stroller and walked down the middle of the field to the coach and assistant coach, and I told them he was calling my son Sambo and I wanted it stopped and if it wasn't stopped I was going to contact the school."

Her husband had already done so. Sam was on a planning board with Morgan Wooten, the school's legendary basketball coach, and told the coach that he was sorry to bother him but that he had a little problem. "He said, 'No bother at all,'" Sam said. The assistant coach was fired shortly thereafter.

Life can grind down people who lack means and connections, rendering them virtually helpless to fend off outside attacks. The day laborer must accept whatever his boss-for-the-day offers. The welfare recipient silently grits her teeth at the probing questions of her caseworker. Minimum-wage cooks, salespeople, and clerks suffer through daily indignities from customers and supervisors to avoid losing their lifeline. But Linda and Sam, self-employed and well-connected, have leverage and they have wielded it—just like others in their position—to open doors and move obstacles out of the way for their children. When the public schools were lacking, Linda and Sam paid for private ones. When their children needed additional tutors, they hired the best. And when someone messed with their children, they took care of it, even if their children didn't always understand, or even want, their intervention.

Sammie, for instance, was steamed at his mother for embarrassing him in front of the team. As he often did after his sports team lost, Linda said, Sammie "blew up like a frog." "I said, 'Sam you have to understand that this was not only an insult to you, it was an insult to me and every black person in that school.' It was inexcusable. I couldn't let it stand."

The intervention continued even after Sammie graduated from college. He wanted to work for Chrysler but never got a call back. His father had a law partner who had a friend in Detroit who was on a corporate board with one of the members of Chrysler's board of directors. Sam passed along his son's resume. Sammie got an interview and then a job as a mechanical engineer. He worked on the hydraulic system for the Viper, and the company later paid for his master's degree at the University of Michigan. Even now, he leans on his parents when he runs into a problem, and he shares an office with them in Philadelphia.

Linda is an early riser, usually up around four in the morning, and on Ashley's graduation day, soon after rising, she sat reading in the lobby of Marriott's Springhill Suites on Virginia Beach. Later in the afternoon Ashley would receive her degree from Old Dominion. The sun was shining bright after an evening of thunderstorms and lightning had cleared stragglers who lazily dipped their toes in the Atlantic for a midnight stroll. Six hours later, the beach was coming back to life, its sand smooth and ready for the onslaught of bare feet, volleyballs, and plastic shovels. This is the time, when others are sleeping, that Linda catches up on her reading. One of her and Sam's favorite authors is Napoleon Hill, a self-improvement author who had grown up poor in West Virginia but went on to became an adviser to Andrew Carnegie. One of Linda's favorite chapters in *The Laws of Success* is called "A Definite Chief Aim." Some of it is a recitation of common sense, but one point in particular sticks with her: Decide your major aim in life, write it out in a clear concise statement, and make specific plans to reach that goal.

It's motivational happy-talk to some. But Linda and Sam, turned on to Hill by Sammie, are hooked. "You have to stay focused on where you're trying to go," Linda said.

Their business, Ashlin Management (named for mother and daughter), has survived for thirteen years by staying focused. They want to provide opportunities for people to grow, and they want to provide social services to people in a humane way. The company hires people they believe in, as well as people who, in their view, deserve a chance to prove what they can do. Some are counselors with doctorate degrees. Others have only high school educations and have been through a few scrapes with the law, but all the employees use their varied backgrounds to service state and federal contracts that require Ashlin to recruit and determine eligibility for summer employment, manage child support cases, and train government employees to perform various tasks.

Linda and Sam approach managing their business the same way they approached raising their children. Sammie and Ashley turned out okay because their parents paid attention to the details, focusing on each child individually, defending them from attacks, and attending all of their outside activities no matter how insignificant they seemed. In business, they are determined not to overextend themselves. They operate on a pay-as-you-go model, afraid of becoming dependent on credit that has become the lifeblood, and death knell, of so many businesses. They don't believe that in order for them to do well, others have to do badly. Linda hires employees whose work history would suggest that maybe she ought not to give them a chance. Sometimes she runs across a foster child whose case handling is so egregious that she and Sam take their personal time to talk to judges or staff to get the situation resolved. They lean on slogans and try to put them into practice. And through their children, they dream about better days. On this day, Ashley was graduating. Her father hustled out to get balloons and flowers.

Families descended on Old Dominion's campus in Norfolk for that time-honored tradition of marching across a stage to get a piece of paper bestowing upon them a college degree. Linda had stationed the family, by chance, where the processional entered the

8,500-seat Constant Center. Championship banners hung around the rafters honoring the men's and women's teams who regularly made headlines for their dribbling and shooting skills. But on this day, academics were front and center. Parents were reminded over the loudspeaker not to have extended outbursts for their children, and to respect the couple of seconds of fame that each graduate had as his or her name was called. Ashley had prepared to crane her neck looking around the capacity crowd to find her parents. But there was no need. As soon as she emerged from the shadows of the tunnel, classmates nudged her and told her to look at a blue placard that read, "Congratulations Ashley Botts. You did it!" surrounded by red, orange, green, and yellow stars.

Ashley hadn't planned to cry, but the moment made her tear up as saw she her parents, two cousins, and her brother cheering her on. Those little moments of triumph and promise and hope that tomorrow will be better than today were evident through the arena. Sam and Linda beamed. They'd adopted Ashley when she was an infant destined for a foster care system that, despite good intentions, chews up children all the time. Linda knew well what could happen to children in the system. As an administrator, she had been responsible for it in Prince George's County, and in her business life, through various contacts, she ran across children in trouble. Sometimes she could help—employing Sam's legal skills—but not always. Adoption and foster care had touched Linda personally. Her father, a country club waiter, gave what he could to the family, but he fought personal demons that, to a child, were often embarrassing. Later in life, her mother would tell her to cut her father some slack: both his parents died by the time he was fourteen, and though family members helped, he was often left to fend for himself. Linda's mother, during her childhood, lived in what's best described as foster care while Linda's grandmother worked as a domestic. She used her earnings to pay the families who cared for her daughter, but they often treated Linda's mother poorly, washing themselves, then passing the soiled rag to her, and taking their children out for excursions and leaving Linda's mother behind.

The memory still scars Linda, and with Ashley, she made sure that history would not repeat itself. So when her daughter was diagnosed with a slight learning disorder as a child, Linda and Sam chastised the white school officials for trying to label Ashley and considered finding another school.

"I didn't want her labeled as having a learning disability," Linda said. "Sam and I spent thousands of dollars having her evaluated by black people because we felt more comfortable. The black folks essentially told us the same thing."

She had to make sure. Once she knew the problem, Linda provided extra support for Ashley in the classroom during her free period, taught her to sit in front of the class and realize that she had to write things down, in addition to listening carefully. Ashley sometimes doubted herself. "I heard from her a lot of times, 'I have to study this hard. Sammie doesn't have to study at all.' At one point she told us she wasn't going to college. What can I say? She is graduating on time with a 3.0 average."

David Gergen, a national commentator who has worked in Democratic and Republican White Houses, received an honorary doctorate at the ceremony as loved ones sat through more than two hours of names being called, followed by handshaking. Angel, Franklin, Natasha, Rachel, Jeremy, Jennifer, Kevin, Sarah, and, finally about midway through, to the delight of her family, Ashley Botts.

Linda instinctively yelled out her daughter's name, even though she had said she wouldn't. Sam snapped pictures. But before the names were called, Gergen tempered the sense of optimism in the auditorium with a dose of reality about the times. A day earlier, on May 8, 2009, the April employment report showed that the nation that month had lost 539,000 jobs, making it a total of 5.7 million lost since December 2007. The unemployment rate rose to 8.9 percent, but the good news was that the job losses were on the decline and unlikely to result in a depression.[12]

"It's the worst job market in a century," Gergen said. "It's going to be rough, and you're not going to find jobs quickly. But you know what we're going to get over this. We're going to get better. With the degrees you have, you're going to have to work hard but you're going to make a good living. The challenge is not how to make a good living but how to make a good life." It's a refrain that Ashley knew well. Her parents had drilled it in, as they shelled out thirty-five thousand dollars a year to pay for her room and board at the school. Gergen's kicker was this: "We don't care if you go home, but you can't stay here."

Old Dominion's campus had become a comfortable cocoon for Ashley. Wherever she went, she'd see friends. They would hang out and talk and go to parties and talk about guys and life. When she'd left home, she was unsure how she would leave behind the friends from her tiny private school in Prince George's and make it in such a large place. Now it was over. And four years later, she was nostalgic about the friends she had made, the boyfriends she had passed on, and the ones who were now telling her that all throughout their college years, they secretly wanted to be with her, never mind the young women they were currently dating. Over a dinner at Kincaid's, a steak and seafood restaurant in downtown Hampton, Ashley said, "I didn't think I would get here."

Family members ate shrimp, crab cakes, creamed spinach, and apple pie and key lime pie as they toasted the youngest, who was preparing to start her own life. Ashley opened cards passed her way, carefully reading them aloud before pocketing the money inside. Her parents allowed Ashley to take off a month before moving to Atlanta to look for a job. She's staying in their gated condominium there. They let her redecorate a little, but they were emphatic: This is not your place and you will have to share when we come to town for business.

They can, and will, intervene with friends to get her a job, but they want her to work for other people before she—*if* she—comes to work for them full-time, to understand that the world won't be as nurturing as they are. Ashley realized that during her internship in her final semester of college. She was working at a domestic violence and homeless shelter for women. "It was a humbling experience seeing these women," she said. "You have this idea of homeless people that they smoke crack or, you just have this idea. Really they just don't have a home. They're people struggling. We had a lot of people coming in who had just lost their house." While there, she also learned about the work world. A supervisor, older than both her parents, yelled at her and made her feel like dirt in front of the staff when she thought Ashley didn't move quickly enough to complete a task.

The woman told her to go home and, initially, not to come back—which would have jeopardized her graduation. Her parents wanted to come down, and possibly sue, if that happened. Ashley calmed them down. The woman had been in a power struggle with subordinates who were later fired. Ashley wanted to tell the supervisor how she felt about her treatment, but ultimately did not, after the woman said she had been a good employee and that she would provide her with a job recommendation.

Ashley held her tongue and decided to move on—a lesson learned.

But she knew that her parents had her back.

Because of her parents, she's sure she will have a job soon. "If worse comes to worse, I can work for my mom, but I don't want to do that. I want to break out, meet new people, get new experiences." Down the road, she might want to start her own business working with children or take over for her parents. The Bottses, clearly, owe their extraordinary success and that of their children to their own hard work, talent, and education.

But how do you turn one family's individual success into something that becomes routine for black children in a county government controlled by African Americans? It's a question that has been asked as blacks assumed leadership roles in Atlanta and Detroit. Linda and Sam were let in on the deal using their political and business connections to win contracts, changing the arc of their careers and that of their children.

This is the way that ethnic groups have historically used politics to get ahead: the Irish in Chicago, the Italians in Philadelphia, the Germans in Milwaukee, and the Cubans in Miami. The dream of those on the outside was to be let in, to be a part of whatever largesse and opportunity had always been available to those in power. African Americans were no different, but places like Prince George's show that political power doesn't ensure advancement for the masses. The repeal of laws that separated one race from another opened doors for educated, skilled, and connected blacks in the post–civil rights period at the very moment that the global economy was closing doors for the uneducated, the unskilled, and the disconnected. Much as it was in South Africa during the post-apartheid era, where some blacks saw their fortunes rise and others descended deeper into poverty, inequality among African Americans in the United States is greater than at any time in history.

In Maryland, and across the nation, the growing influence of corporate cash in elections and policy making, coupled with the downsizing of America's manufacturing base and the labor unions that represent blue-collar workers, has profoundly changed political dynamics in the black community. Old-school black pols like Detroit mayor Coleman A. Young, Chicago mayor Harold Washington, and Washington, D.C., mayor Marion Barry were largely populists, who oiled their political machines with civil service jobs, passable schools, trash collection, *and* contracts for a black constituency that forms the most reliably liberal voting bloc in this country. Many in this new generation of black leadership—Newark, New Jersey, mayor Cory Booker, New Orleans mayor Ray Nagin, and D.C. mayor Adrian Fenty, to name just a few—are less beholden to constituents than to their moneyed donors.

One of Prince George's own, former congressman Albert Wynn, represented Maryland's Fourth District, which includes the county. In 2005, he was one of ten black lawmakers on Capitol Hill to vote for a Republican-led overhaul of federal bankruptcy laws, a measure that is essentially a gift to the credit card industry but hammers consumers. Three years earlier, Wynn voted for a joint resolution authorizing the Iraq War, which was wildly unpopular in his district, save for the defense contractors.

When he lost his reelection bid in 2008, Wynn landed a high-paying job with a prominent D.C. lobbying firm. Wynn may have cashed in, but in his home county a laundry list of problems includes the inequities in the handling of police misconduct, economic development inside the Beltway, and the disparate treatment of children from affluent families versus poor ones in the county's public schools. Resistance often is based on kowtowing to monied interests that finance campaigns. How else to explain Wynn's unpopular support for the war or the bankruptcy bill, which cost him reelection? The choices don't even make political sense. And this has ramifications for Obama, who early in his presidency has pressed ahead with unpopular bailouts for the banks or ignored polls that consistently show that a majority of Americans support a Canadian-style government health care system. Ignoring such sentiment leaves some wondering whether the movers and shakers in places like Prince George's have a basic understanding of what political ascension, and ballots cast, is supposed to mean. It might be summed up this way: "Can y'all count?"

Sam remembers his wide-eyed youth when he wore a beret and a big afro and helped take over the administration building at

Howard University as an undergraduate. He remembers the FBI knocking on his door and wondering what he'd gotten himself into. He laughs at it all now—the posturing and big plans and dreams of a revolution.

He'd initially been drawn to Obama because he was a black man with a real shot at the nation's highest office, and John McCain's decision to pick Sarah Palin as his running mate sealed the deal. Hope and change, he realized, didn't come from catchy slogans but from hard work. But he got teary when Obama won, and early on the morning of the inauguration, he packed up the family and headed to downtown Washington to brave the crowds and the cold. A picture of the new president hangs on the wall of his office. He needed to bear witness. But unlike many in the loud and hopeful throng of supporters, Sam isn't starry-eyed or even in complete agreement with the Obama's vision of how to solve problems.

The young man surely is a masterful public speaker, Sam acknowledged, but one who spent too much time during the campaign harping on the need for higher taxes. It was the "same old Democratic line," Sam said, referring to the pledge to roll back the Bush-era income tax reductions on households with incomes exceeding $250,000 a year.

Sam was wary and grew more so in the early days of the presidency as Obama continued what his predecessor had started, announcing billions to bailout banks and the automotive industry. The numbers were dizzying to Sam and Linda, even though the consulting firm they own forks out between $100,000 and $150,000 a month in salaries. As business owners, they certainly understand how the failure of the financing giants could upend the economy. But it was unclear to them whether the president and his advisers understood that he also needed to shore up small businesses like theirs that gross $10 million or less each year but employ half of the nation's private-sector employees.

"What about us?" he asked.

Sam feeds the homeless on Thanksgiving, hires employees who need a second chance, and volunteers his legal services on behalf of foster children. But he has never believed that the nation's problems could be solved by taxing those who have the highest incomes. Partly as a result, he voted for Ronald Reagan, George H. W. Bush, and George W. Bush (twice). Jimmy Carter got his vote because he was a fresh face and Gerald Ford had shown himself to be such a poor leader. Sam proudly never voted for Bill Clinton.

Obama, meanwhile, felt like new money, something to smile about, after the country had fallen into a lull during the waning days of the Bush II presidency.

Voting for Obama was far easier after John McCain chose Sarah Palin, the gaffe-a-minute governor from Alaska, as his running mate. "I still don't know what McCain was thinking," Sam said. His twin brother, a resident of Florida, voted Republican, and he tells Sam all the time: "It's cool. But that brother is going to run us into the ground."

Sam doesn't think Congress will let him. At his business, half of what they earn goes to salaries and wages. By the time he pays for lights, insurance, and subcontractors, in addition to current state and federal taxes, Sam figures he ought to keep whatever he makes. Sam loves the symbolism of having a black man in the White House, but he would rather that he wasn't trying to lighten his pockets.

"He's talking about $250,000. It's not a lot of money during these times. He has probably never had to cut a payroll check in his life. We work hard. If he were to tax me because I got up early, what is the point?"

| 5 |

Casualty of War

Tee Green in Baghdad

The Negro must not allow himself to become a victim of the self-serving philosophy of those who manufacture war that the survival of the world is the white man's business alone.

—MARTIN LUTHER KING JR.

We regret the untimely death of your son.
The words, on White House letterhead, were supposed to serve as a salve, a gesture from a grateful nation to a grieving family that their child's death was important enough to warrant a personal note from President George W. Bush. But instead of pride in their daughter's service, or some small comfort that she had died for a noble country, in a just war, the letter stoked rage in Garry and Yvonne Green.

It felt like a punch in the gut.

Toccara Renee Green—everyone called her Tee—was the first woman from Maryland to die in the Iraq War, killed just outside Baghdad by a roadside bomb on August 14, 2005. She was posthumously awarded the Purple Heart and a coveted burial plot at Arlington National Cemetery, and her military family had been great to the Greens. But the letter from the commander in chief hurt. This fool of a president had promised to restore honor to the White House but couldn't bother to get her gender right? How dignified was that? Where was the honor in sending other people's children off to die in an unnecessary war, based on lies and half-truths, without even caring enough to ask if an obviously androgynous name like Toccara belonged to a male or a female soldier? What kind of man, what kind of parent, could do this to other people and their children?

As Tee entered boot camp in 2003, a *Washington Post* and ABC News poll showed that blacks were almost three times as likely as whites to oppose the just-started war in Iraq.[1] A CBS Poll in 2007 found that number growing, as 83 percent of African Americans said the Iraq War had been a mistake.[2]

"I have not found a black person in support of this war in my district," Representative Charles B. Rangel, a Democrat from New York told a newspaper reporter in 2007. "The fact that every member of the Congressional Black Caucus—emotionally, politically and vigorously—opposes this war is an indication of what black folks think throughout this country."[3] Black recruits into the army, as a result, slowed dramatically, accounting for 23 percent of active army recruits in 2001 and 15 percent in 2007.

But the army had always felt right to Tee. During Operation Desert Storm in 1991, the Greens were featured on a Baltimore television news program after her brother, Garry Jr., as part of a class assignment, wrote a letter to one of the soldiers serving there. The United States had launched an offensive after Iraq invaded neighboring Kuwait. His letter, coincidentally, reached a soldier from nearby Dundalk. A news station set up a meeting with the soldier's family and the Greens. "Garry was about eleven or twelve," Yvonne said. Tee was thrilled to be on television.

As a child, she was a quick learner. She walked at nine months and was potty-trained by fifteen months. She learned to ride a bike before her brother, who was three years older. "She liked to excel," Garry Sr. said. "She liked being in charge."

When she entered Forest Park High School, known for its ROTC program, she was immediately at home. She wanted to perfect the precision drill routines. "She loved the uniform," Yvonne said. "She liked things being done in order. She liked the whole structure and professionalism and discipline."

She was a frequent roller skater and often had pets, including hamsters and guinea pigs. Tee talked to her parents about men and relationships, and when she was in trouble—for speeding, on more than one occasion—she called her father, who was also a police officer. If it was in Baltimore, invariably the officer would call Garry Sr. first. His standard response was this: "She belongs to me. Read her the riot act and send her home."

After high school, just before the attacks of September 11, 2001, Tee attempted to go boot camp, but there was a discrepancy with her paperwork. The recruiter didn't get back in touch, and her parents persuaded her to try college. She tried two, including nearby Morgan State, but it wasn't what she wanted. In 2003, Tee headed off to boot camp, where she made friends easily, bonding with other black women who formed the BGC, or Black Girl Clique. She was in good spirits after her nine weeks, but she'd lost weight. Her father noticed it despite the black topcoat over her uniform. Her face was thin. Losing weight was easy with all the running and jumping and push-ups and obstacle courses they ran while carrying dozens of pounds of protective gear, food, and water.

"Tee, where the hell are you?" Garry Sr. said. "There was more of you when you came here."

"I have been telling her that food is her friend," said a fellow enlistee. "She doesn't eat."

"I don't believe that," Yvonne said, "because this child is greedy."

"No, because see, in the morning, the food be nasty," Tee explained. "I just eat like a bowl of cereal and peanut butter and jelly. That's all I ate for the last nine weeks. My uniform don't even fit. The first sergeant told me I need to get a Wonderbra. I lost my chest too."

"You got to be kidding," Garry Sr. said, incredulous. "Not my mother's chest."

Tee: "Yeah. I went from a 36-D to a 34-B."

It was a playful weekend, another graduation, and another trip for her parents. They had gotten used to this in high school: Tee in her uniform, traveling from competition to competition. This had the same feel, the banquet, the marching, and Tee, as usual, imitating people, Jim Carrey–like. He was one of her favorite actors, and like him, she contorted her face and body and altered her voice for her impersonations. She could mimic each drill sergeant perfectly, channeling her inner Sergeant Carter, the fictional marine who sought to turn the naive Gomer Pyle into a soldier with plenty of yelling and tough love. "Why are you asking so many questions? Get in formation!" As she had before joining the army, Tee kept everyone in stitches. But near the end of the weekend, Garry Sr., from behind the camera, observed: "I can't get over it. This is not ROTC. This is the real thing."

The point was made even more poignant, right after graduation, when one new graduate was promoted to sergeant and told he was deploying immediately to Iraq. Tee would deploy to Iraq for the first time within months. But war's reality loomed even as she explained the meaning of the pins on her uniform.

"This one is for the grenade," she told her mother. "I'm qualified to throw a grenade now. I'm a first-class grenader, one step under expert." Leaning in for emphasis, she pointed to her rifle pin, "This one means I'm qualified to *kill*."

For all the good feelings and weepy good-byes among friends, boot camp is about training soldiers to survive in the midst of a battle and, when necessary, to kill—and die—in defense of the nation. Less than two weeks after Tee's death, one of her friends from Forest Park's drill team was killed in Afghanistan.

Death is a part of war, but an insult from the man who ordered the war was too much.

"'We regret the death of your son,'" Garry Sr. said, spitting the words and turning to his wife. "Duh! Big-time White House. Do we still have it or did we tear it up?"

"I don't know what I did with that thing," Yvonne said, still bitter four years later. "I was about ready to make news again and call up every news station and show them the letter. As a mother, I was hot. It was not cool, I know that." The slight was almost as painful as getting that dreaded knock on the door: "We regret to inform you that your daughter has been killed in action."

If there is anything that black Americans agree on, almost unanimously, it is their distaste for war. In this regard, African Americans are indeed a monolithic community. At the height of nationalistic fervor, in the weeks after the September 11, 2001, attacks on the Pentagon and the World Trade Center, 44 percent of African Americans supported an invasion of Iraq, compared to 73 percent of whites and 66 percent of Latinos, according to a Pew Research Center poll.[4] By Election Day of 2008, blacks were more united in their opposition to the war—98 percent—than they were in their support of Obama.[5]

The biggest question about Obama's candidacy—from both his Democratic and Republican opponents—was how he would deploy America's might. Would he be tough enough? The Greens, like most African Americans, asked another question: Would he have the courage to walk away from a fight? Did he have the stomach for peace?

Large majorities of African Americans have opposed every American war since World War II. Not coincidentally, virtually all of those military efforts targeted darker-skinned people—Koreans, Vietnamese, Iraqis—and this is the principal lens through which blacks see war.

"Why would they ask me to put on a uniform and go ten thousand miles from home and drop bombs and bullets on brown people in Vietnam while so-called Negro people in Louisville are treated like dogs and denied simple human rights?" Muhammad Ali said in 1966 to explain his refusal to appear before the draft board. "No, I am not going ten thousand miles from home to help murder and burn another poor nation simply to continue the domination of the white slave masters over the darker-skinned people of the world. . . . The real enemy of my people is right here."[6]

The connection that Ali made between racism and militarism was reinforced by Martin Luther King's antiwar stance; the selection of U.S. Army general Curtis LeMay as the vice presidential running mate to rabidly racist Alabama governor George Wallace in his 1968 presidential campaign; and the stories told by black World War II veterans of their mistreatment by white soldiers, and those told by black Vietnam War veterans who said their lives had been spared by North Vietnamese captors as a gesture of solidarity. Perhaps just as telling is the almost reflexive antipathy blacks have traditionally had—even years after his death—for America's greatest military icon, John Wayne.

There is a very real irony here because while African Americans loathe war, perhaps the most revered, mainstream institution in all of black America is the military. Blacks account for 12 percent of the population, yet they make up 21 percent of all military personnel and 30 percent of the U.S. Army.[7] Since World War II, the one opportunity that the United States is perfectly willing to extend to blacks is the chance to die for their country, and blacks, famished for work, starved of respect, and searching for a path to get ahead, have seen in the military—and especially the all-volunteer army—a route for upward mobility. Any reader of *Jet* magazine in the sixties or seventies will recall as heroes of the black community Daniel "Chappie" James Jr., the first African American four-star general, and Benjamin O. Davis Jr., the first African American general in the U.S. Air Force and commander of the all-black squadron of fighter pilots known as the Tuskegee Airmen. With the unemployment rate for black men usually twice as high as that for white men, many blacks often figure, as an African American soldier revealed to her commanding officer in the 1996 movie *Lone Star*, that "this is as good a deal as they let us in on."[8]

But the willingness to join up for the opportunity has always run headlong into an outspoken segment of the black community that argued strenuously that no self-respecting black man should join the white man's military. Often those critics simply point to the way blacks have been treated in the armed services. In *Brothers in Arms*, an account of the 761st Tank Battalion, the first all-black armored unit to see action in World War II, Kareem Abdul-Jabbar, of basketball fame, and Anthony Walton wrote that whites resented black soldiers carousing with Englishwomen and, seeking to impose abroad the restrictions prevailing in the rural South, forced blacks to move off sidewalks to let white soldiers pass and regulated which pubs and theaters they could attend. "They [the black soldiers] considered themselves first and foremost Americans, and were honored to fight in the nation's service," they wrote. "But they also had to internalize and transcend the knowledge that they were viewed, at best, as second-class citizens by the brass and many of their fellow soldiers—and often, far worse, as incompetent and cowardly. It was one of the tragic ironies that African Americans had come to understand as something they just had to live with."[9]

This resentment continued back at home, when black soldiers returning from World War II were routinely denied the right to vote and were prohibited from attending segregated universities in their home states, particularly in the South. Even so, the military remained a draw for blacks because it offered a career and travel when college was not an option. But as quick as blacks are to join, they are reluctant warriors, in part, because of having been on the receiving end of the misuse of government authority. Black people, in general, were against the invasion of Iraq and, after it started, voiced strong opposition.

If Tee was reticent about military service, she didn't tell her parents. She had gotten her love of the uniform honestly. When Tee was little, Garry Sr. picked her up in the paddy wagon and drove her to school, dropping her off a few blocks away so her classmates wouldn't see. And if she begged ("Pleeaase, Daddy?"), Garry Sr. would occasionally turn on the lights of his patrol car and ride her around an empty parking lot, risking his job but winning the heart of his little girl. The two, since she was a baby, would stay up late into the evening watching movies. By her teenage years, Tee was wearing her own uniform as a member of the ROTC drill team at Forest Park High School. She caught the bus every morning at six to arrive in time for early practice, rising through the ranks to become class commander and winning competitions. Her father was always there filming his children's big and small moments— before the prom, after the prom, and, on one occasion, even inside the prom as the teens danced. Batteries charged on his trusty camera, Garry Sr. would wake up at two or three in the morning and listen to the highs and lows of the night and to excuses for being late. "I was an hour late," Tee said, "but it wasn't our fault." Daddy smiled and let the issue go. And when she kept on talking,

118

her father would say, "Tee, I will never get to bed if you don't get out of here."

And she left on this note, "I got to pee like a race horse," knowing that she was skirting the line, but that her parents were tired. "I don't care, I'm a ghetto girl," she would say.

As her last visit with family and church members wound down before she made her final trip to Iraq, Tee cut the grass at home and helped her dad set up the tents for a backyard gathering, where they listened to old soul music and ate barbecue. When she first arrived, Tee's cat, Spartacus, sat on her bed as Tee, kneeling on the floor, rested her torso on the mattress as she unbraided her hair, thankful to be away from sandy Iraq.

"So Tee, you going to get your hair done?" her dad asked.

"I'm going to do something with this stuff," she said. "Look at it. It's a mess. I'm tired of it. Soon as you put the grease in, that sand falling right behind it. So you got like a salt and pepper combination of sand in your hair."

The conversation veered toward death. "The marines don't respect their own kind because when their guys get killed, they don't even send them off. They sit them in the freezer for like two, three days before they send them off. But with us . . . " She stopped midsentence to chastise her cat. "This is my time, not your time."

"For us," she said, turning back to her father, "when guys get killed, they get sent right off, right then and there, within an hour or two they get sent back to the States." The night Tee was killed, she had taken the place of another soldier, her family was told. That was comforting to Garry Sr., but one night soon after her death—his house full of visitors—he drove his SUV to the nearby Home Depot parking lot to have what he described as a "pity party." Alone in his thoughts and sorrow over losing a child, he heard a loud bang and felt a shake. In the empty parking lot, a shopping cart had gotten loose and slammed into his truck. "God said, 'Wake up, Dude!' I said, okay, I'm going home. I got to be strong like the Scripture in the Bible that said don't get sorrowful when you lose a loved one, because when they are saved and with Christ, they're going to be with Him."

"I just started screaming."

This is what Specialist Nicole Coleman told a *Baltimore Sun* reporter over a crackly connection days after Tee was killed on August 14, 2005. "I never lost a best friend before."[10]

Tee was driving one of several vehicles in a supply convoy behind Coleman when the vehicles stopped to refuel and switch drivers near Baghdad. With the sound of the first explosion, Coleman, who was standing outside her vehicle, dropped to the ground. When a second round of blasts went off, she hopped back into her Humvee and waited. The chatter was that there were casualties, and when Coleman got out again, she recognized Tee by her head scarf, lying there in a pool of blood.[11] The two met during basic training in January 2003 and were delighted that they were both assigned to the Army's 57th Transportation Company, 548th Corps Support Battalion, in Fort Drum, New York. The duo sometimes referred to themselves as "Pinky and the Brain," a reference to the Warner Brothers cartoon about genetically improved lab mice. In the cartoon's famous tagline, Pinky says, "Gee Brain, what do you want to do tonight?" eliciting this response: "The same thing we do every night, Pinky—try to take over the world." America's critics around the globe would argue that world domination is the goal of the United States, exemplified by an unjust invasion of sovereign Iraq. But the Bush administration argued that it sent these two young women to advance the cause of freedom and to overthrow the tyrannical Saddam Hussein before he unleashed weapons of mass destruction. Saddam and his sons were killed, but no WMD was ever found. Neither the fictional characters Pinky and the Brain nor their human namesakes would ever conquer a thing. Tee's injuries were so severe that she died before the Medevac unit arrived.

Soldiers in their dress blues arrived at the Green household late that Sunday evening with the devastating news, starting a procession of visitors and well-wishers that would continue for thirty days. Friends and strangers beat a path to their door, just outside the Baltimore city limits, winding past the commercial construction equipment rentals on Pulaski Highway and the Dollar Store on Chesaco Road. On their suburban street are brick homes, with neat yards. The Greens have a rock garden and a gurgling goldfish pond out back. They moved to Rosedale in 2001 after Tee graduated from high school. The neighborhood, about evenly split between blacks and whites, offered mostly peace and quiet.

Childhood playmates who had been like brothers and sisters showed up to tell stories about how Tee would stop everything—jumping rope, hopscotch, or whatever little girls do—as darkness neared. "My father don't play," she would tell them as she scurried home. The tidbits they couldn't remember were captured on hours and hours of videotape that Garry Sr. had accumulated over the years. Memories he had meant for Tee to show to her children when she had them were now more precious than he ever imagined. There is Tee pouting at her middle-school graduation because she had not been voted class clown. Then she's hamming it up for the camera as her older brother, Garry Jr., nervously poses for pictures and prepares to go to his senior prom. Then there's Tee, in 2000, at her high-school graduation party, panning the camera over all of the awards she'd received, and then it moves to a picture of herself in a ball gown and saying, "Gorgeous, isn't she?" The smiling, playful girl and young woman on the tapes seemed incongruous with the new reality that Tee, at twenty-three, was a casualty of war, leaving her parents in shock.

During her last visit home, a friend had asked Tee if she was scared of dying. She replied, "If it's my time, it's my time." She had said something similar to her brother, a marine sergeant at the time, who had also spent time in Iraq and Afghanistan. Garry Sr. had rejoiced when his son joined the marines, certain that it would provide the discipline and respect for authority needed to cleanse Junior of the silliness of "sagging his pants," wrecking cars, and "getting in situations." But Garry Sr., a twenty-three-year veteran of the Baltimore Police Department, did not want Tee in harm's way. She was his baby. "I never thought it would be me in this position," her mother said.

Memorial Drive leading into Arlington National Cemetery is grand and stately, alerting visitors that this place is special. The grass is lush and manicured. This is America's "most sacred shrine," states a sign near the visitor center. "Please conduct yourselves with dignity and respect at all times. Please remember these are hallowed grounds." Cars creep by here, and people walk slowly. The official cars for those who run the place are black Chevrolet Impalas. Tourists file off tour buses silently, taking in row after row of white marble tombstones, letting the gentle breeze wash over them as leaves rustle on the magnolias, crape myrtles, and maples. This is no place for running and jumping. Breaks in the white and green palette of headstones and grass come from what visitors leave behind: flower bouquets, colorful rocks placed atop headstones, and the occasional blue balloon with the yellow smiley face and a message that says: "Thinking of you." The serenity is occasionally punctured by the three quick bursts of the twenty-one-gun salute, followed by the bugler, standing off from the bereaved family, slowing playing "Taps." Those outside of the funeral party invariably stop in their tracks and respect the moment—another soldier being laid to rest. It's the kind of place that brings comfort to families, knowing that their loved ones—many of whom died loud and violent deaths—are in such a peaceful place. This, you can imagine them thinking, is how a nation should honor fallen soldiers. Everything is just so. One of the most popular tourist attractions is the Tomb of the Unknowns, which holds the remains of unidentified soldiers from World Wars I and II and the Korean Conflict, and is guarded 24 hours a day, 365 days a year.

All are reminded at every turn to respect the dead.

The gravestones for individual soldiers are thirteen inches wide by four inches thick. The top curves gently. When one of the fallen is a loved one, when you've heard them laugh and seen them cry, Arlington is not a tourist trap. It's a place to commune, to acknowledge and remember that the once living are now dead. Tee's headstone is in Section 60, site number 8216, near the intersection of York and Halsey drives. To the left is a marker for Sergeant Edward R. Heselton, twenty-three, who was killed three days before Tee, on August 11, 2005. His family called him Eddie, and he left a wife and a one-year-old daughter to grieve. He had a knack for fixing engines. Heselton was from Easley, South Carolina, and died when a bomb exploded near his vehicle as he performed a route-clearing mission in Orgun-E, Afghanistan.[12] To the right of Tee's headstone is one for Master Sergeant Ivica Jerak, who was forty-two when he died. A resident of Houston, Jerak was born in the former Republic of Yugoslavia. As a boy in his tiny village of Debeljak, he stayed on the basketball court, working on his hook shot and spin move to the basket.[13] He was killed along with two other soldiers when an improvised explosive device detonated during combat operations near Husaybah, Iraq, on August, 25, 2005. Three soldiers—a father, a daughter, and a husband—blown up thousands of miles from home, now resting at America's most storied cemetery. The summer they died, U.S. casualties in Iraq numbered about 1,800.[14] By mid-June of 2009, the number had ballooned past 4,300 in Iraq and in excess of 700 in Afghanistan.[15]

On August 26, 2005, Tee's funeral procession made the forty-five-minute trip from Baltimore. A police escort shut down the Beltway that wraps around that city for the procession, which stretched for half a mile. At her funeral, U.S. Representative Elijah Cummings told mourners, "As Americans, we owe a debt of gratitude that we can never repay."

But through memorials and gifts to the family, individuals tried to show their gratitude. One woman had sent a beautiful painting of Tee that now hangs in their living room. Another sent a prayer shawl. Shortly after Tee's death, the Greens participated in a boot ceremony at Johns Hopkins University in Baltimore, where a pair of boots were laid out for every Maryland soldier who had passed away at the time. Tee's death was so recent that organizers hastily put out a pair for her after Garry Sr. and Yvonne inquired about why she was not represented. At a September 11 ceremony in Rosedale, Tee was honored along with other area soldiers who had died. A huge flag—which the Greens could see from their backyard—was dedicated to Tee and the others. Newspaper clippings and a growing collection of plaques and awards started going up on the wall of their wood-paneled basement. There's a photo of Tee sitting atop a military vehicle with a long machine gun attached to the top, giving the thumbs-up. The photograph of them with Bobby Ehrlich, the former governor of Maryland, when they were honored at the state house in Annapolis is there. So is the photo of them at center court at the Verizon Center in downtown Washington. During halftime at a Wizards basketball game, the family was called down from a suite they had been provided to receive the Pollin Award, named after team owner Abe Pollin. Garry Sr. shows the awards to anyone who wants to see them.

To keep her memory alive, the family formed the STG Foundation, which stands for Specialist Toccara Green. So far they have given away nine $500-dollar scholarships in her honor. "We had taken out student loans for Tee," Garry Sr. said. "But when she passed the bill was still there. Those student loans don't go away. So I said 'Let's start this scholarship fund to help these kids go to school.'"

Initially, they said yes to every invitation. As time passed, they realized that soldiers' families were brought in as props to raise money for this or that cause. During some of the national 9/11 celebrations, they felt like tokens, the only blacks on stage to represent a fallen soldier. But they didn't make a stink, they just started being more selective about events, and retreating more often to their basement to relax.

During happier times, Garry Sr. would be down there watching television or working in his office and occasionally yell upstairs for his daughter. "Tee!" he'd yell. When she answered, he'd say, "Shut up!" Mildly upset at having been suckered, Tee would yell back, "You shut up!"

One of his hardest days came a little more than a month after her death. Tee's belongings arrived in two batches. They were the last things she touched, the last things she'd worn, the last things she owned. Garry Sr. spread them across the basement and took account, again on camera. There was a DVD player, a digital camera, books, and uniforms. He opened a closet door where he'd hung up some of her clothes, and his hands lingered on the coat she was wearing the day he saw her after boot camp, when she looked so skinny. "That was almost three years ago," he said. At the time, he was unsure what to do with all of her things, so he cleaned out a closet in the basement and put them all there. "I don't know what we're going to do with all her things," Garry Sr. said. Yvonne does.

"They're going to stay there," she said, looking over at the closet door.

This space in their home—where they eat, wash clothes, watch movies, and entertain guests—has become their personal hallowed space. Looking at all the plaques on the wall, and remembering all of Tee's honors, Garry expressed this wish: that people like his daughter, the grunts, would be recognized while they are alive.

"I guess it doesn't work that way," he said.

Garry Sr. retired from the Baltimore police force the same year his daughter died. He'd never thought about being a police officer until he was laid off from Bethlehem Steel. He started there at age eighteen, making about twenty-five thousand dollars a year. His best friend, who would become Tee's godfather, was going to take the test to become a state policeman. Garry also took the test and scored high, but decided against joining up. Six months later, the Baltimore police offered him a job. Garry was unemployed, so he accepted.

"I didn't even like the police," he said. Two decades later, he was a detective on the warrant squad. When Tee deployed, if Garry got a call at three in the morning while serving a warrant, he knew it was his daughter. He always answered. But once she was gone, he no longer had the heart for the job. The constant knocking on doors got to him. They were an odd reminder of the soldiers who knocked on his door to tell him about Tee. So he retired early. His wife stopped working too. She had been a bank teller, but after the third time she was robbed, she decided to try something else.

Now Garry buys houses, fixes them up, and rents them out. It's hectic work because tenants often abused the properties, forcing him to find ways to "ghetto-proof" them by fortifying screen doors so children wouldn't burst through and placing braces around sensitive pipes so they wouldn't be accidentally broken. He complains, but he enjoys the work and being out back in his tool shed, which has a small television that allows him to get away.

He had never been much for politicians. He was on the security detail for a couple of Baltimore mayors and thought they were all right, but he generally steers clear of politics and politicians.

"They'll tell you one thing, and do another." But he's bullish on Obama.

During the fall of 2008, as the campaign heated up, he began watching the news, and five months into Obama's presidency the Greens were generally pleased. Obama wants the troops out of Iraq but understands that it's harder to get out of a fight than into one. Kind of like what former secretary of state Colin Powell, a retired general, said: You break it, you own it. Garry Sr. also embraced Obama's decision to ramp up activity in Afghanistan. He's not a pacifist. From his time in the police department, he knows that there are times when force must be used to protect the public good. But he had never been a fan of the war in Iraq. "The Bush administration came in there and they made money for themselves, for the rich people, and they used the war as a means to get money," Garry said. "We had no business rolling into Iraq."

The Bush administration seemed too eager to fight, too eager to place the lives of soldiers at risk for a war that didn't have anything to do with the terrorist attacks of September 11, 2001. "Like my wife said, I want the troops out of Iraq, but we went in there and stirred up a hornet's nest. We can't just quit like that. You gotta stay there and try to wean them off our presence because they don't want us there. We don't need to be there."

Like most of America, by the middle of 2009, he thought he'd rid himself of the Bush administration when the forty-third president flew off on the presidential plane one last time after Obama's inauguration. But the former vice president, Dick Cheney, kept rearing his head "like a devil," the Greens said. Just that week, the second in May, Cheney had made the rounds on national talk shows to argue that Obama was making the country less safe by saying that he would close Guantanamo Bay, the U.S. military prison in Cuba, and by publicly saying that the country would no longer use harsh interrogation techniques such as waterboarding, or simulated drowning, to extract information from potential enemies. The former vice president was like too many Republicans, they thought, criticizing without giving Obama a chance.

"I'm not going to put blinders on because he is the first black president," Garry Sr. said. "At the same time, I'm going to support him if he's doing right. He's a lot better than what we had."

He said Obama's election, to many, was a "bitter pill." "They better drink plenty of water and swallow," he joked. Across the street from his own home, one neighbor had started flying a sizable Confederate flag in his backyard. The two had been friendly, but the flag vexed Garry Sr. "Is it racism? Was it about the election? I don't know."

What the Greens want from Obama is for him to eventually bring the soldiers home from Iraq, to finish the job in Afghanistan, and to remember the price that military families pay. Both said they were sympathetic to mothers like Cindy Sheehan, whose son was killed. She camped outside of Bush's home in Crawford, Texas, alienating her husband and her other children. Yvonne met her. Where some saw a crazy woman acting irrationally, Yvonne only saw "a mother who was hurting and trying to deal with it."

On one of Garry Sr.'s tapes, Tee is across the room in her ROTC uniform in high school when she spots her father and waves. "Hey, Daddy," she says silently, just mouthing the words. Instinctively, sitting in his basement with Tee's things, Garry Sr. smiles, raises his right hand and waves back.

"God, I miss her. Every time I see a female soldier in a uniform, it's like I'm looking at her."

| 6 |

White Is Not an Abstract Concept

Angela's Daughters in Appalachia

"Men take advantage of weakness in other men. They're just like countries in that way. The strong man takes the weak man's land. He makes the weak man work in his fields. If the weak man's woman is pretty, the strong man will take her." He paused to take another sip of water, then asked, "Which would you rather be?"

I didn't answer, and Lolo squinted up at the sky. "Better to be strong," he said finally, rising to his feet. "If you can't be strong, be clever and make peace with someone who's strong. But always better to be strong yourself. Always."

—BARACK OBAMA, *DREAMS FROM MY FATHER*

Outside, the air was brisk and damp. There hadn't been much snow in the preceding days, so the narrow winding road up the mountain to Angela's cabin was passable. A good thing, since she'd misjudged and run out of toilet paper. Her home is a real-life tree house, a perch from which to peer over the canopy, to commune with elk, deer, and flying squirrels that pitter-patter over her wooden roof and collect the corn kernels that Angela scatters on her wraparound deck. She sits in her rocking chair, next to the sliding glass door, taking in the trees and blue sky and stillness. This place had once been a bit of a splurge, a getaway from the flatlands of Florida. But now it's home: two Manhattan-sized bedrooms, a postage-stamp loft, a bathroom, a living room with a wood-burning stove smack in the middle, and a small kitchen.

A local handyman helps Angela when things need fixing. She loves it up here, and so do her three dogs—Elvis, Misty, and Bella, whose barks disturb the peace. But just after noon on Christmas, as she peeled sweet potatoes, Angela was mildly vexed.

Her daughter Paloma, down for the holidays, kept getting up from the sewing machine to talk, make tea, and gaze out the window. Electricity, Angela needed to remind her, costs money. "Earth Girl," Angela said, "when not using an appliance, turn it off." Paloma began to mouth a protest but returned instead to her seat at the dining table, and to her sewing, which was a smart move.

Angela is a stickler when it comes to waste. She grew up in London during World War II when clothes, food, and fuel were rationed. She ate crusts of bread, sprinkled with a little sugar, for a meal and was happy to have it. Extra food was available on the black market, but such cheating was frowned upon in her enclave of Irish and Italian immigrants who were well acquainted with making a little stretch for as long as necessary. Even now, sixty years later, she dons a sweater on chilly days rather than firing up the wood-burning stove to save money. She turns off lights. And in an era of drive-throughs and microwave ovens, Angela makes her own jams and tomato sauces, things that keep, bartering the extras for other goods and services.

That's the way she raised her girls. Their father, Oscar McGregor, was a fixture during their early years, when they lived in his native St. Croix. But in the two decades or so since he and Angela divorced, every meal, sniffle, and heartache was Angela's to resolve. A painter and a teacher, she moved for better pay and quit jobs that took her away from the girls. Money was tight, but she made sure that they were well rounded and engaged in the arts, and that they traveled. They survived by living simply, buying off-brands, mending, and reusing.

But at seventy-one, Angela's survival skills were being tested mightily by her growing medical needs. She had liver disease, high blood pressure, and the lingering effects of a debilitating automobile accident that required her to learn to walk again. Her insurance through her former union got too high to keep. Often, she can't afford the medicine she needs, and she has delayed preventative treatment because of steep up-front costs. As a union activist and employee, Angela spent a lifetime fighting for paid vacation, wages, and health benefits. In her glory years, however, she wonders if she'd be better off if her pension and Social Security paid a few thousand less. That way, she wouldn't exceed the roughly nineteen-thousand-dollar cutoff for Medicaid, which would give her a free ride on medicine, doctor's visits, and surgeries.

"Those Medicaid people go to the doctor three or four times a week," she said, longing for the universal health care that residents in her native England take for granted. "They have drawers full of medicine. I only take one drug, for liver disease. I don't take anything for high blood pressure."

Just before her two daughters arrived, coughing and a nasty bout of pleurisy—an inflammation of the cavity surrounding the lungs—kept her up nights, and she felt constantly tired. But she mustered the energy to prepare a holiday dinner complete with sweet potatoes, tossed green salad, and a bottle of red wine. Two baked chickens, purchased already cooked, chilled in the refrigerator, waiting to be heated. Mincemeat pies for dessert, with a crispy brown top, were fresh out of the oven. Paloma eyed them hungrily, but they were for after dinner, so longing glances had to suffice. Both daughters are big eaters, and they know that, for them, their mother went all-out. Regular days are far more meager. In two months' time, facing another costly medical procedure, Angela will start going to a nearby pantry where she qualifies for free food. She reported in a cheery e-mail to Paloma that she had scooped up the fresh fruits and vegetables no one else wanted.

But on Christmas, Angela's home and spirits were festive. An artificial tree was full of ornaments collected over a lifetime. And the white-haired matron wore red pants and whimsical Cat-in-the-Hat-type socks. The mood was playful as Angela chided her other daughter, Patricia, for sleeping too much, kicking off what amounted to an Abbott and Costello routine.

"I've only been here two days," Patricia protested. "I just finished an intense semester of college. You always talk to me at school and you say, 'You always sound exhausted.' I am exhausted. I have not gotten enough sleep. So I come down here to get some sleep, and you say I am sleeping too much. I stay up later than any of you do at night." The last part sounded like an adolescent pout.

"I thought you seemed unusually tired," Angela said. "I said it out of concern, and I get attacked. You can't win."

"Nobody can win," Paloma chimed in.

"Everybody loses!" Patricia said in mock excitement. "Yah!"

The push and pull between mother and daughter is familiar to parents whose independent children are thrust back into their orbits for extended periods. Angela, like most mothers, wants to retain the control she was accustomed to when her daughters depended on her for everything. Her independent daughters, meanwhile, can revert to smart-alecky children. But that's a small part of the McGregor interplay, a rolling conversation that skips easily across centuries and continents—from World War II Europe to early Athens and modern-day South Africa—with each searching for the right tidbit from Greek mythology, pop culture, dance, or gardening to make her point. They finish the others' sentences, sometimes cutting in abruptly. Angela loves to spin a tale, and often she is the brave heart, staring down a bully, castigating a greedy corporate type or taking umbrage at those she considers morally bankrupt.

Angela's daughters, both in their thirties, had recently formed their own art collective known as Angela's Pulse, after their mother. Paloma dances for Urban Bush Women, a Brooklyn-based company that for a quarter century has performed African American–themed works around the world. Patricia worked on Broadway before deciding to attend graduate school. Her work, too, centers on race and identity, what it means to be black, white, or both. But ask the McGregors what defines them, and it's not race but experience, namely Angela's, as a teacher, a single mother, and a cheerleader. Her message to her daughters was simple: You can be whatever you like. Don't let anyone run over you. You are strong. Women are powerful.

It's one of the reasons Angela supported Hillary Clinton during the 2008 Democratic primary. Angela didn't think that Barack Obama was ready to be president. What had he done, she thought, to earn a shot at the presidency? Hillary meanwhile was battle-tested and had spent several years in the Senate, and during her husband's first term she struck out boldly, though unsuccessfully, to alter U.S. health care. Angela admired Clinton for those fights and believes that sometimes the status quo needs to be blown up to make way for change. That's why she signed on with Obama after he defeated Clinton. She knocked on doors for him. She wrote him a check. She cheered when he defeated John McCain. But a month prior to his inauguration, she wondered whether Obama was ready to upset the established order. Doing so meant doing something about health care. Nationwide, about 22 percent of adults have no insurance, compared with 25 percent in North Carolina, the highest in the nation. Another 9 percent, including Angela, have too little insurance to comfortably meet their needs.[1]

"If you don't have a healthy environment, and you don't have health care, everything else is for the birds. I think the pressures now with businesses having to be the sole providers of health care, except for us poor Medicare people—and they're trying to strip us of everything we pay for—that cripples business. It's an unfair burden. They said, 'You don't have to wait in line like you do in England.' I said, 'You don't even get in line because you don't have the money. What the hell are you talking about?' Most people don't have exotic illnesses. You can go and buy the same drugs we all take in Canada cheaper, in Europe cheaper, and in Mexico for dirt-cheap. If you don't have healthy people, you have nothing. I want some very specific things from him. If he doesn't deliver, I'll be on his case. Time is running out for those of us my age and older. I could go north of the border or south of the border and have better health care and have much more bang for my buck."

Angela came to the United States in 1962 aboard a freighter with ten other passengers. A friend of hers, a teacher, had emigrated and married a book editor and sponsored her passage, one reaching back for another. She had dreamed for years of what the place would be like. America's promise is that it provides more opportunity to advance than any nation in the world, allowing foreigners like Arnold Schwarzenegger, a bodybuilder turned actor, to marry into one of this nation's most storied families and to be elected governor of California, the second-largest state. It's this promise—work hard and get ahead—that beckons people to travel across seas and oceans and under wire fences to get to this land of plenty. Angela rode a freighter because it was the cheapest way to travel. The six-day trip took place in the middle of winter, and she remembers it fondly. "We could read and play cards. We were the only ones in the dining room. All of the men got seasick, and we didn't. One time, we were up in the wheelhouse. We were looking out at the ocean, and I saw this huge shape and thought it was a blue whale. It surfaced, and it was as long as the ship we were on. It was awesome." But the highlight was sailing into New York harbor and seeing the Statue of Liberty.

Nearly a half century later—after stops in St. Croix, Hawaii, Florida, and Illinois—she has settled alongside two of the nation's most despised tribes: Native Americans and the people of Appalachia, sons and daughters of Scottish, Irish, and Italian immigrants. The people who live in the mountain ranges of Appalachia have long been judged by their inadequacies. How much education they lacked. How much money they didn't have. How backward and rural they were compared to the urban and suburban masses. She rejects the terms *ignorant*, *redneck*, and *trailer-park trash* assigned to poor whites here.

"It's dehumanizing," she said. She admires the truckers and neighbors from surrounding communities who loaded eighteen-wheelers with cases of jams, water, and food during Hurricane Katrina and defied police roadblocks to get food to the needy.[2] "There comes a time when you have to go through," she said. The people here know what it's like to be needy. They worked hard to coax a living out of the land and left behind them lives that have kept artists and writers coming back to pick at and prod them for new meaning.

Capitalists have long stripped these ranges of their minerals and their young during times of war and peace. A desire for a better life led young people to enlist in droves during World War II, and later flock to industrial centers in the Midwest to help build bombs and seek steady employment, higher wages, and better living conditions than they could have at home.[3] It was an outflow that would continue to the present day as teenagers like Jessica Lynch of Palestine, West Virginia, joined the army in 2000 because her family didn't have the money to send her to college.[4] Lynch never thought she'd see action, but in 2003, soon after the U.S. invasion of Iraq, she became a household name after she was captured. The U.S. government offered her up as a modern-day Rambo who took down enemy soldiers and bravely escaped captivity.[5] Lynch didn't remember firing her gun. But her story and the reasons why she joined in the first place are played out in tiny towns across the United States: the lure of travel, the benefits, a career, a free college education, and an escape from grinding poverty.

Angela identifies with the underdog. "My mother's family came over to England in the potato famine. They were all British citizens. They were looked down upon worse than anybody. I remember as a small child we played in the streets all the time. A city street kid, one of these nasty little boys, started throwing stones at me and calling me a 'dirty Iti.' The Italians were in league with Mussolini. They threw these rocks at me, one of them hit me. Instead of sitting down and crying, I picked the rocks up and socked them right back in their heads. Then I went in and said, 'Mom, what's a dirty Iti?' I didn't know what it was, but I knew I wasn't going to be called that, not without some repercussions."

She now lives on the outskirts of Bryson City, North Carolina, a town of fourteen hundred, adjacent to the Qualla Boundary Reservation of the Eastern Band of the Cherokee and Smoky Mountains National Park. Paloma had worried that the place might not give Angela, a globetrotter, enough access to plays and movies and interesting people. She worried that her mother would be isolated and that might not be good for her. It's also not diverse; nearly everyone here is white. What Paloma hadn't taken into account was how the mountains revived childhood memories. "I have always been drawn to the mountains," Angela said. "Maybe my ancient Irish and Italian ancestors had it encoded in their genes. I do love the sea, but only if it's near mountains. I used to hike in one of the most beautiful areas of England if not the world, the

Lake District, home to Lake poets like Wordsworth and of course the domain of Beatrix Potter, who actually farmed sheep there when she wasn't drawing and writing and spearheading the formation of the preservation effort to form the Lake District National Park. When we lived in flat and humid Florida, I longed to have a small cabin in the mountains to escape the summer heat there. Patricia and I found this place, and I bought it as the price was right and the view was terrific. It is reminiscent of the Lake District but much wilder, of course. Many Scots Irish, the Ulstermen, came and settled here because it reminded them of their Scottish and Irish homelands. In fact, it's known as the Southern Highlands in some circles."

The beauty of the mountains has for decades contrasted with the hard living that was done here. The coal mines, in particular, were a blessing and a curse. They provided much-needed jobs, but the workers had to fight tooth and nail for every wage and safety benefit. The documentary *Harlan County, USA*, for instance, told the story of violent battles between coal miners and the Eastover Mining Company in Kentucky during a strike that lasted more than a year because the two sides couldn't reach an agreement. Those fights, in large part, are a thing of the past. But coal is still on Angela's mind. Coal-fired plants just across the border in Tennessee, owned by the powerful Tennessee Valley Authority, throw off smoke that ends up in her lungs. "We have ozone days here now," she said. "We didn't have that when I moved here."

Angela fires off pithy e-mails about the local comings and goings. In late October 2008, she wrote: "The other day a dead bear was found dumped on the WCU campus with Obama signs stuck all over it. The poor bear was a 75 lb cub shot execution style in the head, and they are investigating if it was one of the many tame ones kept in Cherokee. On all levels this is horrible."

"It's frigging freezing and snowing here but I don't plan on going anywhere," she wrote to Paloma in January. "Two houses in nearby counties slid down their mountains due to the rain, but I understand that one of them was newly constructed and had a very flimsy foundation. It carried its elderly inhabitants clean down the mountain in Maggie Valley but they were unharmed!"

In a perfect world, that would be the end of the story: a senior citizen retiring to a slower-paced place that reminds her of her roots. But this is not one of those stories. Angela came to live in Appalachia out of necessity. She had a nasty car accident in January 2000 that left her body broken. She couldn't work. Bill collectors were calling, and she needed a cheaper place to live. It didn't get much cheaper than here.

The United States spends twice as much as the rest of the industrialized world on health care, $7,129 per capita,[6] but has life expectancy, infant mortality, and immunization rates similar to those of much smaller countries that spend less than a quarter of that amount. Eighteen thousand people die each year because they are uninsured.[7]

The escalation in the use of managed care organizations set off a debate that has continued for decades: either we have private health care like what exists today or a government-funded system like what is offered in Canada, France, and England. There, health care is a right, and it's free. People who get sick go to a hospital, and they are not sent a bill. It's paid for out of their taxes. Today, the people who advocate this version of health care are pushing for what is known as a single-payer system. Doing so, advocates argue, would put an end to the rampant exploitation of poor people in an area that should not be based on ability to pay.

In June 2003, in a radio interview, Obama was an advocate of having the government pay all the bills. "I happen to be a proponent of [a] single-payer universal health care program. The United

States of America, the wealthiest country in the history of the world, is spending fourteen percent of its gross national product on health care. Yet, it cannot provide basic health care to everybody."[8]

But on the campaign trail five years later, Obama's position softened. "If I were designing a system from scratch, I'd probably set up a single-payer system. For those unfamiliar with the terminology, you've got one government-funded program. Medicare would be an example of single-payer if everybody was in Medicare. But the problem is we're not starting from scratch. We've got a system in which most people have become accustomed to getting their health insurance through their employer and for us to immediately transition from that, given that a lot of people work for insurance companies, a lot of work for HMOs, . . . making that transition in a rapid way will be very difficult. And people don't have time to wait. They need help now. My attitude is let's build off the system that we've got. Let's make it more efficient."[9]

Angela and many others argue that it's already too painful for those who need health care and often find it out of their reach. She's hoping Americans will rise up as they did during the Vietnam War, the civil rights movement, and the aftermath of the Great Depression, when workers demanded better wages and better work conditions. Health care, she said, is as important as those issues were. She realized that when the car came careening across the centerline and crashed into her. She didn't have time to react and wound up in a hospital bed, battered and fighting to survive. She had a job. She was covered. But what she realized, like some 250 million Americans, having health insurance doesn't mean that basic treatment or medicine is assured or that trying to access care won't send them to the poorhouse.

"In January 2000, some idiot crossed the median as he was traveling too fast and spun his way head-on into my car as I was going to work at my school in Florida. I spent the next few months in and out of hospitals and rehabilitation, getting multiple surgeries for severe orthopedic injuries and being taught to walk again and use my arms and hands again," she said. "Apart from the awfulness of the injuries and the fact that my insurances had to pay the majority of the costs for it, as the fellow was uninsured and Florida is a no-fault state, no matter if there was negligence involved, I met the best and the worst of medical care and got enormous amounts of help from the Methodist church we belonged to at that time. They filled the gaps that our so-called social services didn't. Paloma was my rock during that time, and I would probably have not had the will to go on if she hadn't been there, especially when the finance offices from Florida Hospital started threatening me, the insult-to-injury method."

This is the part of America she has never liked, our lack of priorities and our desire to have more money, more cars, and more houses even when it's unsustainable. Six years into her stay, as she took the citizenship oath, Angela was already exercising her rights to free speech. By then, she better understood the genocide of Native Americans, the brutality of slavery and racial segregation, and the second-class status of women.

"They asked me why I wanted to become a citizen. I said, 'Because I wanted to bitch legally.' They expected us to say, 'I want to join the greatest democracy in the world.' They asked, 'What kind of country is the United States?' I think they wanted that same answer: 'The greatest democracy in the world.' I said, 'A republic.' They asked, 'Is that all?' I said, 'Yes. There is no guarantee of a democracy. When this country was founded in its present form, this country and the government didn't let women vote. They didn't let black people vote. They didn't let Native Americans vote, whose country it was they stole. There were the smallpox blankets, the outright shootings, and giving them horrible government food, which is enough to kill everybody, Spam and government cheese.'"

America's ideals and its realities have always clashed, and Angela comes down squarely on the side of people like Shirley Chisholm, who became the first black woman elected to Congress the same year Angela became a U.S. citizen. Chisholm adopted the slogan "Unbought and Unbossed" and urged the nation to reject the notion that anything is owed to the traditional power structure that had led the nation astray.

In March 2009, Angela acquiesced to an endoscopy, even though she couldn't afford it. But her bout with pleurisy, a painful infection of the membrane surrounding the lungs, had kept her coughing since early December. Unable to sleep and afraid something could be seriously wrong, she agreed to have a tube fed down her throat. The results showed a hernia. The coughing, her doctor said, was the result of a valve between the esophagus and the stomach being propped open by the hernia. Acid backwash, as a result, was filling the esophagus. Hence her constant coughs.

"They gave me pills to reduce the acid," Angela said. "The hernia is not going to shrink and disappear. They say you have to manage it. They can do surgery if it's really painful or it starts to strangulate. At least I know it's a thing you can deal with."

Angela has a love-hate relationship with U.S. health care, which she said works only for the wealthy or the poorest of the poor, who qualify for Medicaid. She worked for thirty years as a teacher, but when the monthly cost of her insurance through her former union tripled to three hundred dollars a month, she had to let it go. With Medicare, she's on the hook for a thousand if she needs a hospital stay. But she loves her own doctors. One spent fifty-five minutes on the phone with her, talking through a problem. Another helped put her bladder back in place after it fell. And when her insurance company wouldn't approve her drugs, the doctor wrote to the drug company, which charged her the deeply discounted five dollars a bottle. "I have been lucky with doctors, considering how shady the system is," she said of her caregivers in North Carolina. "They swim against the stream."

But she wonders about everyone else. "It doesn't matter how many Hamas rockets are going into Israel. It doesn't matter where Osama bin Laden is. It doesn't matter what the KKK is doing. It doesn't matter how many banks fail. All of our differences, whether philosophical, racial, or whatever, none of it matters if we can't breathe. People are sick of being taken. There comes a tipping point when it just doesn't work anymore."

She thinks of the health care system in the same vein as she does the financial system that neared collapse just as Obama's presidency began. To Angela's dismay, Obama continued what Bush started: pouring billions into Wall Street firms, buying up assets that some considered worthless, and arguing that allowing firms to fail would be disastrous.

In an economic state of the union address in April 2009, Obama addressed the concern of the Angelas of the world. "One of my most frequent questions in the letters that I get from constituents is 'Where's my bailout?' and I understand the sentiment," Obama said during a forty-five-minute address at Georgetown University in Washington, D.C. "It makes sense intuitively, and morally it makes sense, but the truth is that a dollar of capital in a bank can actually result in eight or ten dollars of loans to families and businesses. So that's a multiplier effect that can ultimately lead to a faster pace of economic growth. That's why we have to fix the banks."[10]

Angela is unconvinced. "This thing is beyond repair as it exists," she said. "We're as bad as the countries in Africa and Asia who siphon money off for themselves. There has to be a measure of common sense and control. Call me a socialist, a communist, or whatever you want. The patient is dying. We have to do something about it. I know Obama's style is, 'I don't want to pour oil on the

fire.' But it's like being a parent and you have a screaming child in a department store. You have to remove that child or threaten instant annihilation. They are beyond reason and you have to do something."

Angela is always at the ready to do something, whether it's throwing a rock back at a childhood bully or stepping in front of an out-of-control mother arriving at a high school office with a grievance. At the time she was a union representative for the Hawaii State Teacher's Association.

"You fucking nigger," the enraged woman yelled at the principal, a black man, loud enough that Angela could hear from behind the closed door.

"I heard thumps and the door flew open and out flew this gigantic Hawaiian woman. Hawaiians can get seriously huge, and this woman was insane. She was hauling off at him. She was swinging and everything and she said, 'You fucking nigger!' I don't know why I got up and went right over to her and said, 'Ma'am, why don't you come outside with me and get coffee and a donut.' I said, 'Ma'am, I am sure you are upset but there are better ways to deal with it than to swing at people and call somebody a fucking nigger, and I will not be in the room with someone who calls names like that.' I said if someone was calling you a name like that, I would defend you. She got kind of quiet."

This is one of Angela's famous stories, the ones that her children laugh off as gross embellishments or outright fables. But Angela tells them gustily to make a point: she's always game to stand down a bully, no matter how big or how powerful. At heart, she's a softy who saves stray dogs and sticks up for the weak, but get on her wrong side and Angela goes into what she calls "intimidator mode." The moniker tickles Paloma and Patricia, but Angela is serious. She has the education and the training to be diplomatic, but it's not her nature, which tends toward the Old Testament's eye-for-an-eye philosophy. She believes in treating people and animals humanely. Power, or the perception of it, is what makes the world go 'round. Whether she has it or not, Angela projects power and certitude. And about this she is certain: the Hawaii she saw was not the image that tourists are force-fed through postcards and television ads and news stories of a tranquil, laid-back paradise where leis and fruity beverages are as abundant as smiling natives waiting and willing to make your stay more enjoyable.

In Hawaii, with few black Americans, Angela and her daughters were different. And they began to realize how jumbled the issue of race in America could be. Angela, as a white woman, got used to being referred to as a "stupid fucking howlie." (Her retort? "If we're so dumb, how come we have all your money?") The Japanese hated the Filipinos. The Chinese stayed to themselves. The Puerto Ricans were considered loud and gregarious. And no one knew quite what to make of black people, even those with light skin. One day Paloma went to school with her hair in one big braid, and a classmate told her, "Your hair looks like a piece of shit." A school form asked Paloma to check the box for her race. She didn't know which one to pick. The future president had a similar experience in Hawaii. He was one of few blacks in his school, and he dealt with his share of racial slights, and fights. Bar, as his grandparents called him, bloodied the nose of a seventh-grade classmate who called him a coon, threatened to report a tennis pro who joked that his color might rub off on a schedule of tennis matches, and cursed out a white basketball coach who sought to teach him the difference between black folks and niggers.[11]

Until they arrived in Hawaii, being white or black was never much of an issue in the McGregor household. Angela was white; her daughters were light-skinned blacks. But in the comfort of their home—wherever that was—they were mother and daughters, family, and the racial divide was nonexistent when a diaper needed changing, a math problem needed solving, or hurt feelings needed soothing.

Angela taught them about themselves in more subtle ways with the images she had on the wall: photographs of their white relatives from Europe, alongside black faces from Haiti and Africa. But the world outside the familial cocoon was not subtle at all. Paloma would attend a predominantly black college, Florida A&M University, at her mother's urging. And she would ensconce herself in art projects rooted in African American culture. Wherever she goes—Latin America, Africa, Europe—Paloma is approached by people who think she is one of them. When people ask what she is, the rebel in her is tempted to say, "I am a woman. I am a dancer. I am a human being." Most times, she doesn't bother. But in the United States, in some predominantly black settings, her fair skin remains an issue. She has thrown herself into the creation of art that explores and amplifies the lives of black people. Still, she gets chided sometimes for trying to be "too black," in theory to compensate for her mixed-race heritage—an idea that Paloma rejects. But she struggles internally with her choices about dating. She married, and divorced, a black man. But she wonders whether she could marry a white man. "I don't know what I would do with a white child," she said. When she was in college, she had to distance herself from conversations with black students whose idea of racial justice was to "kill whitey."

"Maybe my experience of being raised in America was different from theirs, and maybe they were subjected to certain things in their lives that were different from mine," Paloma said. "My experience is that white is not an abstract concept or an oppressive outside force. White is my mom. I was able to have a perspective on it that, like, maybe that's not something, kill whitey rants, for instance, I could participate in even while I understand the roots of where that's coming from."

As a child in St. Croix, none of that mattered. But in the paradise of Hawaii, Paloma had her racial awakening. "Hawaii was horrible," she said. "But it was beautiful."

Judging people by skin color or religion breeds intolerance, which is Angela's main knock against organized religion. She fights against it on behalf of her children, and her society. During the 2008 Democratic primaries, the entrance of the Reverend Jeremiah Wright on the national political scene reminded Angela of religion's danger. As pastor of Trinity United Church of Christ in Chicago, Wright had been Obama's pastor for twenty years, presiding over his marriage and the baptism of his daughters. But the pastor caused a stir during the campaign when footage of his more strident speeches made their way around the Internet and then onto the national news. In one sermon, days after the 9/11 attacks, Wright suggested that America itself was needlessly violent and murderous.

"We bombed Hiroshima, we bombed Nagasaki, and we nuked far more than the thousands in New York, and we never batted an eye," Wright said. "We have supported state terrorism against the Palestinians and black South Africans, and now we are indignant because the stuff we have done overseas is brought right back in our own front yards."[12] The clip that got the most traction, however, was Wright's denunciation of the United States for its treatment of black Americans. "The government gives them the drugs, builds bigger prisons, passes a three-strikes law, and then wants us to sing 'God Bless America.' No, no, no, God damn America, that's in the Bible for killing innocent people," he said in a 2003 sermon. "God damn America for treating our citizens less than human. God damn America for as long as she acts like she is God and she is supreme."[13]

Obama resigned from Trinity United during the summer of 2008 and publicly split from Wright. Three months into Obama's term, Wright cautioned a crowd in Selma, Alabama, against putting too much trust in the new president. "Barack's name ain't

Jesus," Wright told seven hundred people gathered at Tabernacle Baptist Church for the forty-fourth anniversary of the Selma-to-Montgomery voting rights marches. "Barack ain't gonna improve your child's reading score. There are things we've got to do on our own."[14]

Obama's relationship with Wright still rankles Angela. "I just thought [Wright] tapped into a very mean-spirited conversation, the kind of stuff I would slap some white person about saying about black people. I thought, if you promote yourself to follow Jesus of all people, this is bullshit. It was pointless. It wasn't helpful what he said. It informed me a lot about Wright, but it didn't inform me about the church he purported to belong to. I've been to black churches. I have been to churches where I have walked out because I thought the preacher was an asshole, and that's basically what I thought he was. I just thought it showed a flaw in Obama. I'm not leery about the creator. But I am leery about churches, nearly all of them. I think they stand or fall on their individual pastor. I was raised as a Catholic, and you were supposed to believe this monolithic bullshit, so I quit the Catholic church even though I like people who are in the Catholic church tremendously. But if you are going to be a leader in the church, you should strive to be a saint. If not, just join the rest of us. I think Obama knew. But I didn't think he knew it would get out and it would be so offensive to people whose votes he needed. I think he could say he wasn't there very often, but I have been to black churches with black preachers who got very lively, which most white preachers don't, for the most part. I thought he tapped into something ugly. I'd like to be in a room with Wright and really take him on."

People like Wright annoy Angela, who believes that the world is at its best when people are cooperative. But when powerful men disappoint, Angela understands and almost expects it. Women are another story. At home her daughters saw their mother take control when their father became a nearly nonexistent figure after the divorce. Angela's proudest stories are of Aunt Kathleen, who during the darkest of days of World War II always had a little "egg money" stashed away. The term originated because the proceeds from selling extra eggs were often the only bit of money available for farm women. But it also became synonymous with a little something extra put away for hard times when the cupboard was bare. Egg money and her aunt's insistence on it had taught Angela a lesson: the men might go off to fight the wars and earn the wages to pay for housing and clothing. But it was the women who held the family together, who kept factories running and the economy humming. What those women knew is the same message that Obama's stepfather had passed along to him when they lived in Indonesia, "Always better to be strong yourself. Always." Paloma was Angela's strength after the accident. She came down to be by her side in the hospital, and then Angela went to live with her before deciding to relocate to her cabin. "I would probably have not had the will to go on if she hadn't been there," Angela said.

But she's also a mother who wants to be a grandmother. Over Christmas, she hectored Paloma, divorced and unattached, about having a child. It's a point that seems anathema to what they have been taught about independence. Even with her girls, she has a tendency to push conversations to a level of brinksmanship.

"Do you want me to just fuck somebody and have kids?" Paloma said in anger. "Is that what you want?"

Cooler heads prevailed and everyone went back to their respective corners, realizing, as usual, that they were on the same side and have always worked in one another's best interests. Angela respects her children, and they respect her as one of the strongest women they have ever met. Like many mothers, Angela lavishes praise on her children's work whenever she has the chance to see it performed live a few times each year. She actually enjoys it when they push back. It's evidence of the strong women they have become. "Women are far more practical than men. For the sake of kids, of our daily lives, we have to be cooperative. In some animal societies the males are the protectors, but the women rule. I don't think I taught them that, I just said, 'I'm not putting up with anybody's shit.'"

This construct that women are hardwired to be more compassionate than men bothers Patricia, who was part of the Broadway production team for *Medea*, a play that is sometimes seen as one of the first works of feminism. The play by Euripides is a tale of jealousy and revenge exacted by a woman who has been betrayed by her husband. Despite their having children together, he rejects her for another wife. As revenge, she poisons and kills the would-be wife and then murders her own children, who helped her in the deed. It was all to spite her husband.

"*Medea* is considered the worst story ever, because how could a woman kill her children?" Patricia said. "Generally in Greek mythology there is a moralizing about when women do it, that is different from when men do it. There is a craze, a female mania. When violence is executed by men, often it is okay. Either it was a bad man who was killed or he was just executing something. I think we have to be careful about not assigning, 'Oh there is a nature element and so that's just the way of the world.' We, as storytellers, have to be really careful."

But Angela is adamant. Of all the horrors—killings, rapes, burnings—associated with apartheid in South Africa, it was Winnie Mandela who fascinated her. Angela said she sat glued to the television screen as Archbishop Desmond Tutu, who headed South Africa's Truth Commission, begged and pleaded with Winnie Mandela to admit to her crimes and say that she was sorry. The fate of the nation, he urged, depended on getting everything out on the table so that the country could move on. It reminded Angela of the Nuremburg trials, in which Nazi leaders were prosecuted after World War II.

"I nearly fell out of my chair watching," Angela said. "It was one of the most high-drama things I have ever seen. I had never seen anything like it. I was riveted. I thought, 'Oh my God, this is like the crux of something.' It didn't solve what had happened, but it gave some kind of feeling that there was a public accounting and there was a public punishment. It wasn't perfect, but it was necessary. I mean somebody has to answer for this shit. I think that what happened with the Truth and Reconciliation Commission was enormously daring and highly Christian. It was like Christ on the cross. It was a morally high ground that few of us could aspire to. But I think somewhere in there, someone should have been taken out to the back of the woodshed and had their ass kicked."

On the second day of a six-day run, Patricia was still tweaking aspects of *Jelly's Last Jam*, a fantastical musical about the legendary Jelly Roll Morton, a New Orleans Creole who claimed to be the inventor of jazz. It was one of several plays during her three years at Yale School of Drama that dealt with the thorny issues of race and class. Patricia had chosen it as her thesis, even as professors counseled her against such a difficult musical, fearing she would not have enough black actors to fill out the production cast. But with the stubbornness of her mother, Patricia pressed on. On a Saturday afternoon in mid-February, before the first of two scheduled shows, she was in mothering mode. One performer was sick and dragging. Drink plenty of fluids, she told him, and then advised the others to support him from afar. She didn't need everyone sick. But her critique of the previous night's opening was that they needed to reach deeper and channel the Roll, as Morton liked to call himself, for his final two-hour performance as he tries to convince the Chimney Man that his soul was worth saving. The central question of the play is this: once we've "given up the ghost," what do we leave behind? Patricia said opening night had been a hit, but something was missing. "We have two hours to save this man's soul," Patricia said. "That hunger has to be there. This is a living, breathing thing. We have to work to make this better."

When she's with her mother and sister, Patricia is the baby of the family, the one who most needs catering to, maybe because Angela once told her that the best genes go to the oldest child. But away from them, Patricia is a leader. She is artistic director for Yale Cabaret, serves on leadership boards, and directs plays that sell out. *Jelly's Last Jam* resonated in her own life. "For me this show is an exploration of some of my favorite obsessions: American folklore, racial intersections, cultural authenticity, and the simple magic of forgiveness," she wrote in her director's note to the audience. Here's Angela's take on the performances she's seen and Patricia's way with actors: "She doesn't scream and yell, but she was clearly in charge. Both of them are very take chargeish."

On the back page of the *Jelly* program were three quotes. From August Wilson: "Confront the dark parts of yourself, and work to banish them with illumination and forgiveness. Your willingness to wrestle with your demons will cause your angels to sing. Use the pain as fuel, as a reminder of your strength." From Chris Rock: "Yeah, I love being famous. It's almost like being white, y'know?" From Angela McGregor: "Your family history is complicated and you have to know it all. If you don't know the soil from which you were sprung, the world's gonna roll all over you."

Angela approaches life with a bludgeon, whacking those who would stand in her way. Paloma thinks her mother's feeling of authority arises from her being white and having come from Europe, giving her an aura of sophistication that allows Angela to dismiss those she considers obstructionists. "I tell them to fuck off and leave me alone," Angela says. Both daughters recognize their mother's contribution to their personal and professional lives, forming Angela's Pulse as a home for their artistic collaborations. But both are more measured, like Obama, in their dealings with the world. Patricia, a member of a Yale diversity committee, understands her mother's zeal but chooses a different path. "There are times when you're like, 'Are you serious?' You want to just shake people and say you're a complete idiot," Patricia said. "But then I would have that fight and it would be done. And I would probably get what I want because I am a pretty strong person. But then I leave behind a group of people who actually need my negotiation skills to kind of move things on in a system I find very frustrating, and so I have to distance myself."

Patricia's biggest worry is that Obama's election will send the wrong message. "There is going to be a lot of fallout of people being, like, 'Yeah but if Barack Obama can become president, why can't you transcend all of these things?'"

But for all the soaring rhetoric during the campaign about change, the kind you can believe in, Obama's election wasn't Angela's ultimate goal as she knocked on doors for him in her conservative North Carolina county. What she wanted was practical change in two areas: health care and the environment. And she wants it now. Just as she told Patricia in the quotation that appeared in her program for *Jelly's Last Jam*, Angela is adamant that "if you don't know the soil from which you were sprung, the world's going to roll all over you." She doesn't want that to happen to Obama. He now has the reins of the nation's economy, the trappings of the most powerful office in the world, and corporate and executive types who will try to convince him that their needs outweigh those of little people. But the soil from which he sprang was fertilized and worked by folks like her who, after eight years of George W. Bush, poured their dreams into a senator from Illinois and now want to see them realized.

| **7** |

Little Men

Jewel and Launnie in New Orleans

Nothing can more effectively contribute to the Cultivation and Improvement of a Country, the Wisdom, Riches, and Strength, Virtue and Piety, the Welfare and Happiness of a People, than a proper Education of youth, by forming their Manners, imbuing their tender Minds with Principles of Rectitude and Morality, (and) instructing them in . . . all useful Branches of liberal Arts and Science.

—BENJAMIN FRANKLIN, 1749

First, a boy: curly-haired, jug-eared, cheeks like Satchmo, impishly handsome. He wears high-top sneakers like his idol Chris Paul of the New Orleans Hornets, watches Tom and Jerry, the Teenage Mutant Ninja Turtles, and anything with Bruce Lee in it. He grooves to Fela Kuti, sings along to Lupe Fiasco, swears he can break-dance, and drives his mama crazy trying to play the acoustic guitar she bought him for Christmas. He has a sense of humor that can only be described as diabolical, a smile so straight and bright and warm that it could melt a glacier, and smooth, golden-brown skin that glows like honeyed lava. He eats peanut butter and pizza and sushi—all at once if anyone would ever let him—calls his mommy "Jewel Bush" when he wants to get a rise out of her, giggles when it works, loves going fishing with his granddaddy, whom he calls Pa Pa, and he will not, will *not*, take a nap. This, Laundale "Launnie" Galmore Jr. will not do. He is six.

And then there is his family: Jewel Bush was twenty-three when she got pregnant, unmarried, a year out of college, but still regularly hauling her dirty clothes to her parents' house to wash. "How in the world is that girl going to raise a child?" her father, Joe Bush, mused. "She's a child herself."

Jewel paid him no mind. Her parents never understood what makes her tick; why she makes everything so difficult; why she asks them not to smoke in their own house; why she tries to guilt-trip her dad by telling Launnie that cigarettes kill people; why she gets so angry about the most casual remark when her little sister will let it roll off, like water off a duck's back.

"If I say dog, Jewel has got to say cat," her mother, Red, often says of the elder of her two daughters. Jewel is the writer in a family of schoolteachers, a vegetarian in a milieu of meat-eaters, the bohemian daughter of a man who worked on the railroad for twenty-eight years. Her ambitions were always bigger than New Orleans, or working a nine-to-five job every day so she could pay the mortgage on a house where she would go home every night and watch television, waiting to die. She wants to meet new people, listen to their music, and understand their culture, and that's why she headed off to Haiti in March of 2009 with a group of artists, her third trip there. Two months later she went to Egypt and the Gaza Strip for a week when an aid-worker friend told her that they had room for one more. Her personal mission statement (yes, she has one) says: "I aspire to travel the world writing about the beauty of places tainted by ill global perceptions; and through this raising international awareness and encouraging movements to improve the quality of life in said places."

This is what she wants for Launnie, a borderless educational experience, not just a diploma from a mediocre school in a state with more than its share of people like that. She wants him to learn *how* to think, rather than *what* to think. So when she evaluates a school, she asks: Will it spark his imagination or subdue it? Will it prepare him for an engaged or creative life, or is its goal simply to help him land a job in which he will toil away for some over-paid corporate robots who reward him handsomely to be a glorified clerk, or worse yet, their "diversity" hire, looking different but thinking exactly the same way as every other clerk.

In this respect, Jewel's views on education are similar to those of Benjamin Franklin 260 years ago, and those of Barack Obama's maternal grandparents, who despite their blue-collar status managed to pull enough strings for him to attend a prestigious prep school in Hawaii along with the island's elites. "For my grandparents, my admission into Punahou Academy heralded the start of something grand, an elevation in the family status that they took great pains to let everyone know," Obama wrote in *Dreams from My Father*.[1]

Launnie's grandparents are just as engaged. Red, his grandmother, managed to help Jewel enroll him in the parochial school where she works as a gym teacher, and Joe waits for Launnie after school to help with his homework before Jewel arrives to pick the boy up and take him to her house. Like Jewel, they see education as paramount for Launnie, but to them, schools are for the basics, where the boy will learn reading, writing, arithmetic, history—the subjects he'll need to get ahead. "Jewel wants him to go to a school where he is exposed to the sciences, the up and trendy school," says Red Bush. "But you can't beat tradition. You start a child in those types of schools, I don't know if you build a foundation."

And, just as important, especially for a black boy in New Orleans, their grandson needs a school that is safe, where they can send him out the door in the morning and have a reasonable expectation that he will return in the evening in roughly the same physical condition. Their central worry is the violence in the schools that is carried out by other youths, but almost as worrisome for black families is the violence inflicted by the schools on their children by "zero tolerance" policies that criminalize children merely for acting like children when their only sin is the darker hue of their skin. What might be considered a boyish prank or schoolyard scuffle for white boys can result in suspension, expulsion, or even arrest for a black boy, like the six black teenagers right up the road from here in the small Louisiana town of Jena, who were arrested when their peaceful protests against the hanging of a noose in the schoolyard led to a string of racial skirmishes. Not a single white youth was charged, even though, by all accounts, it was a white teenager who pulled a shotgun on a group of black youths.

Moreover, some charter schools are permitted to mete out corporal punishment without parental consent. They are quick to diagnose learning disabilities and antisocial behaviors in black kids and can even legally require them to be medicated with numbing, mood-altering drugs.

And so if this family often finds that they are at odds with one another, on this they are in full agreement: New Orleans public schools, by and large, are not in the cards for Launnie. Jewel has considered moving to a wealthier suburb to enroll him in what she considers a suitable school, but for the time being, he attends an integrated parochial school on New Orleans's West Bank, Holy Name of Mary, where 40 percent of the students are African American. "He's getting the basics," his grandfather said one afternoon at Jewel's home, a short drive from the school but just outside New Orleans. "And what he doesn't get there, he gets at home. That's why I take him fishing and get him away from television, all that old rotten shit. All of those video games all the day long. I make him do something."

. . .

New Orleans is in many ways unlike anywhere else in America, and yet in its political and economic development since the 1954 U.S. Supreme Court decision integrating public schools, it is exactly like all other cities. *Brown v. Board of Education* was the thunderclap that began an exodus of whites from the city to the suburbs, which they walled off like fortresses to keep blacks from following them. The 1968 riots accelerated that migration, and the 1974 Supreme Court *Milliken* decision effectively neutered *Brown* by preventing central cities from busing schoolchildren beyond their borders in an effort to comply with desegregation orders. The modern American metropolis was born. By the time that Hurricane Katrina capsized New Orleans in 2005, two of every three people living in the city were black;[2] one of every three was poor;[3] and one quarter of all adults over the age of twenty-five did not have a high-school diploma.[4] Schools, by and large, were dangerous and dysfunctional.

Still, the New Orleans African American community has known for years that the whites who abandoned the city want it back. Louisiana is in the heart of the slaveholding Deep South, and the dispossession of black labor, land, and liberty courses through its veins like bad blood. New Orleans is where Dred Scott disembarked from a train and claimed that he was a freed slave, only to be told no by the Supreme Court, because no descendant of Africa could be recognized as a citizen and Scott's liberation would deprive Scott's white owner of his property. In the 1977 mayoral campaign, Ernest "Dutch" Morial captured 95 percent of the black vote to become New Orleans's first black mayor, narrowly defeating white city councilman Joseph V. DiRosa, whose campaign slogan—"Take Back the City"—was only a thinly veiled appeal to racism. "I got jungle bunnies coming out of the woodwork to help Morial," DiRosa told a newspaper reporter. "It looks like Idi Amin has sent in troops."[5]

The declining tax base of cities like New Orleans left inner-city school districts with fewer resources to educate children who are poorer, sicker, and in much greater need of expensive remedial intervention. The quality of education worsened, as did the quality of mercy. The rate of school expulsions of black students is typically triple that of whites, despite evidence that severe punishment increases the likelihood that students will drop out.

Before Hurricane Katrina touched down, the nexus of the charter school movement was Washington, D.C., or Chocolate City, which saw the number of charter schools increase from 3 in 1999 to 131 campuses in 2008.[6] One in every three schoolchildren in the District attends a charter school.

What does D.C. have to show for a decade-long love affair with charter schools? Not much. Nearly one in four public high school freshmen drops out of high school, and standardized test scores at the city's charter schools are lower than the systemwide average, though that figure is incomplete because most charter schools are not required to report results of tests mandated by No Child Left Behind legislation.[7] Permitted to skirt the contract with the teachers' union, charter schools have hired teachers who are less likely to be certified, at lower salaries and with tenuous job security.

Thanks to the destruction of its school system—along with everything else—New Orleans recently supplanted the District as ground zero for school privatization. Within days of Katrina, Louisiana's Democratic governor, Kathleen Blanco, convened a special session of the state legislature to discuss a takeover of the Orleans Parish Schools District and its half-billion-dollar budget.[8]

"This meeting took place while there were still people on roofs and at the Superdome waiting to be rescued," one education activist later told a reporter.

Within two months of the storm, state lawmakers had approved the takeover, and by the fall of 2008, more than half of all public schools in New Orleans were operated as charters. The overseer of this effort is Paul Vallas, a Republican accountant, who was installed as the CEO of Chicago's Public Schools by Mayor Richard M. Daley in 1995 after Daley seized control of that city's schools. Over the next six years, Vallas closed dozens of underperforming schools—typically in the city's poorest neighborhoods—barred the teachers' union from going on strike or negotiating on issues such as charter schools or class schedules, and managed to hike students' scores on standardized tests with a maniacal focus on teaching to the test. Vallas became the face of school reform in the United States, twice earning praise in President Bill Clinton's State of the Union address, but he left behind a Chicago school system that graduated only half its students and saw gains in test scores evaporate almost as quickly as they appeared. For every one hundred black and Latino freshmen who enroll in a Chicago public school, only three earn a diploma from a college of any kind within ten years. Education, one Vallas critic in Chicago said, isn't just a matter of "yelling louder and applying sanctions harder."[9]

As opposition to Vallas's imperial style, abrasive personality, and political ambition mounted, he resigned to lead first Philadelphia's public schools, followed by those in New Orleans. In his place, Daley named a then thirty-six-year-old Vallas protégé named Arne Duncan, who seven years later would be appointed the nation's secretary of education by President Barack Obama. Duncan's approach, which did not differ significantly from his predecessor's, represents Campbell's Law, which posits, essentially, that the more you focus on a single indicator, the more corrupt that indicator becomes. The preoccupation with test scores rather than learning does nothing to change the fundamental divide in public education in the twenty-first century, which the writer Jonathan Kozol describes as this: "In wealthy school districts, white students are taught to think, and to be the future leaders of America, while in the impoverished school districts in the inner-cities, the black and brown schoolchildren are taught to *obey*."

. . .

Weeks after Obama's election, Jewel and Launnie attended a Kwanzaa celebration with Jewel's friend Gia and two of her boys, who are eight and five, at a New Orleans park. The two single mothers are always saying that they should get their boys together more often, but there never seems to be enough time. Still, Jewel and Gia marveled at how well their kids played together, watching them chase after a football as they ran off into the park. And then, there was a pregnant pause, followed by a moment of almost dread. At that exact moment, as both women recalled later, Jewel and Gia recognized that their three sweet, well-mannered little black boys would, in only a few years, be the embodiment of America's long-standing boogeyman, feared and hated like nothing else in the popular imagination of this country.

"We just looked at each other and said: 'Ohmigod, people are going to be so afraid of our little men,'" Jewel would say later. "And that scared us. It just struck us at the same time that we were raising black *men*, and there is so much fear attached to black men that it makes you fearful of what this world will want to do to them."

A 2005 national survey by the Yale University Child Study Center found that black boys in pre-kindergarten are expelled at three times the rate of white children.[10] That's *pre*-kindergarten. This fear extends far beyond school walls, or more precisely, infects the schools from the outside in. For many New Orleanians, there's no more poignant reminder than what happened following Hurricane Katrina on the Crescent City Connection, which links downtown New Orleans to what locals call the West Bank. A small sliver of the city, including Algiers, where Launnie attends school, is there. The West Bank is also home to the majority-white towns and neighborhoods of Jefferson Parish. Jewel grew up there, and her parents still live there.

On September 1, 2005, as thousands were still stranded, hungry, and thirsty, the bridge connecting the two sides of the Mississippi River became a dividing point. Even today, there are conflicting reports of exactly what happened that day. But this much is not in question: After two days of people streaming across the bridge on foot, authorities in Gretna, the second exit off the bridge, formed a line of mostly white officers, shotguns in hand, and told the overwhelmingly black crowd of thousands of men, women, and children to turn around and go back downtown, where conditions were even more desperate. At one point—some say after threats were made against the refugees—a black Gretna police officer with a shotgun fired what authorities describe as a warning shot at the crowd, forcing them to retreat, conjuring up images of Bloody Sunday on the Edmund Pettus Bridge in Selma, Alabama, forty-some years earlier.

Patryce Jenkins, a 911 operator for the New Orleans Police Department, lived on the other side of Gretna. For two days after the hurricane hit, she had wandered the city hungry and tired, passing bodies and looters. She wanted to get home. The police department headquarters had been evacuated, so she couldn't camp out there. "I was just trying to get to safety," Jenkins told the *Chicago Tribune* three years later. "I had my driver's license to prove where I lived. But those police didn't even look at my ID. I was called racist names. . . . I was just crying in disbelief. I couldn't understand how people could be so heartless to force me back into the hell I had just escaped."[11]

Authorities said they were just protecting their small community of seventeen thousand from descending into chaos; it didn't have resources to help everyone. "I'm sure that there were very good people," the town's mayor, Ronnie Harris, would say later. "There were scared people. There were desperate people. And, unfortunately, contained within that crowd was a criminal element. That criminal element burned, looted, stole, threatened and terrorized."[12]

This irrational, dehumanizing fear of the black menace is a weight-bearing pillar on which America and its dysfunctional educational system is built.

In New Orleans and across the nation, blacks have taken a dim view of privatizing education, seeing it as a house on fire, with the No Child Left Behind Act as its accelerant, a multipurpose fuel source designed to shift resources from poor pupils to affluent ones, deepen gentrification, stifle democratic dissent, and undermine the teachers' unions and their heavily black and Latino rank and file. Since the 1990s, educational reform efforts like the one proposed by Obama in his first hundred days in the Oval Office have introduced the idea of competitive pressure, bottom-line numerical quotas in the form of standardized test scores, corporate models of leadership that have promoted the hiring of businessmen like New York public schools chancellor Joel Klein (an investment banker with no previous experience in education), and union busting by those who posit teachers and their unions as chiefly responsible for failed schools. Apparently undeterred by studies that show that black and white infants score nearly identically on intelligence tests (with blacks scoring slightly higher) when prenatal care is adjusted for, dozens of school districts, including the nation's largest in New York City, have hired as a consultant the African American Harvard economist Roland Fryer, whose explanation for the racial gap in test scores centers on the idea that there are both cultural and genetic differences in the innate intelligence of blacks and whites.

A decade into this nationwide experiment, there is no statistical evidence that the free market can fix our schools, and yet charter schools continue to proliferate.

Before Katrina, about 2 percent of roughly 65,000 public school students attended charter schools in New Orleans.[13] By June of

2008, the number had blossomed to 53 percent of 33,200 students.[14] One Washington-based critic told the *Washington Post* that Louisiana had "opened a flea market of entrepreneurial opportunism that is dismantling the institution of public education in New Orleans."[15] Some parents were overjoyed, particularly those whose children were enrolled in the handful of schools whose contracts rewarded them with per-pupil funding—funding that in some cases was more than twice that of "regular" public schools. But the waiting lists for those schools is long, and the systemwide results—as least as they relate to test scores—have shown modest gains at best. And the charters have not been immune to the same type of dysfunction that the public system had long been criticized for. One example was the launch of Lafayette Academy of New Orleans by a real estate developer named James Huber.

"I don't know the first thing about running a school," he told parents as he wooed them to his school in the late summer of 2006.[16] But he promised parents "a great product." They signed up in droves.

Huber partnered with one of the national for-profit management firms that, at the time, ran ninety charters nationwide. The result was a mess. More than half the staff quit. There were few textbooks and supplies, and nearly two-thirds of the ninety-two fourth graders failed the state test required for promotion to the fifth grade. The school's leaders, including the chief executive officer, had little interaction with teachers and students. A month into the school year, teacher Catherine Stone got her first visit from her leader.[17]

"One of my first graders ran up to me like, 'Ms. Stone, there's a white man in the room. Who is that?'" Stone told the *Times Picayune*. The company was fired, and a new principal was installed. He greeted students at the door.[18]

These types of tales nag at parents like Jewel. She is all for the innovative and the new. But she also wants to know that the place has high standards and isn't selling parents a bill of goods, and isn't just looking to teach kids on the cheap. The combination of fear for her child's welfare and the transparent profit motive of the schools motivates parents like Jewel to create a school checklist that goes well beyond the curriculum. "Is this a school that will just look at my son and say, 'Oh, he's going to end up in jail anyway so teaching is really a waste of time?' And Launnie is a typical boy. He's energetic and active and curious. Will some school say that he has a learning impairment because of that? Will they try to say he has [attention deficit disorder] and try to put him on Ritalin or some other bullshit drug to calm him down? Public schools nowadays—and I'm including most of the charter schools in this—are just crazy. My heart just bleeds for little black boys who have to go through that gauntlet."

Jewel's trepidation is perhaps best encapsulated by authors Jennifer Hochschild and Nathan Scovronick in their book *The American Dream and the Public Schools*. "Americans want all children to have a real chance to learn, and they want all schools to foster democracy and promote the common good, but they do not want those things enough to make them actually happen."[19]

Launnie's grandfather Joe often takes the boy to Lebeau, a Louisiana town with a population of 149, about 140 miles northwest of New Orleans. Joe was born there, and whenever they go, Launnie falls right in with his cousins on the farm. There are horses and pigs there. "They ask me why I let him get muddy," he said. "I said, 'I didn't let him get muddy. He got muddy.' He has to learn how to fit in." Joe would never lay a hand on the boy, but he practices gruff-love, meant to toughen the skin and teach a boy how to be a man, a black man, in an unforgiving world. What Joe understands is that a good part of Launnie's education, a part of any black boy's education, is survival training. The world is a dangerous place, more so if you are black. Even the good ones don't always make it through. When Launnie went through a cursing spree a few months back, Jewel was incensed, but Joe gets angry only when he senses real danger. "I took him fishing the other day. I had to get on his ass. The river high right now, and he want to play in the goddamn water. He likes the outdoors."

For Joe, it's about teaching his grandson the responsibility and hard work that manhood requires, something he won't learn from watching a Lil Wayne or 50 Cent video or listening to tales of their sexual exploits or latest purchases.

If Launnie doesn't listen, Joe makes him stay inside or takes away a video game. "That kills him," he said. But the real goal is not to chastise Launnie but to show him by example. Every May, the men in the family—professional and blue collar—take their sons on a long fishing weekend where they eat, drink, play, and allow the boys to be boys. They run around and fish and get dirty, with no women there to scold them for being boys. Launnie, the youngest participant, has gone for three years and looks forward to seeing his older cousins. This, according to Joe, is what boys need. In that environment, little boys learn not to mess with the bigger boys, or else they'll get thumped. They learn boundaries; they learn that there are times when you are on your own, when you have no one to back you up, and you have to get by with your wits. They learn that the only real safety in the world is understanding that there is no real safety in the world. Minor scrapes from the inevitable fall or the errant fish hook draw a passing glance from the men, but there is no sense of urgency like there would be if women were around. Boys learn that sometimes they just got to shut up, listen, and figure stuff out on their own.

On a spring Sunday afternoon, Joe was lazing in his living room recliner sipping Jack Daniel's when Jewel and Launnie burst through the door. They had just come from a street festival.

"Goddamn, boy, you got makeup on?" Joe asked.

"That's not makeup," Launnie said. "That's paint."

"You know men don't wear makeup," Joe said, as his grandson disappeared into the bathroom to clean the red smudges from his face.

While the boy is away, Jewel tells her parents that Launnie married one of his classmates, a white girl, on the school playground not long ago, and later the two went on a play date.

"He likes those little white girls," says his grandmother.

Joe protests. "Don't put nothing on nobody. You don't know that."

This is a source of tension for Joe. He knows firsthand that navigating race will be one of the most difficult things, if not *the* most difficult thing, his grandson will ever do in his life. White folks you think are your friends will almost always think they're better than you or harbor some kind of resentment that comes out at the worst time or when you least expect it. Joe's cousin, for instance, told him a few years ago that he went on a hunting trip on the Bayou with a few of his white coworkers and after a few drinks one night, they started telling "nigger" jokes.

Working on the railroad for twenty-eight years, Joe always had white friends. Some years back, he befriended a subordinate named Cliff, who was eighteen when he moved to Louisiana from Illinois looking for work and a place to stay. Joe gave him both; Cliff often slept at Joe's house, and Joe treated him like a son. When Cliff's mother called to inquire if her son was drinking, Joe replied, "Not to my knowledge," even as Cliff held a beer in his hand.

One night Joe and Red and Cliff were visiting one of their white neighbors in a New Orleans suburb when Cliff said he wanted to learn to dance. The host put on some music, and Cliff blurted out: "No. I don't want to hear that nigger music." That remark sucked the air out of the room.

166

"He was very apologetic," Red said. "I didn't hold it against him because he was so apologetic. He said he was sorry and if he could take it back he would because he didn't mean to hurt us, to offend us, and that he appreciated us for letting him stay here. At the end, I felt sorry for him."

But Joe is not so forgiving. It taught him a lesson about what white people, even poor white people whom you bend over backward to help, think about you. But in the black community generally and New Orleans specifically, there is not just the issue of what whites think about blacks, but there is also an internal conflict that polarizes blacks from one another. Launnie's grandmother, Red, who is on the lighter side, has always struggled with this as she went from all-black schools to integrated schools. At one place, everybody was black. Then, in an integrated school, whites shunned her for being black. Later, at another school, because of her skin color, blacks accused her of being white.

"She think she a white girl. She look like she white. Oh, she high yellow," she said, mimicking the former classmates. "So what am I? I was a black nigger at the black school. At the other school I was too bright. So what am I?"

Launnie will have his own moments of rejection and uncertainty, and his grandparents plan to be there to guide him. Joe, especially, feels a sense of responsibility since Launnie's father is not a regular fixture in his life. Somebody has to teach him to be a man.

Two weeks later, Jewel is sipping on a margarita at a bar in the French Quarter and talking about what Obama means to black America. The nation's first black president could have a dramatic impact on how black men see themselves, she says. That black boys and young men will have as a role model a black man who is intelligent and articulate, dotes on his daughters and his wife,

A Day Late and a Dollar Short

and pummels adversaries with his mind rather than his fists, these are all good things, Jewel says. "I admire the fact that he's given so many people hope."

But will Obama reassure the white women who will see Launnie fifteen years from now and grab their purses tighter or lock their doors? Jewel doesn't think so. Will Joe Bush, because there is a black head of state, forget to teach the teenage Launnie that if he ever gets stopped by the police he should grab the steering wheel with both hands and move very slowly and let the officer know that he is reaching into his back pocket for his wallet and not a gun? Jewel can't see it. Will Jewel be a little less afraid to see her boy leave the house every morning because the threats against him are dramatically reduced under a black president? Absolutely not, she says. Does she expect that Launnie will have some kind of problem down the road with a teacher or principal or boss who feels threatened by a smart, independent, freethinking black youth or man? You betcha she does.

Obama, for all of his triumphs and obvious gifts, she says, represents incremental change, not revolutionary change. "That's what we need," she says. "That's what I want for my son."

She smiles as she takes another sip of her margarita. "I guess that's the problem, hunh?"

| 8 |

Dandelions

Eddie's Freedom in D.C.

Freedom of mind is the real freedom. A person whose mind is not free though he may not be in chains, is a slave, not a free man.

—DR. BHIMRAO RAMJI AMBEDKAR, INDIAN ORATOR

For a time, Tiger Woods kept Eddie Ellis going. The damnedest thing he'd even seen before Obama was elected was watching a black man beat the pants off the country club set at their own game. When Tiger was on television, the word spread like wildfire, forcing black men across the nation to flip between basketball and golf during the spring and summer. No matter the lack of physical contact in golf, Tiger was a warrior, rising to achieve what no one expected.

Earl Woods, born and raised in Manhattan, Kansas, had practically willed his son to become one of the world's greatest golfers. Eddie remembers watching one tournament on a Sunday as Woods tussled with Phil Mickelson. To seal his victory, Woods hit a meandering putt of forty yards or so that curved wildly, then straightened, disappearing into the bottom of the cup. Every black man within earshot erupted. "It was like we won something," he said.

After eight years of fear and warmongering by the Bush administration, black America, especially, needed a change in the White House. In the best of times, their issues were on the periphery, but under Bush/Cheney, their concerns weren't even given lip service.

Eddie, at thirty-two, needed to believe more than most, having spent half his life in prison, where guards controlled his movement, the lights, the showers, and the food he ate. In such an environment, the mind stagnates, reality becomes perverted in order to make peace with everyday abnormalities: a society of only men, an existence in which one day is just like the next, where it feels as if time is standing still. Loved ones on the outside, the ones who still accept your collect calls or send letters, have stories of new adventures, hardships, and the latest music and technologies. You soak it up, but limit what you share because no one, not even your mother, really wants to what know goes on inside a prison. They assume it's difficult and leave it at that.

"It helped me not to focus on the conditions I was in," he said. "I understood somebody could lose their life. I understood where I was at. It was a bad situation. I was not around my family. I was around mofuckas that could kill me, that I might have to kill, that I would have to be around for years. So what could I do? It started messing with my mind."

In this environment, a golf tournament, won improbably by a man who is near your age and who looks like you, is special, a rare connection with the outside world.

Almost as if you had won something.

The first time they sent Eddie away, he was fifteen. The year was 1991. Crack cocaine was coursing through black America, and Barack Obama was graduating from Harvard Law School and preparing to move back to Chicago, where he had worked for several years as a community organizer. Police in Washington, D.C., snatched Eddie up for trying to rob someone at gunpoint. Eddie, by then, had become a headache for his mother, selling drugs and carrying a gun for protection, or provocation, when necessary. But he insists, even to this day, that he was innocent of that *particular* crime.

His namesake, Eddie B. Ellis Sr., was killed while robbing a liquor store. Eddie was two, and remembers his father only through the stories he was told later in life. His mother did all she could working as a secretary to pay for tennis lessons, send him to the Boys and Girls Club, and move him out of harm's way to a nice apartment in D.C.'s Maryland suburbs. But Eddie had already begun taking his cues from the streets. He first saw somebody blow cocaine in the suburbs and, against his mother's wishes, gravitated to Washington's mean streets, where idle, unemployed men pass on what they were taught: how to dish out punishment, and how to take it.

Eddie learned early on what was expected. He must've been eight, maybe nine, years old playing sandlot football at a local elementary school.

"I got an interception and was running it back," he said. "I tried to jump over a guy, and my leg got caught on his shoulder. It felt like my hip came out of place. The first thing I heard people say was, 'Get up, you can do it.' They don't know I'm hurt. I got up instead of crying like I wanted to do. We don't want to be considered a nerd or square. To show emotion is to be gay. If it wasn't meant for you to cry, you wouldn't have tear ducts. A drop of water can crack a rock. You holding that stuff in, it's going to come out the wrong way at some point."

He ended up on the block, a term in many neighborhoods across America that has become synonymous with hustling, making ends meet, and getting that money, understanding, even in

171

the preteen years, that being on the block typically leads to a stint in juvenile lockup and eventually an adult cell block, if a bullet doesn't find you first.

Eddie wasn't convicted of the robbery—a juvenile judge dismissed the charges—but not before he'd spent six months at the District's juvenile detention center at Oak Hill, Maryland, known as "The Pound," because the mostly black and Latino boys there were treated like stray dogs by the guards there. Eddie doesn't talk much about his stay there, but he left even angrier, even harder, than when he came in. "They didn't even apologize," he said. "They didn't say nothing. I didn't care anymore."

Six months after his release, Eddie shot and killed another teenager during an argument. He said it was self-defense, but he was convicted of manslaughter. He tells the story as though he is a court reporter reading a police affidavit: "On December 20, 1991, me and my codefendant were going to a party. We went to an apartment building, found out the party was canceled, so we come back out the apartment building and the deceased, he's there with two other friends. When we see each other, he said, 'What the fuck are you doing?' He pulled out a gun. I pulled out a gun. I had a chance to be killed or to protect myself. I fired one time, and he was shot and he passed away. I didn't know he had been killed until the homicide detective said, 'Mr. Ellis, you have killed someone.'"

On that day, in the eyes of the law, Eddie became an adult. He was sixteen.

Growing up in prison meant that Eddie, if he had any hope of surviving, would have to become even tougher and much, much smarter. Initially Eddie was sent to Lorton Correctional Complex, the District's prison in northern Virginia. It was close to home, and in many ways familiar. Prisoners and guards were from the District, and many of them had grown up in the same neighborhoods as friends and rivals. But it was that incestuous environment that led to volatility, leaving Lorton crowded, violent, and corrupt, even more so than most correctional facilities. Eddie learned quickly that in prison, you have to size people up immediately. Why did so-and-so ask me that? What angle is the prison guard playing? What's *not* being said in this exchange? All he heard at sentencing was this: "Twenty-two years."

"I said, 'I don't know how I'm going to do twenty-two years,' and I started crying," Eddie said. If he could have, he would have leaned on his mother, who was in the courtroom watching.

But his mother, twenty-one when Eddie was born, was torn. She loved Eddie, but she also knew that another mother, another black woman, was feeling at that moment the worst hurt she'd ever know, and it was her son who was the cause. She held back her tears in deference. "I didn't even feel worthy to cry," she would say years later. "I didn't think I had a right to cry because of the devastation to the other family."

It was a thought that she didn't share with her son the entire time he was locked away.

She also didn't share her prayer: Lord, she thought to herself as Eddie's image tugged at her heart across the miles, keep my son in prison until he has changed.

Many nights, in the early days, he called home asking for help. "Eddie, you got to deal with it," she said sharply. "Baby, I can't help you. You got to do it or you're gonna kill yourself."

He had ignored her all those times when she was telling him to straighten up, but now he was angry that she couldn't help him adapt to prison. Still, "I didn't want to kill myself," he said. "I had to grow up. I had to become a man."

Eventually Eddie learned to focus on what was in his control. He read books and wrote letters to men and women, often strangers, whose responses from the outside would allow him to dream.

He began to work out, pray, and shed friends who still embraced a hustling, "get-over" mentality. The rules were simple: Make better choices in general. Choose your friends more wisely. Be respectful. Be a leader. Instead of complaining, do something.

He searched for inspiration wherever he could find it: Tiger Woods on the golf course, spirituality, the dandelion that poked through the concrete outside one of his jail cells. Gardeners would not have been surprised. They curse the dandelion's deep roots and feathery seeds that ride the wind like gypsies in search of a nesting place. Its survival instinct outwits herbicides, shovels, bare hands, and, yes, even concrete. What Eddie saw that day was a picture of himself and how he could salvage the rest of his life.

"This goddamn flower that you call a weed is growing out the goddamn concrete," he said. "I said to myself, 'What makes this flower any more resilient than I am?'"

"What helped me a lot was not taking prison seriously. I tried not to allow the conditions to get to me. It could destroy you. I fantasized about the fun things I did when I was a kid, when I went to camp, when I played football, when I went to school, when my mother took me out, when my grandmother took me out, where I used to play. I thought about that. It helped me not focus on the conditions I was in. I decided, I got to educate myself. I got to work out. I got to try to keep my spiritualness going. I got to focus on going home."

To many African Americans, Obama's election was a fulfillment of Jesus' declaration in the Gospel of Matthew: "The last shall be first and the first last." But Maya Wiley, the head of a New York City nonprofit, says: "Maybe, if you graduate from Harvard Law School."

Far more likely, in this, the era of the first black president, is that a black man is far more likely to spend time at a correctional facility than at a four-year college, let alone an Ivy League one. The United States incarcerates, at any given time, 2.3 million of its own citizens,[1] more than any other country in the world, more even in sheer numbers than China, an authoritarian state with a population five times that of the United States. Nearly 44 percent of America's prisoners are black.[2] What this means is that in Chicago, librarians on the South Side of Chicago, Obama's adopted hometown, contend that youths most commonly use computers at the facilities there to look up the release date of relatives, friends, and neighbors. And in many neighborhoods in the District of Columbia it can be difficult to find an African American household where at least one man isn't behind bars, on parole, or on probation. In the nation's capital, which Obama now calls home, as many as sixty thousand D.C. residents—one in ten—are felons, with fifteen thousand of them under active court supervision.[3]

The Emancipation Proclamation freed from involuntary servitude all classes of citizens save one: those doing time. Since Reconstruction, the United States has used its penal policies and jails as a way to profit from African Americans, using the "convict leasing" system's chain gangs initially to supply southern plantation owners with the cheap labor that the Emancipation Proclamation had deprived them of. In more recent years, the privatization of prisons has turned into a multimillion-dollar industry, with corporations' stock prices based largely on how many inmates their facilities hold.

With good, decent-paying blue-collar jobs disappearing, things fall apart: families unravel, communities dissipate, homicide rates rise. The downfall, for many, starts in elementary school, and the typical offender at Washington's juvenile jail is a sixteen-year-old black male who lives east of the Anacostia River, the poorest, blackest, sickest, and most crime-ridden part of the city. During the year preceding their incarceration, most of these boys seldom, if ever, attended school. Forty percent have a mental health issue that requires medication or some other form of intervention.[4] Most of those who come in the door suffer from what a local administrator calls the "big five": family dysfunction, drug use, mental illness, a lack of education, and difficulty finding a job.[5] It is this rot, which so often ends in death—physically on the streets or spiritually in a jail cell—that best juxtaposes the state of black America with the black head of state. And the question is this: Does Obama's success help to heal this diseased limb like a dose of strong medicine? Or does it merely obscure the pain, like a dose of morphine before everything goes dark?

D.C. mayor Adrian Fenty, who like Obama is biracial, is a strong believer that if he makes all parts of city government work better, he will improve the lives of everyone, regardless of their race. A week before Obama's inauguration, Fenty was on NBC's *Meet the Press* when the moderator asked Fenty about young urban kids who might look at Obama's life and say, "No, no, that's not me. That's not my life. That's not my path."[6]

It took some journalistic prodding to get Fenty talking about disconnected youth in neighborhoods like Congress Heights, Benning Terrace, or Trinidad, which so often make the news. But instead of shining a light on the tumor, Fenty, instead, went for the trite: "I really think that Obama connects with this generation of Americans in a way that few presidents ever have," Fenty said. "These shots of him, you know, preparing his young daughters to go off to school, I mean, these are just going to resonate through the psyche of, I think, people in Washington, D.C., and other cities. And you know, someone said to me . . . in an Obama fund-raiser one time, he was a white gentleman in his fifties, he said to the crowd, 'You know, to all of us he'll be the first black president. But to our kids and the younger generation, he's just the president.'"[7]

Representative James Clyburn of South Carolina, the House majority whip, went even further, proclaiming that "every child has lost every excuse."[8]

That's an astounding statement, given the depth of the maladies in many neighborhoods. Op-ed columnist Charles Blow in the *New York Times*, four days after the inauguration, urged black leaders to "cool this rhetoric lest the enormous and ingrained obstacles facing black children get swept under the rug as Obama is swept into power." Blow cited, as an example, a report by the National Center for Children in Poverty indicating that 60 percent of black children live in low-income families and a third live in poor families, a higher percentage than any other race. "Most of these kids will rise above their circumstances," Blow wrote, "but too many will succumb to them."[9]

Black men are six times more likely to be slain than whites. Those aged fourteen to twenty-four were the most vulnerable, accounting for 15 percent of the nation's homicides in 2002, despite being only 1.2 percent of the population.[10] And black men were three times more likely to serve time for their first conviction for selling drugs than were white men who sold the same amount.

Eddie said it was in the affluent Maryland suburbs that he first saw white classmates "blow" cocaine, but to his knowledge none of them had done any time.

For many offenders, however, going in isn't half the problem that getting out is. About two thousand prisoners come back to the District every year—an average of five a day. They arrive at the homes of relatives, at halfway houses, and at shelters. One-third end up homeless or close to it. Seven out of ten have abused drugs. Half don't have a high school diploma.[11] Employers, landlords, and even family members often avoid them.

Most emerge ill-equipped to stay out of prison. Two-thirds are rearrested within three years. Forty percent are sent back to prison. This means more crime, more victims, and more money spent to send them through the justice system again and again.[12] Eddie left prison the same month that Obama announced that he was running for president in January 2006. He was thirty years old and, by that time, had spent half his life locked up.

The District, a federal enclave, is the only jurisdiction in the country where the federal government has direct authority for housing its felons. When Eddie went in, the District was in a financial shambles, and town houses in many neighborhoods could be had for a song. But two mayors and fifteen years later, the city was booming. Downtown was back. The area around the Verizon Center had become a mini–Times Square, and the Metro—the underground subway system—was by now as central to the city's daily life as air. White people were walking dogs in neighborhoods that Eddie remembered as all-black and infested with drugs and crime. He was a stranger in a world that had moved on without him. His family hardly knew him. He couldn't drive, didn't know how to use the subway system, and was nervous in crowds. He had no job, no money, and a felony record that jumped out at potential employers like a red flag. He longed for some sense of normalcy—nostalgic momentarily for the three squares, the stark cells, and the regimentation of prison life. It was all a bit much to take. In the days and months following his release, Eddie would become so overwhelmed that he would simply close himself up in his room, making his mother wonder whether he was upset.

"It was weird. I was just trying to learn to live on the outside again," Eddie said. "I had been locked up so long that I was paranoid in crowds. I didn't know if I should smile or laugh. I wasted my money taking cabs because I didn't know how to use the Metro. One time, I panicked and got off. Everything had changed." During particularly rough patches he would think to himself: "It's easier for me to go back in there and live that life because it's less responsibility. Out here, things are harder."[13]

Then he remembered the chill that rippled through him every time the steel doors slammed shut. And he kept going.

.   .   .

Eddie had done the last six years of his sentence at Supermax, where there are two sets of doors on every cell, both locked and heavy. Typically, an effort is made to gradually move inmates to less restrictive institutions as their release date nears. That didn't happen in Eddie's case. He was sent straight home to the District. Realizing the error, the agency that oversees returning felons in the District sent Tosha Trotter to intervene. Her mission was to convince Eddie to spend another thirty days in a residential treatment facility, where leaving without permission can get residents hauled before their parole officer for possible sanctions.

"You need time to adjust, so we're strongly suggesting that you spend thirty days in the reentry center for those fighting addiction," Trotter told him. "It's a residential treatment center. It's not prison."

"I don't have a drug problem," Eddie protested.

Trotter knew that, and she was aware that he had not yet spent a night with the wife he married while in prison. But Trotter also knew that Eddie needed to ease into his freedom after so many years. Thirty days of around-the-clock counseling, along with job training assistance, would give him time. She was right. Eddie was thankful for the slowdown. The wife he was anxious to see is now an ex-wife, and Eddie reluctantly notes that the experience has helped him to understand addiction better.

"Drugs incarcerate you too," he said. "Some people really don't understand the seriousness of it. Being around all these dope fiends, crack heads, like that, learning how drugs really affected them. Before I'm out in the streets selling drugs here and there, I knew it messed them up, but I ain't know it was like that. Alcohol affects people in different ways. Some people can have two or three beers. Some people can't. I recognized my own triggers. That's why I don't go to clubs and happy hours. I don't want be around a lot of BS. Somebody get drunk and say something out they mouth."

Impressed with Eddie's determination and skills as a communicator, Trotter asked Eddie to talk to returning inmates and, on occasion, to help train parole officers. It works like this: Trotter places Eddie's criminal history on an overhead projector and asks the men and women—whose job is to determine reentry plans for ex-offenders—to develop a plan. Some ask why such a monster is out on the street. Eddie, listening the whole time, rises to tell them about his experience in prison and on the outside afterward. "It allowed them to see you're not dealing with a piece of paper," Ellis said. "I let them know that all of us are not monsters."

This basic premise, that people exiting prison are people with needs, led him to his first major project after he was released in August 2006. He started working immediately on *The Window of Opportunity Pre-Release Handbook*, designed to help others make the transition. His fifty-two-page manual is filled with contacts to help the newly released, or those about to be released, find housing, jobs, and government agencies that assist ex-offenders. He spent a year researching the book and self-published it in February of 2008. It sells for twenty-five dollars.

The handbook's news-you-can-use is mixed with encouraging words to lift the spirits of men and women who've become accustomed to being told when to eat, sleep, work, and go outside for recreation. Eddie sees the manual as a bridge to freedom.

"Transitions are hard," Eddie said. "It's hard for people to transition from college to work. Imagine what it's like coming out of prison, this man-made dehumanizing environment. These places were thought of before they were made. They used therapists, psychologists, nutritionists, people who know about lighting to affect behavior. They know how it's going to affect people. But we expect people to just get out and get a job and everything is just going to be all right. It doesn't work that way."

One constant bit of advice is something Trotter told Eddie when he got out: Slow down. Stop worrying about other people, and focus on you.

"We must put in overtime and work to keep our lives on track in order to remain free," he writes in the booklet. "There are a lot of programs out there that can be of some help to us, and so we must use those programs to help get our lives back on track."

Ellis said that although inmates can't change how others view them, they can maintain a positive attitude and keep knocking on doors until someone takes a chance on them. In addition to his book project, Ellis works at a cleaning job and also speaks regularly to criminal justice classes at colleges in the District. He mentors those just out of prison and tells them that even in rough times, individuals must keep their own counsel. "The parole board, the police can't make us do right," he says. "You have to want to do right for yourself."

A decade earlier, it was hard to imagine Eddie as anyone's mentor. It was hard for him to imagine walking free again. He was in Ohio, at a private prison that was particularly violent, with more than forty assaults, two fatal stabbings, and six inmate escapes over the course of a year.[14] The place was eventually closed after a review by then attorney general Janet Reno found lax security, inexperienced and poorly trained staff, and an improper mix of medium- and high-security inmates housed together.

It was during this period that Eddie was implicated in another homicide. Another inmate confessed to authorities about the killing, but Eddie refused to say anything about it. He was charged as an accessory and, if convicted, faced a lifetime in prison. Again, he said, he was innocent. But who would believe him, considering the crime for which he had been locked up? Eddie felt sick, just as he did as a juvenile, sitting in Oak Hill for a crime he didn't commit. But he took the plea anyway.

Parole was coming up on his initial charge, but the new charge meant he would have to do at least another seven years.

"I did it so they wouldn't take my whole life from me," he said. "I realized that I didn't have control of anything."

As angry as he was—and still is—about the injustice of doing time for somebody else's crime, Eddie now says, "I lost and I gained." At the time, he still hadn't changed his life or his mindset, at least not the one he thought he needed once he returned to the streets. His new home, for six years, was the Supermax prison in Florence, Colorado, considered the most secure federal prison in the United States because it has two layers of doors on each cell and houses people such as Zacarias Moussaoui, the so-called twentieth hijacker in the September 11, 2001, attacks, and Theodore J. Kaczynski, the Unabomber. A young kid from D.C., Eddie was rubbing shoulders with mob bosses, terrorists, and gangbangers, whom he calls "cowards." A couple of people he recognized from seeing their faces on TV.

What he had there, more than anything else, was time to think.

Obama, like Tiger and the dandelion, was another inspiration. Sitting in the Supermax prison in Florence, Colorado, Eddie paid close attention to what was going on in Illinois in 2004 as the Republican governor, George Ryan, a former death penalty supporter, commuted the death sentences for everyone on death row. A commission had found that death sentences were given disproportionately to poor ethnic minorities and often relied on informers' testimony. More than a dozen people had been wrongly convicted and later released.[15] Watching those developments led Eddie to Obama's unlikely rise from community organizer to the U.S. Senate. Eddie wrote asking for a copy of *Dreams from My Father*, and though he never received a response, he didn't hold it against the boyish-looking senator. The man was busy.

So on the eve of the 2008 election, with prison in his rearview mirror, Eddie was like a kid at Christmas, too anxious to sleep, texting after midnight, peeking at the clock until it was time to get up. He is naturally impatient, working on a book project, writing a play, setting up speaking engagements, wanting to finish them all at once.

"Man, do you know how big this is?" he asked, expecting no answer as he carried on a one-way conversation in his head.

It was just before seven on an overcast Tuesday morning in November 2008. There were eighty-five people in front of him, and hundreds more fell in behind. Doctors, lawyers, entire families on bicycles, people who had brought along small children to be a part of history. In the nation's capital, which is overwhelmingly Democratic and left-leaning, it's a foregone conclusion that the Democratic nominee gets the city's three electoral votes.

But Eddie had to be there, voting. It was a quiet moment, marked with a smile and a thumbs-up. He saved his "I Voted" sticker, wanting its sticky back and his memories to always remain fresh. One man. One vote. In the final tally, Obama drew 92 percent of the 265,853 votes cast in the presidential race in the District.[16] Among those voters was Eddie, a citizen, casting a ballot for a man who considers himself a bridge builder.

On the Saturday before Father's Day 2009, the president took his two daughters to get custard, a photo opportunity to augment a three-day focus on fatherhood and the responsibility fathers have to their children. Seven blocks from the White House, at the Martin Luther King Memorial Library, Eddie also was preaching responsibility.

Slim and clean shaven, Eddie was the featured speaker, and the mid-afternoon crowd swelled to about a hundred, many of them ex-offenders, some fresh out of prison, all of them looking for a roadmap for their life ahead. Since coming home, Eddie had served as a consultant and an actor in a play about prison and street life. He began getting speaking engagements, and his audiences at places like Georgetown University were dumbstruck. People with money send their children there, aware that they will have the opportunity to interact with the best and the brightest and start out on solid footing. In December 2008, the estate of a former alumnus donated $75 million to the school,[17] which is located in a ritzy section of the District with upscale shopping, million-dollar homes, and little crime. And when Eddie visited on three or four occasions, the students' eyes always say: *So this is what a killer looks like as he stands before me, with a starched white shirt and jeans, looking as though he could be one of us.*

Their questions come rapid fire: What did you do in prison? "I went to school a lot. I worked out." Do you keep in touch with the family of the person you killed? "No. But on the victim impact statement his family asked for leniency. Me apologizing now won't bring him back. It happened. I can't change that." What was prison like? "It was a lot of things, people who lift weights, people stabbing people." Ever see a rape? "It's not like you see on television. I never witnessed a rape in prison. I wouldn't say it didn't happen. I was just never around it."

There is always some version of this question: How does it feel to take a life?

Eddie pauses before saying, "Ken Lay, he didn't take nobody's life but he took people's life savings. You make that choice to drink and kill somebody, you could be that person."

In these settings, his message is like Obama's, direct but filtered enough so that he doesn't come off like the angry black man. To the students, Eddie is their glimpse into a hidden world.

But the King Library crowd knew Eddie. Many had been behind bars and could relate to the obviously homeless men and women who sit quietly for hours in the library's reading rooms, lugging their possessions in tattered suitcases and grocery bags until the shelters reopen for the evening. Eddie talked about his own frailties, learning humility, learning to trust again, and talking weekly with a therapist about his feelings. As he shared, the men opened up: "I have been in prison more than I have been out." "I see a psychiatrist, too." "I'm in a shelter now." "I don't know how to forgive myself for my crime."

Eddie said he could relate. "I can't bring him back. I still wrassle with it because somebody lost their life. It kills me everyday. But I had to forgive myself."

In one regard, Eddie stops short of offering advice when a man or a woman asks him what they should do next to get their lives back on track. But about this he is clear: don't allow yourself to become a victim. Yes, he's been turned down for jobs because of his record. Yes, some people think he ought to still be in jail. Yes, politicians talk a good game about what they're going to do and often disappoint. But his solution, in each case, focuses not on the obstacles but how he can get around them, channeling Obama's charge to Americans to focus on what binds us together. "The system is what it is," he says. "Prisons weren't made to rehabilitate you but when you understand that, you try to rehabilitate yourself."

This he knew from prison: nobody likes a whiner. One man who became a friend, he recalls, was always talkative and in good spirits. One day, he allowed Eddie to look at some of the paperwork from a case he was fighting. Eddie looked up in astonishment. "It says you have six hundred years," Eddie said. "How you got six hundred years and you don't complain?

"I am going to fight," the man said. "I am going to live my life."

That same man, from Indianapolis, has served as an inspiration ever since, even though they are not in touch. People get so focused on their own troubles, Eddie said, that they forget to look around. It's a pet peeve of his on the outside. He meets single young women with no children who earn upward of $60,000 a year but always complain about not being able to make ends meet. He can't listen. "Don't complain," he said. "Do something about it. If you're not going to do something about it, be quiet. My grandmother told me, 'Don't cry about nothing you ain't trying to change. You wasting breath.' You can't pay a light bill. You're about to lose your apartment. This man looked at me and said, 'I would love to have your problems.'"

Obama had grumbled mildly, soon after his election, of the difficulty of living inside a bubble. Everyone is watching, and there is no place to hide and be normal. That pressure Eddie understands better than most, and it's the reason, despite his joy at Obama's election, that he did not join family members who trekked down to the Mall to watch Obama being sworn in. It's not that he didn't want to be there. But standing in a crowd, even now, is a mask he can't stand to wear. It makes him feel boxed in, like a prisoner.

It's a feeling he never wants to have again.

His assessment, as a free man, of Obama's first six months: so far, so good.

| 9 |

Watermelon Man

Cecil, Jon, and Ryan in Indianapolis

The paper tiger hero, James Bond, offering the whites a
triumphant image of themselves, is saying what many whites
want desperately to hear reaffirmed: I am still the White Man,
lord of the land, licensed to kill, and the world is still an empire
at my feet.

—ELDRIDGE CLEAVER

What I remember is that it was summer; the windows were open, the sun was shining, and I could hear the sound of lawnmowers buzzing outside. It was 1971, maybe 1970, which means I was five or six, and my father would've been roughly forty, a few years younger than I am now. The two of us were lying side by side on twin beds in the tiny bedroom that I shared with my older brother, a sliver of parquet flooring between us, our feet facing the north wall. We were watching the small black-and-white television with a misshapen clothes hanger for an antenna, perched atop an unfinished pine dresser.

My father worked so much when I was young—by day making engine blocks at the Chrysler factory on the west side of Indianapolis, then as a night janitor cleaning up at a Nabisco cookie factory—that I seldom saw him during the week and got to know him, really, by lazing with him on weekend afternoons, watching him watch television, studying his gestures and responses to the images that appeared on the screen. What I learned early on was that my father adored this loud, rhyming boxer named Muhammad Ali and a bearded, cigar-chomping, funny-talking soldier named Fidel Castro, because whenever they materialized on the screen, my father would rise quickly to his feet, no matter how weary he may have seemed fifteen seconds earlier. He would approach the dresser—which stood at his chest—lean in close to the screen as though he was either half-blind or hard of hearing, and he would cheer them on, mumbling unintelligibly and laughing in that guttural, baritone howl of his that seemed to rumble like an aftershock through his body and the ground beneath us. I remember wondering if my father *knew* Ali or Castro personally.

What sparked my question this particular afternoon, I can only guess. Maybe it was something I'd heard in school that week or a photograph I'd spied somewhere, like in the thick family encyclopedia that I was always thumbing through in my pre-Internet childhood. In any event, the twenty-sixth president of the republic was on my mind.

"Daddy," I called out to my father.

"Yes," I recall him answering, drawing out the word with this cloying, indulgent sweetness.

"Was Teddy Roosevelt black?"

My father chuckled, but it was unlike any laugh I'd heard from him before. There was something joyless, cynical, almost menacing in his tone, as though I'd touched a nerve or exhumed some sinister family secret.

"Boy," he said, "if you had called Teddy Roosevelt black, he would've spit on you."

Years later, I asked my father if he remembered this exchange, and he did, instantly, though I think largely because it cemented in his mind his notion of me as a peculiar boy, full of odd, fanciful thoughts. But I remember it for two very different reasons. First, it was the seminal political thought that I can recall, this idea that race mattered, a lot, so much in fact, that people did not like black people, disliked *us* so much, in fact, as to react violently to any suggestion that they were in any way like us, or Mr. Brookings, who was a deacon at our church and lived two doors down and would oil my bicycle chain if he heard it squeal as I rode by, or Curtis, who was my best friend at the time and the funniest kid in my class and the only one I knew who could do that farting thing with his armpit.

But even more astonishing for me, as I untangled my father's words and tone in the moments and years to follow, it revealed to me my father's anger and bitterness and disillusionment. It was the first time I can recall contemplating my father as someone who was more than just my daddy, as someone who had a life distinct from my own, that began before mine, and in that other life, he had suffered mightily at the hands of white people and, at the midpoint of this other life, he was bracing himself—and me—for more.

Until that moment, I had known my father only as a gentle man, good-humored, almost lighthearted. He doted on me and my three siblings and his nieces and nephews. I almost never remember him raising his voice to any of us. He would draw cartoons for us, read to us, take us out for ice cream, picnics, art museums, attend parent-teacher conferences, and roughhouse with the other kids in the neighborhood. He never seemed to meet a stranger. The one time that he threatened to spank me, he aborted the mission when I showed up for my punishment with a book "hidden" underneath my pants. "Go on boy, get out of here," I remember him saying through raucous laughter. Years later I would watch *The Cosby*

Show and recognize in Bill Cosby's depiction of Heathcliff Huxtable my own father, playful and affectionate and self-sacrificing.

But from the day when I first raised the question of Teddy Roosevelt's race, I came to gradually get to know my father as a black man, an African American Everyman, far more complicated than my early assessments of him, by turns rakishly mirthful and mercurial, irascible. In his estimation, America, its people and its institutions, had failed him, time and time again, and he had grown to loathe it, this country of his birth.

Maybe two or three years after our exchange, I remember my father pumping gasoline at a self-service gas station while my mother, my two brothers, and I waited in the car. I can't recall if my sister, the oldest, was there, but it was summer again, and from the car's back seat I watched as my father and the cashier, a white woman, began to argue. He accused the woman of cheating him out of the change he was owed; the cashier insisted that he had given her a ten-dollar bill rather than the twenty dollars my father said he had handed to her.

My father grew angry, then livid, then white-hot with rage, swearing and pointing his finger at the woman who was behind the glass cage.

"Sir, I am going to have to call the police," I remember her saying over the loudspeaker.

"Go head," my father said defiantly. "I'll be right *he-ah*."

When the police officer arrived a few minutes later, the woman told her story, my father his. The officer, also white, unsurprisingly chose the cashier's version of events. Towering over my father, the police officer extended his hand to return the change that the cashier said he was owed from his ten-dollar bill.

"*Motherfuck your change, peckerwood*," my father said, simultaneously slapping the change from the officer's hand. I remember the hollow sound of the coins pelting the concrete like tin rain, and watching the officer place his hand on the holster as though reaching for his gun, and not only can I remember, but I can actually relive, the feelings of dread and resignation from fearing that at any second I was going to see my father gunned down like one of the black men I had heard about on the local television news. It would not be the last time I experienced that same flash of emotion.

"Cecil," my mother called out, afraid but mostly embarrassed, from inside the car, "C'mon. Let's go." She had, by this point in their marriage, seen this before.

After a few more terse words, my father did as my mother instructed, but the image of my father, exploding in what seemed like some kind of biblical anger, battered but undefeated, trying to hold on to the last scrap of dignity he had left, is fastened to my consciousness. Once, a bill collector harassing my mother by phone called her a bitch. This rattled my mother, and when she mentioned it to my father, he calmly piled me and my older brother and sister into our station wagon as though we were going on a school field trip, then drove to the bill collector's office, and *exploded*, taking a swing at the cowering agent. It missed its mark, but sent the man and his coworkers, all white, scattering.

When I was an adolescent, my father would shuttle me to an old prewar gymnasium to play pickup basketball, and if we made that trip two dozen times, I swear he told me the same story twenty-four times, each time apparently oblivious of the previous trip, as though he were in a trance. The story was this: when he was a child of maybe eleven or twelve, he had tried to play there, walking the nearly two miles from his family's shotgun house to the gymnasium, only to be turned away by a white man not long after he had walked inside and began shooting baskets with the other boys, all of them white. As he trudged back home in the heat of a summer day, a few of the boys who had seen him at the gym passed him by as they rode in the back of a pickup truck. "Nigger," they snarled as they doused him with a paint bucket they had filled with their piss.

As I grew older, my father, and all his complexities, came into sharper focus for me. Once when I was eight or nine, we were shopping one weekend morning at a downtown Indianapolis farmers' market, just the two of us, when an old, frail black man in a suit and tie wobbled up to my father, almost mumbling as he grabbed for my father's hand to hold as if pleading for forgiveness.

"I'm sorry," I recall him saying to my father, over and over again, as if it were some kind of mantra. "I'm so sorry."

My father, obviously embarrassed, tried to comfort the man.

"No, no, no," I recall him saying, to the man, grasping his tiny outstretched hand with his right hand, and patting his shoulder with his left. "It's okay, Mr. Goodloe. It was an accident. We never blamed you."

When the man finally ambled off, I asked my father who Mr. Goodloe was, and he told me that in 1938, when my uncle John was fifteen, he was wrestling with a friend atop a horse cart filled with hay, parked on the side of the road in the black section of town known as Haughville. The uncle, who by then was already playing catcher for the Indianapolis ABC's in the Negro Baseball League, fell from the cart just as Mr. Goodloe was driving by in his Ford. My uncle and namesake died instantly. Mr. Goodloe, a pharmacist and ironically one of the few blacks in Haughville who could afford a car at the time, never got over it, and my father said that he had been apologizing to him and his remaining siblings for nigh on forty years by that time, every single time he ran into any of them.

The darker side of my father began to surface more and more at about this time as well. He seemed to start drinking more, disappearing, sometimes for entire weekends and returning with the smell of cheap whiskey oozing from his pores. I must've been around fourteen when my father, following one such lost weekend, shared with me the story of how he had just been passed over for a promotion to supervisor at the Chrysler plant where he worked. At the time, he was the only black skilled tradesman at the factory. He'd always had a head for figures, but still, he studied hard, and aced the exam for a supervisory position, scoring the highest of the group. Weeks went by and he heard nothing, so finally he asked his boss about the promotion. The boss acknowledged my father's high score on the exam, but said he couldn't give him the job because his white coworkers would never accept following orders from a black man.

My father seethed, railing against uneducated, "dumb rednecks" like the ones he worked alongside; phony liberals who talked a good game but had no heart, like Jimmy Carter; venom-spitting racist conservatives like Ronald Reagan; puffed-up, boorish tough guys like then Indiana University basketball coach Bobby Knight; and even cartoon characters who reminded him of the racist "Black Sambo" books that he remembered being taught in elementary school. If I or my brothers were watching an old Tarzan movie or some Looney Tunes cartoon, my father's remarks became so predictable I would often mouth the words mockingly behind his back as he said them: "These niggas been living in the jungle all their lives and the lion roars once and they get all bug-eyed and run off into the bush. And here comes the brave white man to save the day. Boy, boy, boy. What kind of sense does that make?"

I remember asking my father why he liked Castro on a few occasions, probably in the late seventies or early eighties. Once he extended his middle finger and said: "Because he's been doing this to the United States for twenty years." Another time he spoke of how Castro stayed at a Harlem hotel on his first official visit to the United Nations,[1] and once or twice he spoke admiringly of how Castro had chased wealthy whites like Desi Arnaz from the island for their mistreatment of black workers there. (I discovered years later that Arnaz and his family left Cuba well before the revolution.)

My father's resentments were not merely a matter of black and white, however. His vitriol was grounded in shared experience more than in any kind of simple racial allegiance. When a white man named Tony Kiritsis lost his property in foreclosure, he went to his mortgage broker's office in 1977 armed with a shotgun and used a wire hanger to attach the muzzle of the weapon to the back of the man's head.[2] Much of the sixty-three-hour standoff with police was broadcast live on Indianapolis's local news stations, and I vividly recall my father and the old black men in the neighborhood barber shop expressing empathy for Kiritsis, whose exploitation they identified with. Similarly, I could sense, even as a child, my father's very deep affection for our pediatrician, Dr. Bertram Roth, who overlooked it when my father couldn't afford his health plan's copay. Once Dr. Roth even chastised his secretary for dunning my father about a past-due bill, explaining to her that he and "Mr. Jeter had an agreement." I remember Dr. Roth as the only man in my youth whose kindness rivaled my father's. Sometimes the two men would laugh and banter on for fifteen minutes after Dr. Roth had finished looking me over, and I remember specifically one conversation when my father jokingly asked Dr. Roth when he was going to follow his white neighbors who had left his comfortable middle-class neighborhood for the suburbs when blacks began to move in.

"The house still works," he said to my father. "I'm not going anywhere." I swear my father swooned like a schoolgirl.

Black people were not spared my father's wrath. Jimmy Walker's Stepin Fetchit–like minstrelsy portraying JJ Evans on the sitcom *Good Times* did not go over well in our household. And if he caught a glimpse of the comedian's shoe-shuffling "Kid-Dynomite" routine, he would sometimes demand that we change the channel. "Just turn it, turn it," he would say, his face disfigured by aggravation. "That boy is a damn fool." When the actor Ben Vereen performed at Ronald Reagan's inauguration in blackface, my father flew into an expletive-filled rant that I had only before heard in his confrontations with police officers or bill collectors. Long before I understood what an Uncle Tom was, I knew from the way my father spat the words out like bile that it was nothing you wanted to be.

As I've grown older and had my own son, I've come not just to understand why black men are angry, but to feel it as well. I've watched my father's rage flicker like a light, while mine has grown a little more each year, and to this day, I love Ali and Fidel. Now in his late seventies, my father no longer drinks but stays home most of the day reading, watching C-Span and cable news. He dotes on his grandchildren the way he once doted on me and my siblings, but he is not nearly as talkative as he once was, and usually, when I call home, he will merely say, "Hey, Jon, you doing okay?" and quickly pass the phone back to my mother after I've assured him that I am. But not on Election Night 2008 as he watched vote tallies roll across the television screen and scenes of African American revelers in Harlem as they celebrated the election of our nation's forty-fourth president, a century after Teddy Roosevelt left office. I heard my father demand the phone from my mother with the TV blaring in the background.

"Hey, hey, Jon," he said with an enthusiasm that I hadn't heard from him in years. "Well, I guess we ain't niggas today, are we?" And then he laughed, deep and loud and long, as though a curse had been lifted, and finally, he was free.

Ten years earlier, I was working as a newspaper reporter and on assignment in Omaha, Nebraska. I don't remember what story bought me to Nebraska, but at a press conference in the city, I struck up a conversation with two black men who lived in Omaha, and they mentioned that Jimmy Walker, the ersatz JJ from the television show *Good Times*, was working as a local radio talk show host, spouting the kind of conservative up-by-your-bootstraps dross that became commercially popular on the airwaves in the nineties. Curious, almost incredulous, I asked one of the men: "What is *that* like?"

One of the men rolled his eyes, glanced over his shoulder to see if anyone was listening, and said, in a voice slightly above a whisper: "He's *still* embarrassing us."

I chewed for days on what JJ meant to black Americans and contemplated writing a feature story for the newspaper on Walker's reincarnation as a radio personality, even going so far as calling the station to request an interview with him. A representative returned my call a few days later to deny my request, but in that interim, I remember discussing the idea with a friend of mine, a black woman raised in the Deep South who worked as a journalist in Minneapolis. We talked about how we recognized, even as children, that Walker's portrayal of JJ Evans was buffoonish, a caricature of black men as cowardly, sexually promiscuous, and childlike. He was a buck-dancing jigaboo mugging it up for white America, and it was well known to readers of *Jet* magazine that John Amos, who played with dignity the role of James Evans, the stern but protective patriarch of the Evans family, had quit the show in disgust after the third season, at least partly because he was unable to tolerate the vaudevillian minstrel show that Walker's character had turned *Good Times* into.[3]

"Why does JJ loom so large in black popular culture?" I asked my friend, trying to get a handle on how to frame a feature story on Walker.

"Because," she said without hesitation, "he killed the black father."

And so he had. Amos's depiction reminded me of my father and maybe a dozen other men that I knew from the neighborhood and church. He was dark-skinned, hardworking, even, like my father, a Korean War veteran, and he was the first recognizable black man anyone of my generation had ever seen on a weekly television show. He was slain, almost literally, by this clownish, Hollywood avatar of a black man, since the show's writers attributed James Evans's absence in the fourth season to a fatal car crash (which led to perhaps the most famous catchphrase from television in the history of black America, Florida Evans's angry, mournful crescendo—*"Damn. Damn. Damn!"*—when she broke a plate after learning that her husband had died).

It would be nearly ten years before another black man who even remotely resembled my father or any of the black men I knew from the neighborhood or church appeared regularly on television, in the form of Bill Cosby's Heathcliff Huxtable.

This is no small thing, nothing to be dismissed or trivialized as mere "political correctness." Dating back to *Birth of a Nation*, Hollywood's infantilization of black men has fed racist attitudes, savage inequalities, and lynching, and has held up African Americans as objects of ridicule, unworthy of either respect or fair treatment. By turns immature and menacing, America's celluloid version of the black man has, like a gust of wind to fire, fanned both violence against, and exploitation of, real black men. Walker's JJ was folklore, an illusion purposefully sustained to justify a nation's most wretched misdeeds. Do you hire someone who is recklessly irresponsible? Why wouldn't you jail someone who is criminally inclined? How much do you spend to educate someone who is dumb? What percentage of your tax money goes to support someone who's fallen on hard times because he is lazy, undisciplined, and undeserving of help?

In this context, stereotypes are tantamount to pornography, reducing humanity to folktales and garish, titillating fables that reflect and direct the poison that courses through our body politic like parasites, taking on, ultimately, a life of their own. The social psychologist Claude Steele posits that our popular cultural narrative conditions people to buy into the stereotypes that have been assigned to them. In a series of experiments conducted by Steele, female students performed far better on math tests when administrators instructed them that the exam was merely to help researchers study their problem-solving ability, and far worse when they were told beforehand that their scores would be compared with those of a group of white male students. The same was true for black students. White youths fared worse when they were told their scores on a science test would be measured against those of a class of Asians taking the same test. Steele even discovered that whites ran slower hundred-yard-dash times when they were told that their times would be compared to those run by youths who attend a nearby all-black school. When researchers told the youths their times would be compared to times recorded at a neighboring all-white school, the sample group ran faster times.[4] Just as telling, perhaps, is an investigation into who does not internalize oppressive stereotypes, among them, women raised under the Communist regimes of the Eastern bloc, which mandated that half of all managerial positions be staffed by women and flooded their airwaves with propaganda, but not the kinds of stifling, subliminal code that dominates the airwaves in the United States. Steele found that these women had built up a certain immunity to what he calls "stereotype threat," and their math or science scores were virtually unchanged by what they were told in advance.

The thread that binds the quilt of American mythmaking is the motivation: it sells. Cloaking commerce in comfortable iconography that the mainstream culture reflexively recognizes as truth sells movie tickets, television ads, and even political candidates. Much as JJ's minstrelsy sold a lot of dish soap, potato chips, and aspirin, Barack Obama continued the American political tradition of using demagogic images of black men to peddle his billion-dollar campaign to white voters. In this rhetorical approach, he perhaps struck the most strident tone in his June 2008 Father's Day address to a conservative, all-black Pentecostal church on Chicago's South Side, in which he lectured black men about their shortcomings as parents. These are excerpts:

> [But] if we are honest with ourselves, we'll admit that too many fathers also are missing—missing from too many lives and too many homes. They have abandoned their responsibilities, acting like boys instead of men. And the foundations of our families are weaker because of it. You and I know this is true in the African American community. . . . We need fathers to realize that responsibility does not end at conception. We need them to realize that what makes a man is not the ability to have a child, but the courage to raise one. . . . It's a wonderful thing if you are married and living in a home with your children. But don't just sit there and watch SportsCenter all weekend long.[5]

The speech was met with applause from parishioners and fawning from gleeful media columnists and on-air personalities who were heartened that Obama had the cojones to give the black community the tough love they needed, and rattle them from their complacent culture of aggrievement. Many blacks, my father included, found Obama's remarks sophomorically reductive or took issue with his pious, condescending tone, but chalked it up as a necessary evil if he was going to win the White House. "He *has* to say that, Jon," my father corrected me when I voiced my displeasure over the remarks in a telephone conversation that same Father's Day after the speech began to pop up on evening newscasts. "You know that's all white folks want to hear."

Still, what Obama did in his speech was to essentially summon JJ back onto the national stage for an encore, describing, yet again, this character who is as farcical as the Loch Ness Monster but still amuses and comforts America. To be sure, there are irresponsible black fathers, just as there are irresponsible white and Latino and Hungarian and ambidextrous dads, and everyone would be better off if they got their act together. But research by Boston University social psychologist Rebekah Levine Coley found that black fathers not living in the family home are more likely to be involved in their children's lives than fathers of any other racial or ethnic group. Moreover, Coley found, black men typically move out of the home because their inability to provide the financial support their families need drives them to despair and a sense of shame that they cannot, like James Evans, fulfill their fatherly obligations.[6] Maybe some people will find fault with that, or see it as a sign of weakness, but it does not support the conventional view of the black man as nihilist, moving from woman to woman to plant his seed and sauntering off yet again as soon as the going gets tough. Indeed, with black unemployment rates historically twice those of whites and as many as half of all able-bodied black men in urban areas like New York City out of work by the spring of 2009, black fathers, more often than not, are playing with pain. And it has not gone unnoticed, even by black men who supported Obama, that during his campaign he never singled out for criticism the men who truly need lectures on personal responsibility— the predominantly white Wall Street traders whose reckless, selfish, immoral behavior capsized the entire global economy.

"We're not electing him," said the University of Maryland political science professor Ron Walters, who worked on Jesse Jackson's 1988 presidential campaign, "to be the preacher-in-chief."[7]

Seen in its entirety, the Obama campaign painted a portrait of black men that is straight out of central casting. He often publicly scolded blacks for their homophobia, though he rarely ever mentioned any other group, and seemed in fact to be saying, "Do as I say, not as I do," when he invited a white man who was a virulent homophobe to deliver the invocation at his inaugural. Early in his campaign he addressed a cadre of black South Carolina state legislators and said: "In Chicago sometimes when I speak to the black chambers of commerce I say, you know what would be a good economic development plan for our community, would be if we were to make sure that people aren't throwing garbage out of their cars." Speaking to a mostly black audience before the Texas primary he said: "Y'all got a Popeyes in Beaumont? I know some of y'all, you got that cold Popeyes out for breakfast. I know. That's why some of y'all are laughing. You can't do that. Children have to have proper nutrition."[8]

But perhaps most dangerous was Obama's proselytizing that racism is dead in America, and that black grievances were overwrought, if not wholly illegitimate. He was fond of saying during the campaign that "blacks were ninety percent of the way to equality," and he used his much-praised campaign speech on race to dismiss as nothing more than unwarranted "anger and bitterness" the assessments of America made by black men of Reverend Jeremiah Wright's—and my father's—generation.

Several years ago, when I was working as a foreign correspondent in South Africa, I had dinner with Reverend Wright, who was then visiting the country with a parishioner who was a friend of mine. Over the course of three hours and a bottle of South African Shiraz, I found him witty and charming, a first-rate raconteur who was also passionate about ending injustice, be it in Chicago or the Middle East. He expressed anger, but nothing I hadn't heard before from black men who've been baptized in American racism and hypocrisy, and he also articulated a sort of global solidarity with oppressed people everywhere. He was nothing like the portrayals of him in Obama's famous speech and the mainstream media's campaign coverage. His church was one of the few in Chicago—black or white—to marry gay couples, and rather than encourage his parishioners to live a quotidian existence devoted to consumerism and "middle-classness," as so many black prosperity preachers do today, Wright exhorted his flock to deepen their intellectual and spiritual commitment to their families and community, from the city's South Side to Soweto, Gaza to Ghana, and Harlem to Haiti. I remember thinking at the time that Reverend Wright, while about fifteen years younger than my father, reminded me of him nonetheless, and that the two men would hit it off famously if they ever met.

Because I had worked and lived in Chicago, the three of us that evening spoke specifically of politics in the city—this was well before Obama leapt onto the national scene, maybe late 2000—and I recall Wright's noting the scorn that some of Chicago's Jewish community heaped upon Louis Farrakhan, the Nation of Islam leader who is often branded by the media as an anti-Semite. Wright, who is a friend of Farrakhan's, acknowledged he didn't agree with everything that came out of Farrakhan's mouth, but many of the worst quotes attributed to him—such as the allegation that he had called Judaism a "gutter religion"—have been proven false, and in all his years of knowing the man he had never heard him say anything openly contemptuous of Jews, nor had he ever heard him use any kind of slur. The same could not be said for Chicago's former mayor, Richard J. Daley, or his son, Richard M. Daley, who can be seen, in a widely broadcast videotape of the 1968 Democratic Convention, very clearly shouting from the floor at Connecticut senator Abraham Ribicoff—who in his address had unexpectedly launched into a denunciation of the Chicago Police Department's use of "Gestapo tactics" against young protesters—"Go home, you fucking kike," and "Fuck you, you Jew son of a bitch."

"Now everyone in Chicago has seen that video at least a dozen times," I recall Wright saying, "but the Jewish community gets along quite well with the Daleys. You never hear Rahm Emanuel calling the Daleys anti-Semites. You never read in the [Chicago] *Tribune* that the Daleys are anti-Semites. They call him their friend.

But I guess it's not a good story if it's the white man in City Hall who is the vulgar racist and the black guy in a bow-tie selling bean-pies is actually the thoughtful one leveling legitimate criticisms at a community. He [Farrakhan] veered from the script, and white folks get confused."

Obama seldom goes unscripted, almost never breaks character. And in his reproach of Wright and other more anonymous black boogeymen, he plays the role of the good black, the straight man to the Jacksons, Sharptons, and Wrights of the world, who, in white America's narrative, are snake-oil salesmen, shuffling, whining, and testifying to injustices that are not there. Obama's casting in this role owes first and foremost to his fair skin, slender build, and clean-shaven face, which marks him in the mind of many whites as unthreatening, avuncular, almost sexless. The scholar Cornel West notes that as gifted as Obama is, he would never have gotten so far if he resembled, say, the dark-skinned actor Danny Glover. There is a certain narcissism in Obama's appeal, in that whites can look into his face and see one of their own, rather than the aboriginal menace represented by a politician like former Detroit mayor Kwame Kilpatrick, a collegiate football player with imposing physicality, flashy clothes and jewelry, and fiery, confrontational rhetoric.

Studies show that there is a reflexive component to this. Blacks, generally, are distrustful of emotionless presentations, while whites, for the most part, are suspicious of emotion in public forums. Obama's robotic, almost unflappable demeanor is calculated to reassure whites, to allay their fears of the "fire next time." His is the blackness that dare not speak its name, and in his diminishment of black grievances, he signals to whites that he can be trusted, almost like the overseer on a plantation. "There's reasonableness about him," Robert Harmala, a Washington, D.C., attorney and top Democratic power broker told *Harper's* magazine's Ken Silverstein.[9]

Ironically, Obama, in his 1995 book *Dreams from My Father*, acknowledges how America assigns roles to blacks and whites. When he was in high school in Hawaii, he and one of the only other black men at the school decided to take two white friends to a black party. Obama drove. Though no one much worried about the white classmates' presence, he noticed that the two stuck together in a corner, uncomfortable. After an hour, they asked to be taken home, just as the party was getting started. Here's where the story picks up in the book:

> In the car, Jeff put an arm on my shoulder, looking at once contrite and relieved. "You know, man," he said, "that really taught me something. I mean, I can see how it must be tough for you and Ray sometimes, at school parties being the only black guys and all."
>
> I snorted. "Yeah. Right." A part of me wanted to punch him right there. We started down the road toward town, and in the silence, my mind began to rework Ray's words that day with Kurt, all the discussions we had had before that, the events of that night. And by the time I had dropped my friends off, I had begun to see a new map of the world, one that was frightening in its simplicity, suffocating in its implications. We were always playing on the white man's court, Ray had told me, by the white man's rules. If the principal, or the coach, or a teacher, or Kurt, wanted to spit in your face, he could, because he had power and you didn't. If he decided not to, if he treated you like a man or came to your defense, it was because he knew that the words you spoke, the clothes you wore, the books you read, your ambitions and desires, were already

his. Whatever he decided to do, it was his decision to make, not yours, and because of that fundamental power he held over you, because it was preceded and would outlast his individual motives and inclinations, any distinction between good and bad whites held negligible meaning.[10]

A few years ago, I was interviewing an African American actor for a magazine article I had planned to write but never got around to. He did not want to be identified because he was still a working actor, auditioning for bit parts in television shows, movies, and commercials, but for the purposes of this book, we can call him Darryl. A Northwestern University graduate, Darryl has been in Hollywood for more than fifteen years, though he has struggled to find work, and when we met, he was working as a hotel parking attendant to pay the bills. Darryl had come to believe firmly that Hollywood, much like the slaveholding South, was an institution determined to explain white superiority as a way of maintaining a moral equilibrium in the world. To that end, angry black characters usually died as a reminder of what happened to rebel slaves. The good black, on the other hand, was rewarded for his pliancy and servility with survival, and maybe even a white woman at the end. The angry black man was boorish, impulsive, angry, promiscuous, of ample size, and often—though not always—darker-skinned, while the good black was smaller in size, polite, sophisticated, dispassionate, and the voice of reason. He also tended to be slightly effeminate, or kind of nebbishly uninterested in sex. Think, for example, of the rival black drug dealers, U-Turn and Conrad, in the cable show *Weeds* or the boyish-looking African American actor Dulé Hill, who played a presidential aide on the television show *The West Wing* and the stalwart best friend of a private investigator in the television show *Psych*.

"I would say that in probably close to half of all the roles that I have auditioned for, they are looking for this kind of androgynous, or almost a eunuch-type, character, or they want a flaming gay or even a cross-dresser," Darryl said over drinks at a hotel bar near Chicago's O'Hare airport in early 2007. He recalled an essay that appeared in *Essence* magazine early in the acting career of the African American actor Isaiah Washington, in which he bemoaned the numerous times he'd been asked to audition for roles in which he had to dress in drag. In his early forties, Darryl had a steady girl-friend, and while he was not a big man, at maybe five foot nine and 180 pounds, he had a look that was hard to place in a Hollywood context. Recently, he said, he'd noticed that many of the roles he auditioned for were going not to small, androgynous-looking black men but to big, broad-shouldered, dark-skinned men who all but leaked testosterone. But the reasons for that, he thought, were per-verse: "They want them for roles in which they are subservient to white men, like a bouncer or a personal assistant or a driver. They like the image of this big black guy being bossed around by the little white guy."

The stock black characters that Hollywood returns to repeat-edly are, of course, patches in a quilt that, once sewn together, rep-resents the "America that never was, and must always be," as the poet Langston Hughes once wrote, a series of stick figures that are intended to redeem the sins of white patriarchy and paint white men as the cultural norms of heroism, decency, intelligence, and even sex appeal, locked in mortal combat with the forces of wickedness and mediocrity. The portrayals of Scottish immigrants to Appalachia as backward, incestuous, and uncivilized "hillbillies" for instance, pro-vided the mining and logging robber barons with a narrative to jus-tify both their rape of the land and the paltry wages they paid to have it done, similar to the depictions of Africans in the European press during the colonial era. Women didn't fare well either. Film historian Neal Gabler has noted that pioneering Jewish studio executives of the early part of the twentieth century favored star-lets (and wives) with soft, WASPish features (think Norma Shearer) to cast in their movies because it appealed to their unspoken desire to assimilate. Fast-forward the industry and its moguls eighty years, and it's easy to understand how the id of the modern studio executive is the main culprit in young girls' horrifically negative images of their own bodies, or the tendency to cast Asian, Latino, and dark-skinned women as sexually available, while white and fair-skinned black women are more likely to be cast as respectable, almost virginal, characters, whose sexuality is like treasure, fetishized but forever out of reach. A perfect example of this is the wildly popular 2004 movie *Sideways,* in which the actress Sandra Oh, who is of Korean ancestry, plays a promiscuous woman who is shown on screen in every manner of undress and in almost cartoonish sexually explicit poses while the blonde actress Virginia Madsen never removes her clothes and is almost Victorian in her coyness. I once read an obituary of the actor Anthony Quinn that noted his swarthy looks resulted in early movie roles that seemed to consist largely of being punched out by every white leading man in Hollywood.

Said Darryl: "Hollywood is very much into emasculating black men and men of color."

Cecil Nathaniel Jeter was born December 22, 1931, in Indianapolis, the seventh of eight children His mother died when he was four; his father, who died when I was a year old, was a gruff but good man, to hear my parents, aunts, and uncles tell it, who towered larger than life over his clan. Born in 1884 in Union City, South Carolina, the industrial heart of the slaveholding South, he jumped on a train headed north by northwest in 1901 when he was seventeen, hoping to make it to Chicago to escape life as a sharecropper. His money ran out in Indianapolis, and so he stayed, caught on at a factory that made transmissions for tractors and other farm equipment, married, had a family.

There's a story my father likes to tell about his father. A few years before my grandfather's death, my father was driving him to a doctor's appointment when he had to stop suddenly. Accustomed to having young children in the passenger seat, my father instinctively extended his right arm as though to stop a toddler from crashing into the dashboard or the windshield (this was before car manufacturers were required to install seat belts and children were required to ride in car seats). The car lurched forward, and then back, and when it was clear that the danger had passed, my father turned to my grandfather and realized that his arm was draped across his frame, his elbow planted firmly in his chest. There was a pregnant pause, with my grandfather sizing up the situation and staring at my father in disbelief. And then he barked: "Boy, have you lost your mind? Do I look six years old to you? I don't need you to protect me."

The car exploded with laughter, my father recalled, and he would guffaw as well whenever he told that story. I love the story because, while I've always thought my father extraordinary, I know, really, that he is quite ordinary in an anthropological sense, and his story represents what I've always known black fathers to be: not shoveling cold fried chicken down their kids' throats, or slouching on the sofa with their hands down their pants watching SportsCenter, or shirking their responsibility, but rather, using whatever they had to overcome a basic lack of equipment in their car, or a nation's fundamental design flaw, to make everything okay, to protect their own, beating back the Devil with one arm tied behind their backs. For most black people, black men aren't the menace; they are its antidote.

When I was a kid, there were two surefire ways to get my father riled up. My father and I have the darkest skin in the family, and when we were kids, my older brother and sister used to tease me about this. I honestly can't remember what they said, but I do remember that when I went running to complain to my father, he would become quite exasperated with me. "Boy, you can't pay no attention to what people say about you. You're going to be called a lot worse names than that. Don't ever be ashamed to be black."

The other thing that drew my father's ire was if we backed down from a fight. Once when my older brother was a lanky eighth-grader, a bigger high school boy picked a fight with him for no apparent reason and slugged him in the jaw, knocking my brother to the ground. My father was upset that my brother hadn't fought back, and he let me know, in no uncertain terms, that not standing up for yourself was unacceptable.

One of the first authors I remember reading as a child was James Baldwin, and in his 1963 essay "The Fire Next Time," Baldwin pens a letter to his nephew, in which he says that his nephew's father, Baldwin's brother, "spent much of his life half-believing what white people said about him."

It was always clear to me that this was not the case for my father, and for the old black men who peopled the barbershop, and my friends' dads. And this was why they fought back, getting up every day that God sent and going to work, trying to do the right thing because they knew that slip-ups reflected badly not just on you but on your neighbors and your kids and your neighbors' kids, and when all else failed, and you were facing someone bigger than you, then you went to war, because your dignity was all you had, and goddammit, you weren't going to let them have that without a fight.

This is why my Dad blew his fuse like a madman when he thought the gas station cashier was trying to cheat him. He figured that she was trying to call him either stupid or a thief, and he was neither.

My son, Ryan, was born in 1987, one hundred and three years after my grandfather's birth. He is, like my father and me, dark-skinned and broad-shouldered. Like my father, he is smart, likes to read, and can charm the pants off people. When he was younger and I took him to visit his grandparents, he would lie next to my father on the floor, where my father rested because of an on-the-job leg injury in 1977 that made it difficult for him to sleep in a bed. And they would talk for hours, and laugh, deep and loud and long. The greatest joy I've ever known is hearing them laugh like that, so free and safe and unafraid. When Ryan was about nine, my father told him a joke while they lay side by side on the floor, and Ryan jumped up to repeat it to me, laughing so hard I feared he was going to hyperventilate.

"Dad," he said to me.

"Yes," I answered.

"What did Abraham Lincoln say on the morning he woke up with a hangover?"

"What did he say?"

"He said: 'Say that again. I did what? I freed who?'"

When he was a teenager and we were driving somewhere and someone innocently cut me off or stopped suddenly in front of me, I would ask Ryan jokingly: "Do you know why they did that?" And he would answer, in a tone that mockingly suggested a conspiracy: "Cuz you're a *black* man," and sometimes he would prosecute the offender with a jab of his finger. Other times, if we walked into, say, a doctor's office and there was no one there to greet us immediately, Ryan would repeat a line uttered by the actor Martin Lawrence from the black buddy-cop film *Bad Boyz*: "Don't be alarmed, we're Negroes." And he loved to deliver the line that Jamie Foxx uttered as Muhammad Ali's tragic muse Bundini Brown in the film *Ali*, commenting on his conversion to Islam: "I can understand giving up white women, but *pork*?"

Once during his sophomore year at Howard University, he called me from the bookstore to complain that they didn't have any copies of J. D. Salinger's *Catcher in the Rye*—one of his favorite books—but they had various titles by the likes of E. Lynn Harris and Rachael Ray. "I just don't believe that," he said, sounding wounded by the disappointment. When we see each other nowadays, we often debate who was the more seminal revolutionary figure, Fidel or Che. I, of course, argue Fidel. He is a huge Che fan and knows everything about him.

But in recent years, particularly since he's grown dreadlocks, Ryan has changed. He sees the world differently because he understands, increasingly, that the world sees him differently. On a few occasions he's been harassed by police while walking or sitting in public with a group of friends. He laments that some of the white college students he met while working one summer on Capitol Hill don't seem to understand that racism exists and shapes the world profoundly. In the summer of 2008, I went to visit him in Rhode Island, where he was working as a camp counselor for poor minority kids. There were twelve counselors, all college students, most of them white, and all of them had access to a lockbox containing a petty cash fund. One morning a woman who was one of the counselors' supervisors noticed twenty dollars missing from the lockbox, and there was no receipt left to account for its absence. She approached Ryan while he was busy trying to organize a basketball game for the kids. "Ryan," he recalled her saying, "did you take twenty out of the lockbox?"

Distracted by kids buzzing around him, he answered simply, "No, I haven't been in there."

Apparently, she didn't believe him, and a few hours later, she approached him again, but this time, more confrontationally.

"Ryan, are you sure there's not something you want to tell me?" she said.

Understanding what was not being said, Ryan answered slowly, drawing the words out to make it clear that he understood. "No. Is there something you want to ask me?"

"I still haven't found that twenty dollars," she said to him.

"And I still don't know where it is," he responded. He turned to catch up with a group of kids he was shepherding to the elementary school's gymnasium, when she grabbed him, forcefully, by the elbow and started to say something.

Ryan cut her off and withdrew his arm from her grasp firmly, but not violently. "Look," he said. "You might want to ask someone else. I told you; I have not been in the lockbox." He paused for effect. "Ever."

She backed off and later found that another camp counselor, a young white man, had taken the money and had innocently failed to leave a receipt. Later, as Ryan retold the story, he said he'd wished he had told her: "I can *get* twenty dollars."

The woman never apologized to Ryan, and he said then he would not return to work at the camp, which he had enjoyed so much previously. He has expressed an interest in going to law school, and, he has confessed to me at least once, considered running for political office in the future. When he finished telling me the story of his camp run-in, he smiled and asked me: "You don't think Obama ever had to deal with this sort of thing, do you?"

|1 0|

The Front Man

Lee Moves from South Africa to Brooklyn

It doesn't matter if a cat is black or white, as long as it catches mice.

—DENG XIAOPING

The twenty- and thirtysomethings gathered inside the cramped, third-floor Brooklyn walk-up resemble a Benetton ad, frolicking and laughing and passing, clockwise, around the room a bag of Cheetos and a bottle of Johnny Walker Blue Label that's been stowed away for months waiting for a special occasion. When Barack Obama ambles to the podium at the Democratic National Convention in Denver to accept the party's nomination for president, someone turns up the sound on the forty-six-inch television set in the corner, triggering a barrage of "Shhhs" and "Be quiet, it's starting." The chattering abruptly stops, all movement is suspended, and a reverent hush descends upon the room like a fine mist until Obama utters the final word of his address. Then, as if on cue, there is this deafening exhalation—even the walls seem to exhale—and the room erupts in spasms of almost evangelical joy.

Christina, the black twenty-five-year-old fashion writer, high-fives Brent, the white twenty-six-year-old schoolteacher. Bea, a twenty-seven-year-old graphic artist and writer from an Iranian family living in Norway, jumps in the air to chest-bump Erica, the black twenty-six-year-old MBA student from Chicago. Bea's husband of one month, Jelsen, who is twenty-four, a graphic artist and a dead ringer for the comedian Chris Rock, drops to the floor in a comical break-dance routine as Obama's wife and daughters join Obama onstage to raucous applause from the crowd.

Lee Alexander is the only one in the room who does not budge. Amid the chaos, he sits motionless on the chaise, elbows perched on his knees, hands clasped in front of his face, body pitched forward, staring intently into the television as though it is a bomb that needs defusing.

He is twenty-eight and grew up in South Africa, but he has made New York City his new home. He describes himself as an African American with a particular emphasis on the African. In just a few months, he and Erica plan to marry and, with any luck, start a family soon. For the time being, he washes dishes at a dimly lit bohemian restaurant in Brooklyn and works weekends at an antiques store while studying for his marketing degree at New York University. His future, his family, his friends, are all right here in the United States, and so, more than ever, Lee has a horse in this American presidential race. He is overjoyed that his adopted country may soon elect its first black president, just as the country of his birth did fourteen years earlier. Much as the world looked to Nelson Mandela when South Africa elected him that country's first black president—in their first truly democratic election—it now turns to Obama as the vessel of all their hopes, a symbol of all that is possible.

But watching Obama take this giant stride toward the White House, Lee can't help but also feel an almost immobilizing sense of anxiety. Déjà vu washes over him, as though this is the opening scene of a bad movie that he has seen before. He was fourteen in 1994 when South Africans of all races went to the polls for the first time, and although he was too young to vote, he celebrated anyway, walking the half-mile to the elementary school in his all-black township outside of Cape Town just to stand outside with his friends for hours, watching the people stand in line to cast their ballots and emerge looking curiously at the bright red smudge on their thumb that was the election board's way of preventing fraud. He remembers everything from that day, as though he lived those hours in a state of heightened awareness: how strong his grandma made that morning's coffee; the pattern of the headdress worn by the poll worker who emerged from the schoolhouse every hour or so to bark instructions at the crowd; the pungent, pleasing smell of the sea in the air; how he was so giddily hopeful that a new day had finally arrived for South Africa's black majority that he actually caught himself skipping on the walk home.

But fourteen years in, Lee has come to accept the fact that his lofty expectations of the country of his birth had been unmet, and so many hopes, like stars, had plummeted to earth. The emancipation—from want and fear and violence—that he had hoped for for South Africa remains elusive and out of reach, like an apparition. Materially very little has changed for his black countrymen since they vanquished white minority rule in the nation's first democratic election. Unemployment is higher than ever, economic disparities have grown, the crime rate has soared, schools are crumbling, and the farmland—the country's most valuable resource—remains almost wholly owned by whites just as it was during the days of apartheid.[1] Walk into any nice restaurant in Cape Town and see who sits and who serves; who drives their Mercedes to work and who rides the bakki, the fleet of crowded microbuses that swarm Johannesburg and Cape Town and Durban like angry, buzzing bees; who owns the house and who cleans it. Mandela has come and gone from the main stage, and voters are preparing to elect their third black president in just a few months, but the defining truth of his native land, now as always, is that the darker your skin, the poorer you are. What good does it do a prisoner if your jailer looks like you but does not set you free? Black South Africans turned to one of their own to govern but wasted the opportunity to transform the values imposed on their country by outsiders, and Lee can hardly bear the thought of Obama repeating the mistake in his adopted country.

In South Africa's case, Lee believes, the mistake was in looking to the West generally, and to Washington, D.C., specifically, to solve the problems of African people. And as was the case with apartheid, there's nothing in Americans' fetishism for either democracy or the free market for people of color. What is it that the Cubans say? Each day in the world 200 million children sleep in the streets; not one of them is in Cuba. Can America say that? While Lee is watching, Obama takes a huge step closer to the presidency, and an African proverb comes to mind, one that his black countrymen often trot out to describe their dilemma in the post-apartheid era: Got a stone but didn't get a nut to crack; got a nut but no stone to crack it with. South Africa's black majority government built new homes for the people but left them without money to pay the rent; provided them with running water but shut off the tap when they couldn't pay the bill; replaced the names of bullheaded white segregationists on the public schoolhouses with those of black liberation heroes but didn't replace the shoddy roofs; ordered companies to hire blacks but permitted them to slash their wages.

And so it goes for the new South Africa, where a small white minority continues to inhabit a splendid country that is, for all intents and purposes, Canada, while three-quarters of the population resides in a country with living conditions similar to those of Kenya or Zambia. It's almost as though black South Africans, in vanquishing apartheid, only applied a fresh coat of paint to a house on fire. The architecture of their oppression remains intact.

Is this what an Obama presidency holds in store for black Americans? Does Obama represent real change, or merely diversity, which, in the lexicon of white Americans, Lee has come to understand, translates as people who look different but think just as "we" do? He is impressed with Obama's obvious intellect and his skills as an orator. "He has a Ford chassis but a Porsche engine," is how he often describes Obama's unassuming demeanor and buttoned-down style. But he wonders why, so far, he has not deployed his considerable talent to champion the cause of creating opportunities for blacks or Latinos or even poor whites. If he accomplished nothing else, Mandela helped South Africans find a way to talk about race, and that foundation provides at least one reason to believe that things may one day improve. There is no such conversation in America, Lee has noticed, and when Obama addresses race, it is usually to publicly upbraid black fathers for their irresponsibility or single out black mothers for their recklessness or to warn that it would invite "moral hazard" for the government to help homeowners in trouble—who are disproportionately black—pay their high-interest mortgages. Isn't it moral hazard to reward larcenous bankers who gambled on bad loans to people who couldn't afford to pay, Lee wonders? He suspects that Obama is "clever," a term that South Africans use to portray someone who is brilliant but coldly manipulative.

"I like Obama, but I'm just not that into him," Lee says later. "Yes, he is black, but I believe he has a white mentality because he was raised in a household with his grandma spouting all that Ronald Reagan garbage."

For at least sixty years, black South Africans and black Americans have seen in one another their avatars, though no slaves from that country ever landed ashore in the United States. Jim Crow laws were not very different from apartheid's strictures; the catechism of the assassinated African American icon Malcolm X was the model for that preached by the assassinated South African icon Steve Biko; both Mandela and King found inspiration from Gandhi and Ghana's liberation hero Kwame Nkrumah; America's potent anti-apartheid movement was largely set in motion by black Americans like Randall Robinson. And South Africa's Afrikaners—white settlers of Dutch and French extraction who initiated the formal apartheid state—are the spitting archetypical image of America's white southerners: both groups have invented folkloric tales of how they conquered hostile lands and hostile, dark-skinned people, delivering civilization, religion, and technology to welcoming savages. (South Africans translate the Afrikaans word *Boer* colloquially as "redneck.") And there is a popular story told in South Africa, usually firsthand by more progressive whites, and secondhand by their black friends. Who knows whether it's apocryphal or not, but it goes like this: A white South African traveled to the United States in the mid-eighties and landed at O'Hare International Airport in Chicago. At customs, a white American immigration officer thumbed silently through the South African's passport for a minute or two, prompting the white South African traveler to ask the beefy, middle-aged officer if there was a problem.

"So, you're from South Africa?" the officer asked, without looking up.

"Yes, I am," the traveler answered, expecting the worst.

The immigration officer stamped his passport, lifted his head to look the South African in the eye, smiled, and returned it to him. "We like the way y'all handle your niggers over there," he said, and waved him through.

In a recent conversation with a black American journalist friend and a South African friend who is a university professor in the United States, Lee recalls that the three of them, in a wide-ranging discussion, stumbled onto a heartachingly tragic statistic. In 1961, the year that Obama was born and Mandela formed the armed wing of the African National Congress (ANC), black Americans earned, on average, fifty-four cents for every dollar earned by white

Americans,[2] and 100 percent of all South Africans living in poverty were black.[3] Forty-seven years later, 99 percent of all poor South Africans are black,[4] and African Americans' earnings have inched up to fifty-seven cents for every dollar earned by white Americans.[5]

"These are not political and economic structures that are designed for black people to get ahead," Lee says later in describing his private thoughts while the room around him celebrated Obama's acceptance address. "They are designed to exploit black people, and without addressing that, any change is just cosmetic." At roughly that moment in his thoughts, his friend Jelsen, whose parents hail from Haiti, surfaces from his dance, grinning broadly.

"Lee," Jelsen shouts at his friend.

"Yes, brother," Lee answers.

"We're about to do this," Jelsen shouts, pounding his chest twice for emphasis. "Shock the world. Shock the world. South African style, baby. South African style."

"Yes," Lee says calmly, removing his eyeglasses to wipe them with a handkerchief. "That is exactly what I am afraid of."

"The United States is fond of labeling many African countries 'failed states,' but what you must understand is that from an African perspective, from the perspective of the Global South, America is the failed state." This is Lee's friend Sean, more than a month after Obama has been sworn in as president. Sean and Lee are sitting in the one-bedroom, $1,300-a-month apartment in Bed-Stuy—good-sized for the money and for Brooklyn—that Lee shares with his new wife. Sean is a professor of communications at a Midwestern university who, just today, was offered a similar position in New York City. They are sipping from tumblers of Bushmills and discussing South Africa's likely next president, Jacob Zuma, a former political prisoner at Robben Island with Mandela.

"The verdict is still out on many African countries," Sean continues. "You must remember that most African nations have only been free to define themselves for a generation and, in South Africa's case, less than that. And they are trying to answer the question of what they want to be while they are saddled with this heavy colonial baggage that has left Africa impoverished and underdeveloped," he says.

America, on the other hand, has been free for 230 years, industrialized for 150, and the world's leading superpower for nearly 100 years, Lee says. And yet, the state is unresponsive to the needs of its citizens. America's institutions exist largely to exploit the commonwealth rather than serve it. There is nearly as much poverty, as much sickness, as much violence and despair in the 'hood in New York as there is in Guguletu, Lee says, invoking an all-black South African township that is known for its crime, tin shacks, high incidence of HIV/AIDS, and overall poverty.

And yet America ignores its ghettoes and its poor as if they are invisible. He notes that while South Africa is home to nine official languages, the standard greeting is *sawabona*, or merely the abbreviated *sawa*, which is translated from the Xhosa tribal language to, literally, "I see you." "Poor people in America are invisible," Lee laments. Why, Sean asks, does the United States, alone among the industrialized nations of the world, not have a national health care system? It is clear from all the polls that most Americans want that. Why does the government insist on defying the wishes of the majority by giving $800 billion of the taxpayers' money to Wall Street speculators?

Why, he continues, does the country allow politicians to control the election apparatus in states like Ohio and Florida rather than establishing a nonpartisan professional elections commission to provide the system with credibility, as is done in South Africa and Britain and Japan? It is not unreasonable to say what most of the world recognizes: America is the world's leading superpower, and it has failed the world. And African countries are failed states only to the extent that they mimic the failings of American democracy and American capitalism. "You see," Sean says, "this is what I think Barack has to address, has to at least begin to address, to be America's successful first black president."

Lithe and handsome, with a neat beard, glasses, and hair cut close, Lee is boyish-looking, smooth-skinned, and the color of wheat. In the apartheid government's caste system, he was designated "colored," which meant ostensibly "mixed race." This afforded him fewer privileges than whites, but more than blacks—or Bantus—in education, housing, jobs. Assigning racial categories was always tricky—usually the job was left to a white physician following childbirth who used such arbitrary criteria as your zip code, skin tone, or name—and so it is not unusual to find, even today, biological brothers and sisters raised under the same roof by the same parents but one is categorized colored, the other Bantu. (This, Lee says, illustrates the fundamental insanity of even the concept of "race," which seeks to assign differences where biology says emphatically that there are none.) But many of South Africa's coloreds are embittered, from both their experience before apartheid's collapse and the affirmative action–like policies that followed. "Too black before, too white now," is a commonly heard refrain from coloreds.

Like many both in and outside the colored community, Lee thinks this kind of thinking creates artificial fissures and unrealistic expectations. Too many coloreds have accepted whites' narcissistic definition of who they are, and that definition was intended to parse blacks from one another, to fracture a sense of community and weaken dissent. It is not uncommon to hear a colored South African lament the loss of relative privilege in the bygone days of apartheid. This narrative strikes Lee as not only shortsighted but reflecting a particularly Western notion of individualism, and antithetical to the African value known as *ubuntu*, or solidarity. We are people through other people. Individuals can't prosper if the group suffers. Coloreds, in other words, don't always understand who they are, according to Lee. And so it is in colored townships like the one he was born into, Mitchell's Plain outside Cape Town, where you see the greatest increase of drug use, alcoholism, domestic abuse, and violent crime

A notoriously brutal gang based in Mitchell's Plain is known as the American Boyz, and as you might expect of a gang with such a moniker, they are flashy, gun-toting, loud-talking young men who brag about their women, their jewels, and their cars.

"There is an identity crisis, you see," Lee says. "They don't understand the community they come from, or they don't value the community they come from and so they run from Africa to re-create themselves in the American image of success, of glory, of individual aggrandizement. They run from who they are, which is African at the root."

This is important, Lee says, because he has noticed that many fair-skinned black Americans behave and are treated like the coloreds in his homeland, given better education, better jobs, and better homes than their darker-skinned countrymen. When they believe they are special, that their privilege is because they are smarter, harder working, more moral, or more God-fearing, then it leaves other "Bantus" more isolated, worse off, and more resentful.

Lee ran with a bad crew when he was a teenager growing up on the mean streets of the Cape Flats, smoking a lot of weed, rapping, smoking more weed. Lee still writes lyrics, although he prefers to rap in his native tongue, Afrikaans, the harsh-sounding, Flemish-influenced language spoken by South African coloreds and by the Afrikaners, the descendants of Dutch and French Huguenots who migrated to Africa four hundred years ago. "The language for me accentuates my blackness," he said. "It's the language I speak to the people I most love in all the world and a reflection of who I am, my history, who I choose to be and what my surroundings have chosen for me."

Once, he and some friends discussed robbing a white drug dealer in Cape Town of his stash of marijuana—"weed is worth more than gold in South Africa"—but backed down when they feared that one of their crew might kill the guy. Shaken up by that, Lee made up his mind to get out of the hood, and found work as an aide in Parliament, which is located in Cape Town. This, he says, helped him, by expanding his consciousness, introducing him to people outside his milieu, helping to finish him, like a block of wood that God is carving, slowly, into a work of art. "It's like working in the antiques shop now. I didn't know anything about antiques before but now I've been introduced to something new." But, he insists, his roots remain African, like jazz and rap music. Eminem is a great rapper, he said, by channeling his inner Tupac, his African center. Nothing wrong with that, says Lee, who sees Tupac as an almost prophetic voice.

"I want to know if Obama likes Tupac," he says. "I think Obama will be a great president if he finds the Tupac inside of him."

Had he been born in South Africa, Obama, with his Kenyan father and white mother, would almost surely have been designated colored. And, Lee says, he's not sure whether Obama would believe he is colored, and not Bantu with a lighter complexion.

"Who are you? This is the question I would ask Obama if I were to have an audience with him. It's clear that he has had some advantages, especially in education, over most black Americans and I would want to know if he sees this as a function of a dysfunctional system or of his own superior initiative. You see, for me, growing up, my grandparents, they were very clear that this 'colored' trash was *kaack*," he says, using the Afrikaans word for shit. "Our parents wanted us to obey the laws to encounter the least amount of resistance but they wanted us to know that we belonged to a community and we are responsible for our community."

.   .   .

223

In April 2009, South African voters went to the polls in their third democratic election and chose Zuma to be South Africa's third black president, following Mandela, who stepped down after one term, and Mandela's onetime deputy, Thabo Mbeki. Mbeki was forced to step down near the end of his second term because he had worn out his welcome with his "Thatcherite" economic policies, which left millions of blacks living in extreme poverty, and an almost Nixonian ruthlessness, which led him to encourage what many South Africans saw as trumped-up charges of rape and corruption against his rival Zuma. Zuma, who served as Mbeki's deputy president, is a hero of the liberation movement, and his political biography, in some ways, is more similar to that of the Republicans' 2008 presidential nominee, John McCain. He was a political prisoner of the apartheid regime, an illiterate twenty-one-year-old when he was jailed at Robben Island alongside Mandela in the sixties. With the help of his comrades and fellow inmates, he emerged from prison eleven years later literate. As a member of the Zulu tribe, he assumed an important role in the Xhosa-dominated ANC. Mindful of the party's Xhosa leadership—Mandela and Mbeki are Xhosa, for instance, and South Africans sometimes jokingly refer to the ANC as "La Xhosa Nostra"—Zuma was the party's interlocutor with its powerful rival.

A bear of a man, Zuma has a public profile quite different from that of Mbeki, an economist educated at Sussex University in Britain and the son of an iconic ANC leader who was a peer of Mandela's and also imprisoned on Robben Island. Mbeki lived in exile for thirty years, and like many of the exiled ANC members, he is viewed with some suspicion by his black countrymen, regarded as an intellectual, but aloof, lacking, as it were, the "street cred" of many ANC leaders—like Winnie Mandela or the assassinated Communist Party leader Chris Hani—who stayed and fought the apartheid regime at home. In some ways, Mbeki's conservative economic policies represent the triumph of the ANC exile faction, and while their approach has won the government fans at the World Bank, the International Monetary Fund, and the White House, it has left black South Africans grappling with an unemployment rate hovering near 40 percent, and soaring costs of fuel, electricity, water, housing, and food. The ANC's land reform effort, based on a "willing-buyer, willing-seller" principle, requires the government to buy land from white landowners, and not surprisingly, has redistributed only a trickle of farmland to the black majority.

"They came back wearing London Fog coats and armed with the ideals of outsiders," Lee said.

When black squatters in 2001 settled on vacant farmland outside Johannesburg, Mbeki sent in police in riot gear, helmets, and bulldozers to demolish the tin and wood shacks they had built. Mbeki defended the move, saying that foreign investors would avoid a country that did not respect the rule of law or property rights, but it was a terrible move politically, reminding the ANC's black electoral base of how the apartheid government razed whole black neighborhoods to move blacks out and whites in. Moreover, many blacks said aloud, what good is the free market if it doesn't even help put a roof over the heads of poor families?

Zuma was South Africa's deputy president during the evictions and, at least publicly, did not raise any objections to Mbeki's market-friendly policies. That didn't happen until Mbeki was elected to a second term in office in 2004 and Zuma, by all accounts, began to contemplate, for the first time, whether he had a future as South Africa's president.

It was during this period that prosecutors filed rape and corruption charges against Zuma, and Mbeki ousted his deputy president. The charges didn't stick, and in newspaper accounts, ANC officials openly accused Mbeki of pressing for the prosecutions in order to beat back an internecine party challenge from Zuma for the presidency. If so, the plan backfired. Unbound from the obligations of the deputy presidency, Zuma strengthened his relationship with South Africa's labor unions, honed his reputation as a populist, and outmaneuvered Mbeki in bitterly contested internal ANC elections to head the party. (South Africa's parliamentary system is modeled on the British system, in which voters choose the political party and the party puts forward its presidential nominee.) Indeed, when voters in South Africa did go to the polls in 2009, the ANC nearly won three-quarters of the vote, and Zuma was easily elected the nation's president.

Within the South African political context, Lee is far from a radical or a communist, but he sees, in Zuma, Obama's twin: an opportunistic politician who offers eloquent, rhetorical nods to "change," but a close examination of his policies indicates very little change from the previous administration. "I think that black Americans and black South Africans have gotten so little from their leaders, they've sort of learned, subconsciously, to expect very little from their leadership," Lee says. "Zuma and Obama really represent a failure of black political imagination around the world."

When asked to describe his own politics, Lee says he considers himself a Pan-Africanist, like Biko or Malcolm X, which, in his interpretation, means only that Africans everywhere are best served by African solutions to their problems. And while he insists that he does not believe in any kind of racial superiority, he believes that Europeans and Africans see the world very differently and that this influences all things political from slavery to apartheid to the civil rights movement in the United States. Whites, generally, exalt the individual and private property; blacks exalt the community and collaboration.

There is a story that every South African learns as a child, not unlike the story of the pilgrims in the United States. In 1837, Pieter Retief, a wealthy Afrikaner farmer, led his delegation of covered wagons over the Drakensburg mountains into Kwa Zulu Natal along the Indian Ocean coastline, where he entered into negotiations with Dingane, a chief who became king of the Zulus

226

after he murdered his brother Shaka Zulu in 1828. In the popular Afrikaans version of the meeting, the two men signed a deed—historians agree it was written in English—bequeathing lands to the Voortrekkers if Retief recovered some cattle stolen by a rival tribe.[6]

Retief's repatriation of the cattle was feted with two days of feasting by Dingane and his chiefs, but the king turned on Retief and his diplomatic party, killing them, then sent his forces to massacre about five hundred Afrikaner men, women, and children camped nearby.

Blacks, by and large, tell a different story. Dingane's was not an act of betrayal but of self-defense when it became clear that there had been a misunderstanding between the two men. Dingane had intended for the Voortrekkers to farm the land, not own it. An argument ensued. Retief threatened Dingane with a musket. The idea of property rights was foreign to Africans. No one owned the land, not even Dingane. The land belonged to everyone and was to be parceled out—leased, if you will—as the king, its caretaker, saw fit. In a communal agrarian culture that valued collaboration over competition, you could no more own the soil beneath your feet than you could the sky or the sun or the water.

The confrontation between Retief and Dingane formed the template not just for apartheid, but for the enduring relationship between tribes of the global North and South over private property and the community's well-being. Around the world, Lee believes, blacks and whites have been at war ever since.

The irony is that Lee is unsure whom either Zuma or Obama is siding with. Obama positions himself as a peace candidate, but since his election the U.S. Senate has voted in favor of every bill to continue funding of the Iraq War, promises to continue the U.S. military presence in Iraq, and rattles sabers at Iran, Pakistan, Afghanistan, and Russia. And, like Zuma, Obama has expressed an unsettling fealty to the market, which, in Lee's view, represents the continuing exploitation of people of color.

The day following his victory over Mbeki in the ANC internecine elections in January, Sean said, Zuma met with mostly white
foreign investors in South Africa to assure them that, for all his
populist appeal, he had no plans to do anything they would object
to, like raising rates on corporate taxes, strengthening labor laws,
or nationalizing industries. Zuma's populism seems as thin and
calculated as Obama's antiwar stance.

Zuma's meeting with foreign investors following his defeat of
Mbeki reminds Sean of Obama's address to the American Israel
Political Action Committee the day after he had sewed up the
Democratic nomination for president, assuring the audience of his
steadfast support for Israel and even further expansion of Israeli
settlements into Palestinian's occupied territory. He notes that
the industry that has donated the most money to Obama's campaign is Wall Street, and when Obama held a press conference
in September to discuss the collapse of the economy and housing
market, it was Robert Rubin—a former Goldman Sachs chairman,
Clinton's treasury secretary, and a principal player in the deregula-
tory legislation that left America with both NAFTA and the housing bubble—who appeared at his side.

"Another critical question that black people in this country
should be asking about an Obama presidency," Sean says, "is this:
Who will have Obama's ear?" To illustrate the point, he recounts
the story of the ANC's efforts to privatize the state-owned airline, South Africa Airways. Wanting first to transform SAA into
a moneymaker so they could attract lucrative bids from investors, ANC officials were almost gleeful in 1998 when they hired
an American turnaround specialist, T. Coleman Andrews III,
to run the carrier. A Republican and a former candidate for governor of Virginia, Andrews was hired to nudge SAA into the
global marketplace with some good old-fashioned American
business know-how.

He did just that, immediately sizing up the competition and setting his sights on Sun Air, a small but nimble regional airline. Slashing fares and flooding the skies with cheap flights, Andrews bludgeoned Sun Air into bankruptcy within a year of his arrival, leaving SAA to gobble up most of its passengers and expand its share of the regional market.

But that enraged the ANC. Sun Air was their baby, the government's first successful effort at brokering a deal to create a viable, black-owned company after decades in which blacks had been legally banned from owning property.

Within three years, Andrews had worn out his welcome, leaving the country with a $24 million severance package—the largest in the country's history—and the company with as much red ink as when he arrived. The $40 million profit that Andrews claimed on the carrier's 2001 balance sheet evaporated after auditors discovered an Enron-like accounting scheme that reported as profit the onetime revenues from the sales of planes and equipment. Those auditors say the airline actually lost about $73 million in 2001, roughly the same as in the year before Andrews arrived, when adjusted for currency devaluations.[7]

"You see, I support both Obama and Zuma, but I worry that both men are playing the same role in this corrupt neocolonial democracy," Lee says, as he finishes his coffee in the campus café. "And that is the role of a front man."

"They're puppets," says Sean.

"Yes," Lee says, snapping his fingers excitedly. "The white man is still pulling the strings, and as long as that is happening the black man is getting the short end of the stick."

"Because the white man uses capitalism and democracy to bludgeon dark people," Sean chimes in. "They use it to exploit Africans for their labor, Palestinians for their land, Iranians for their oil. That's what the Cold War was all about. Not East versus

West, but North versus South and which white man was going to reap the benefits of plunder."

Intuitively, blacks see war for what it is: white people trying to take shit from people of color, or, inevitably, people of color going to get back what was stolen from them, Sean says. "This is why I cringe when I hear my brother Barack Obama say that he will escalate America's prosecution of the war in Afghanistan."

Lee: "But I believe he will be a far better president than [John] McCain. He is trying to be objective, trying to be all things to all people, and that's cool for now. But what I want to see is that African side of him come out. Barack is a black man, and he can't help but see the world as a black man. I understand that maybe he has to campaign as something a little different than what he truly is to win votes from white people."

This is what Mandela did, in recreating himself as this great conciliator, without anger or bitterness.

"He was a warrior when he went to prison, branded a guerrilla terrorist by the apartheid government," Lee says. "But he sees the world as a black man, an African, and at the end of the day, I think Obama will come home as well."

Lee pauses for a second, then flashes a broad grin. "I hope so. Even an African like me wants to live the American dream."

Notes

1. Daisy Mae on the Bayou

1. *Historic Structures Survey*, St. Mary Parish, Louisiana Division of Historic Preservation. www.crt.state.la.us/hp/nhl/parish51/scans/51024001.pdf.
2. 1860 U.S. Census Slave Schedules for St. Mary Parish, Louisiana, National Archives and Records Administration microfilm series M653, Roll 432.
3. Barack Obama, *Dreams from My Father* (New York: Three Rivers Press, 1995), 15.
4. Paul Henslee, "The Francis Family—An Athletic Legend,"*St. Mary and Franklin Banner-Tribune*, January 5, 1973.
5. Ibid.
6. "McCain Favored by State Voters,"*St. Mary and Franklin Banner-Tribune*, November 5, 2008.

2. Made in America

1. Paul Frymer, *Black and Blue: African Americans, the Labor Movement, and the Decline of the Democratic Party* (Princeton, NJ: Princeton University Press, 2007).
2. John Ramsey and Sarah A. Reid, "Smithfield: Race and the Union,"*Fayetteville (NC) Observer*, December 21, 2008.
3. Sandra Jones, "Runoff Elections to Determine Future of Wal-Mart in Chicago,"*Chicago Tribune*, April 15, 2007; "Mayor Vetoes Chicago Living Wage Ordinance Aimed at Big Retailers,"*USA Today*, September 11, 2006.

4. James R. Green, *Death in the Haymarket: A Story of Chicago, the First Labor Movement, and the Bombing That Divided Gilded Age America* (New York: Pantheon Books, 2006), 266–271.

5. John Schmitt and Dean Baker, "Unions: Ensuring Social Justice for African Americans," The Center for Economic Policy and Research, April 2, 2008. www.cepr.net/index.php/publications/reports/unions-and-upward-mobility-for-african-american-workers/.

6. Livingstone Tourism Information, *Destination Zambia—History and Culture*, Livingstone, Zambia, 2002.

7. Adam Hochschild, *King Leopold's Ghost* (New York: Pan Macmillan Press, 1998).

8. Boris Fausto, *A Concise History of Brazil*, trans. Arthur Brakel (New York: Cambridge University Press, 1999).

9. Frymer, *Black and Blue*, 37–39.

10. Ibid.

11. Steven Fishman, "Anger Management: Why TWU Honcho Roger Toussaint Still Blames Bloomberg—and Still Believes Striking Was the Only Answer,"*New York Magazine*, January 1, 2006.

12. Ingrid Eckerman, *The Bhopal Saga: Causes and Consequences of the World's Largest Industrial Disaster* (India: Universities Press, 2004).

13. "World's Most Unionized Countries," Progressive Policy Institute, www.ppionline.org, January 31, 2007.

14. Peter Gottschalk and Timothy M. Smeeding, "Cross-National Comparisons of Earnings and Income Inequality,"*Journal of Economic Literature* (June 1997), 21.

15. Ibid.

16. Associated Press, "Rally at Pier in Protest of South Africa Apartheid," December 1, 1984.

17. Gary Rivlin, *Fire on the Prairie: Chicago's Harold Washington and the Politics of Race* (New York: Henry Holt and Company, 1992).

18. Ibid.

19. Carol Doherty, "Attitudes toward Immigration in Black and White," Pew Research Center for People and the Press, April 26, 2006.

20. See www.OpenSecrets.org; and Campaign Finance Institute annual reports by candidates and donors at www.cfinst.org.

21. Lindsay Beyerstein, "Economist: One in Five Union Organizers Get Canned,"*Washington Independent*, January 14, 2009.

22. David Oshinsky, *"Worse than Slavery": Parchman Farm and the Ordeal of Jim Crow Justice* (New York: Free Press, 1996), 116.

3. He Doesn't See What We See

1. Lillian Williams, "Washington's Doctor Debunks Foul Play Talk," *Chicago Sun-Times*, March 9, 1988.

2. Annette Gordon-Reed, *Thomas Jefferson and Sally Hemings: An American Controversy* (Charlottesville: University of Virginia Press, 1997), xiii.

3. The Department of Justice, Office of the Inspector General, *The CIA Contra–Crack Cocaine Controversy: A Review of the Justice Department's Investigations and Prosecutions*, December 1997.

4. Harriet A. Washington, *Medical Apartheid: The Dark History of Medical Experimentation on Black Americans from Colonial Times to the Present* (New York: Harlem Moon Press, 2007), 3–16.

5. U.S. Census Bureau, annual tables, 2007, at www.census.gov.

6. *Eyes on the Prize II: America at the Crossroads, 1965–1985*, Episode 12, "A Nation of Law?"

7. Jim Schaefer and Ben Schmitt, "Detroit Mayor Charged with Assault after Jail Order Lifted," *Detroit Free Press*, August 8, 2008.

8. Liz Beavers, "England Back in Mineral County: Army Reservist, Notorious Face of Abu Ghraib Scandal, Out of Prison," *Cumberland (MD) Times-News*, March 25, 2007.

9. Oliver Mackson, *Times Herald-Record (Middletown, NY)*, "Four Newburgh Men Indicted on Terrorism Charges," June 2, 2009.

10. Saul Landau, "Bush's Anti Terror-Record: Don't Look Too Hard," *Foreign Policy in Focus*, November 1, 2006.

11. "N.C. State Bar Files More Ethics Charges against Duke Lacrosse Prosecutor," Associated Press, January 24, 2007.

12. Rob Waters, "Medicating Aliah," *Mother Jones*, June 2005.

13. Martha T. Moore, "Bombing in Philadelphia Still Unsettled," *USA Today*, May 11, 1985.

14. Alexander Cockburn, "A Federal Witch Hunt: The Prosecution of Sami Al-Arian," *Counterpunch*, March 3, 2007.

15. Nikki Giovanni, *Hip Hop Speaks to Children: A Celebration of Poetry with a Beat* (Naperville, IL: Sourcebooks, 2008), introduction.

16. Holly Sklar, "Minimum Wage Raise Too Little Too Late," MS. Foundation for Women, July 22, 2008, www.ms.foundation.org/wmspage.cfm?parm1=562.

17. *San Francisco Bayview Newspaper*, "Police 2, Oakland Residents 4," March 24, 2009.

18. Abhi Raghunathan, Casey Cora, and Christina Silva, "Details of Teen's Shooting Death Revealed," *St. Petersburg Times*, June 10, 2008.

4. Where the Grass Is Greener

1. Robert E. Pierre, "For Curry and P.G., the Road Is Filled with Promise and Pitfalls," *Washington Post*, November 13, 1994.
2. Robert E. Pierre, "Curry Event Raises Funds, Reinforces Upscale Image," *Washington Post*, May 22, 1998.
3. Robert E. Pierre, "The Process and the Price of Budget Decisions," *Washington Post*, May 17, 1997.
4. Robert E. Pierre, "In Prince George's, an Apartment Housecleaning," *Washington Post*, December 18, 1997.
5. Ibid.
6. Terry M. Neal and Robert E. Pierre, "P.G. Man Beaten by Police Wins Little Sympathy; Case Recalls Painful Past," *Washington Post*, June 11, 1995.
7. Ovetta Wiggins, "Boulevard at Capital Centre Struggles," *Washington Post*, March 29, 2009.
8. Maryland Department of Housing and Community Development, Property Foreclosures in Maryland Fourth Quarter 2008, January 2009 (citing RealtyTrac). www.dhcd.state.md.us/Website/home/Document/PropForeclosureEvents08Q4.pdf.
9. Valencia Mohammed, "Washington Deluged by Liquor Stores," *Washington Afro American*, May 12–17, 2007.
10. Ovetta Wiggins, "County Still No. 2 in Maryland for STDs," *Washington Post*, March 25, 2009.
11. See www.keyschool.org/about_key/index.asp
12. Peter S. Goodman and Jack Healy, "Unemployment Still Growing, But at Slower Pace," *New York Times*, May 8, 2009.

5. Casualty of War

1. Chip Johnson, "Some Blacks Dubious of Politics behind War; They Say Corporate Greed the Real Motive," *San Francisco Chronicle*, March 31, 2003.
2. "Armed Forces Better Think Again If They're Waiting for the Few and the Proud to Be Black," *Jacksonville (FL) Free Press*, October 11–17, 2007.
3. Thomas Philpot, "Military Update: Black Army Recruits down 41% since 2000," *The Capital (Annapolis, MD)*, March 4, 2005, sec. A.
4. Chaka Ferguson, "Among Black Americans, Support for War Is Lagging," Associated Press, February 24, 2003.
5. Source: Civilian data from Bureau of Labor Statistics Current Population Survey File, September 2008.

6. Howard Zinn and Anthony Arnove, *Voices of a People's History of the United States* (New York: Seven Stories Press, 2004), 431.
7. Derrick Z. Jackson, "Blacks Have Good Cause to Oppose War in Iraq," *Boston Globe*, February 26, 2003. www.commondreams.org/views03/0226-07.html.
8. *Lone Star*, directed by John Sayles, 1996, Columbia Pictures Corporation.
9. Kareem Abdul-Jabbar and Anthony Walton, *Brothers in Arms: The Epic Story of the 761st Tank Battalion, WWII's Forgotten Heroes* (New York: Harlem Moon, Broadway Books, 2004), 73–74.
10. Anica Butler, "She Loved Her Country and Died Serving It," *Baltimore Sun*, August 16, 2005.
11. Ibid.
12. Lila de Tantillo, "Soldier Remembered as Ready and Willing," *Washington Post*, August 17, 2005.
13. Justin Ward, U.S. Army Corps of Engineers, "In Memory of Ivica Jerak," Northshorejournal.org, northshorejournal.org/in-memory-of-ivica-jerak.
14. Jennifer Loven, "Bush Gives New Reason for Iraq War," *Boston Globe*, August 31, 2005.
15. "U.S. Military Deaths at 4311," ABC News, http://abcnews.go.com/International/wireStory?id=7818771, June 7, 2009.

6. White Is Not an Abstract Concept

1. "In North Carolina, Recession Breeds a Health-Care Crisis; Job Losses Leave State with Highest Percentage of Uninsured," *Washington Post*, April 20, 2009.
2. "Faith Based Organizations Mobilize Quickly to Aid Hurricane Victims," *Miami Herald*, October 30, 2005.
3. Ronald D. Eller, *Uneven Ground: Appalachia since 1945* (Lexington: University Press of Kentucky, 2008), 12.
4. Osha Gray Davidson, "The Forgotten Soldier," *Rolling Stone*, March 23, 2003.
5. Ibid.
6. "Consumer Unease with Health Care Grows," *USA Today*, October 16, 2006.
7. Insuring America's Health: Principles and Recommendations, Institute of Medicine, January 2004, www.iom.edu/?id=19175.
8. "As Obama Hosts Summit on Healthcare, Marginalized Advocates Ask Why Single Payer Is Ignored," Democracy Now.org, March 6, 2009, www.democracynow.org/2009/3/6/as_obama_hosts_summit_on_health.

9. Ibid.
10. "Obama Says Changes Are Needed to Help Recovery Take Hold," *Los Angeles Times*, April 15, 2009.
11. Barack Obama, *Dreams from My Father* (New York: Three Rivers Press, 1995), 80.
12. "Obama's Pastor: God Damn America, U.S. to Blame for 9/11," ABC News.com, March 13, 2008.
13. Ibid.
14. "Rev. Wright Cautions: Obama 'Ain't Jesus,'" Associated Press, March 5, 2009.

7. Little Men

1. Barack Obama, *Dreams from My Father* (New York: Three Rivers Press, 1995), 58.
2. U.S. Census Bureau, quickfacts.census.gov/qfd/states/22/2255000.html.
3. Ibid.
4. Ibid.
5. Raymond Strother, *Falling Up: How a Redneck Helped Invent Political Consulting* (Baton Rouge: LSU Press, 2003), 100.
6. "Fixing D.C. Schools, The Charter Experiment," *Washington Post*, projects, www.washingtonpost.com/wp-srv/metro/specials/charter/index.html, December 13, 2008.
7. Lori Montgomery and Jay Matthews, "The Future of D.C. Public Schools: Traditional or Charter Education?" *Washington Post*, August 22, 2006.
8. Leigh Davis, "Coming to a City Near You," *Counterpunch*, August 30, 2006.
9. Alexander Russo, "Paul Vallas Pays the Price of Leadership," *Education Next* 3, no. 1 (Winter 2003), 30–37.
10. Robert E. Pierre, "The Young Apprentice," *Washington Post*, June 9, 2006.
11. Howard Witt, "Katrina Aftermath Still Roils Gretna," *Chicago Tribune*, September 4, 2008.
12. Carol Kopp, "The Bridge to Gretna," CBS News, December 18, 2005.
13. Jay Matthews, "Charter Schools' Big Experiment," *Washington Post*, June 9, 2008.
14. Ibid.
15. Ibid.
16. Amy Waldman, "Reading, Writing, Resurrection," *Atlantic Monthly*, 299, no. 1 (January 2007), 88.

17. Sarah Carr, "About Face: New Principal Reaches Out to Teachers and Pupils," *New Orleans Times-Picayune*, January 19, 2008.
18. Ibid.
19. Jennifer Hochschild and Nathan Scovronick, *The American Dream and the Public Schools* (New York: Oxford University Press, 2003), 4.

8. Dandelions

1. Bureau of Justice Statistics, United States Department of Justice, Office of Justice Programs, *Prison Inmates at Midyear 2008—Statistical Tables*, June 30, 2008.
2. Kevin Merida, ed., *Being a Black Man: At the Corner of Progress and Peril* (New York: Public Affairs, 2007), p. 239.
3. Robert E. Pierre, "Back from Behind Bars," *Washington Post*, September 2, 2007.
4. Ibid.
5. Ibid.
6. Federal News Service, Inc., Transcript of NBC's *Meet the Press*, January 11, 2009.
7. Ibid.
8. George Rush and Joanna Rush Molloy, "It's Time for Strength, Say Stars," *New York Daily News*, January 19, 2009.
9. Charles M. Blow, "No More Excuses," *New York Times*, January 23, 2009.
10. James Alan Fox and Marianne W. Zawitz, *Homicide Trends in the U.S.*, Bureau of Justice Statistics, United States Department of Justice, July 11, 2007.
11. Pierre, "Back from behind Bars."
12. Ibid.
13. Robert E. Pierre, "After Prison New Sets of Barriers," *Washington Post*, July 10, 2008.
14. Cheryl W. Thompson, "Prison's Dangers Ignored, Aide Says," *Washington Post*, August 27, 1999.
15. Robert E. Pierre and Kari Lydersen, "Illinois Death Row Emptied," *Washington Post*, January 12, 2003.
16. D.C. Board of Elections, 2008 Certified Election Results, December 2008. www.dcboee.org/election_info/election_results/election_result_new/results_final_gen.asp?prev=0&electionid=2&result_type=3.
17. Ian Shapira, "$75 Million Bequest from Alumnus Is Georgetown's Biggest-Ever Gift," *Washington Post*, December 11, 2008.

9. Watermelon Man

1. Christopher Gray, "Fidel Castro Slept Here," *New York Times*, April 30, 2009.
2. "I'll Have Vengeance." *Time*, February 21, 1977.
3. "Bad Times on the Good Times Set," *Ebony*, September 1977.
4. Sharon Begley, "The Stereotype Trap," *Newsweek*, November 6, 2000, 66–68.
5. See www.youtube.com/watch?v=Hj1hCDjwG6M
6. Rebekah Levine Coley, "Comparing Father and Mother Reports of Father Involvement Among Low-Income Minority Families," eScholarship at Boston College, 2007.
7. Perry Bacon Jr., "Jackson Incident Revives Some Blacks' Concerns about Obama," *Washington Post*, July 1, 2008.
8. Lynn Sweet, "Crowd Cheers Advice to Turn off TV, Skip Popeyes for Breakfast," *Chicago Sun-Times*, February 29, 2008.
9. Ken Silverstein, "The Birth of a Washington Machine," *Harper's*, November 2006.
10. Barack Obama, *Dreams from My Father* (New York: Three Rivers Press, 1995), 84–85.

10. The Front Man

1. Statistics South Africa, Statistics South Africa Household Surveys, 2008, www.ssa.gov.
2. U.S. Census Bureau. 2008b. Table 4, Poverty Status of Family, by Type of Family, Presence of Related Children, Race, and Hispanic Origin: 1959 to 2008. Washington, D.C.: U.S. Department of Commerce.
3. Statistics South Africa, Statistics South Africa Household Surveys, 2008, www.ssa.gov.
4. Ibid.
5. U.S. Census Bureau. 2008b. Table 4, Poverty Status of Family.
6. Allister Sparks, *The Mind of South Africa* (New York: Knopf, 1990), 91.
7. Sahkela Buhlungu, *State of the Nation South Africa 2007* (Johannesburg: Human Research Sciences Council).

Index

Index

244